REVOLUTION

REVOLUTION

RUSSELL BRAND

CENTURY

Published by Century 2014

4 6 8 10 9 7 5

Copyright © Russell Brand 2014

The author is grateful to quote from the following:

Homage to Catalonia by George Orwell
Published by Martin Secker & Warburg Ltd.
Reprinted by permission of The Random House Group Ltd

Tomgram: Noam Chomsky, America's Real Foreign Policy
Copyright 2014 Noam Chomsky

Subterranean Homesick Blues by Bob Dylan
Copyright © 1965 by Warner Bros. Inc.; renewed 1993 by Special Rider Music

From *Joseph Campbell and the Power of Myth* with Bill Moyers;
courtesy of Apostrophe S Productions, Inc.

Every effort has been made to contact the copyright holders. The publishers will be glad to correct any
errors or omissions in future editions.

First published in Great Britain in 2014 by
Century
Random House, 20 Vauxhall Bridge Road,
London SW1V 2SA

www.randomhouse.co.uk

Addresses for companies within The Random House Group Limited can be found at:
www.randomhouse.co.uk

The Random House Group Limited Reg. No. 954009

A CIP catalogue record for this book
is available from the British Library

ISBN 9781780893051

The Random House Group Limited supports the Forest Stewardship Council® (FSC®), the leading international forest-certification organisation. Our books carrying the FSC label are printed on FSC®-certified
paper. FSC is the only forest-certification scheme supported by the leading environmental organisations,
including Greenpeace. Our paper procurement policy can be found at www.randomhouse.co.uk/environment

MIX
Paper from
responsible sources
FSC® C016897

Typeset by Palimpsest Book Production Ltd, Falkirk, Stirlingshire
Printed and bound in Great Britain by Clays Ltd, St Ives plc

To the divine, mischievous spark in you.

ACKNOWLEDGEMENTS

I suppose I should acknowledge some of the people without who this book would have been impossible. I mean, I'd like to take all the credit ideally but if this Revolution is going to have legs, I have to be a fair, upstanding, decent fella, not a gluttonous narcissist gobbling up other people's credit like, I dunno, Wonga.

So Ben Dunn is the editor of the book who I argue with about whether or not the stuff I write conveys its intended meaning, which, let's face it, he's better qualified to comment on because, I'm me and I know what I mean already. I appreciate and am grateful for Ben's enthusiasm and patience. Plus he's West Ham and done my Booky Wook an all, so he's got form.

Thanks to Nicola Schuller for feeding me, running with me, caffeinating me and encouraging me, taking care of me and forcing me to write.

Cheers vegan cannibal Nik Linnen for reading it and believing in me and helping me not to sound like an out of touch lunatic writing from Cloud Cuckoo Land.

Gareth Roy for keeping it light and funny and giving me football coaching. Thanks Gal.

Thanks to Francesca Pathak at the publishers for saying I come across as a racist because I reference 'brown people' even though the next two people I'm acknowledging are black.

Thank you James for keeping me on point with the fellowship and being there in the twisted moments of dark doubt (and for being black to shut Francesca up).

Thanks Gee for being on this journey and providing a sounding board and compadre who will forever go forwards.

Marco, Jonathan and Cecilia thanks for feeding me and taking care of me when Nicola was away doing her other jobs.

Thanks Alain de Botton for being such a cherry lipped clever clogs and nudging me towards the light and away from town square executions.

Johann Hari you tireless, brilliant, adrenalized busy body, your research, passion, advice and constant interfering and advancement of your own gay agenda has been thrilling and helpful and I know your book "Chasing The Scream" will be a hit.

John Rogers, you druid communist, thank you, thank you for keeping the red flag flying and never being afraid to hurt my feelings.

Andrew Antonio, without your warm hearted Cypriot accountancy and guidance this book would be a pointless scribble in the abyss.

Mick. You are irreplaceable. Heart is more valuable than head, comfort more important than speed.

Tino, thank God you refuse to die no matter what cancer throws at your brain, your brain is invaluable to me.

Manya, thanks for listening and advising and putting me in touch with that lovely teenager.

Moira Bellas you are elegant and kind, serene and wonderful; the anti-Thatcher.

Shepard Fairey thank you for sharing the tussle between commerciality and communism with me, you monochrome Matisse of our time.

Eckhart Tolle, you are from another dimension and clearly

don't need thanks but one has to be polite, thank you, thank you for the clarity.

Adam Curtis you are so important and influential you propagandist for the righteous, I'd like to keep you forever in that straw hat, musing with staccato ingenuity.

Mum and Dad, well done for providing the genetic material required for my existence then sustaining me and teaching me to be compassionate and determined.

Gordon Bosworth, bone bending Gandalf, smashing my spine into compliance with merriment.

Karl T for forever quibbling with my mashed together theories and giving me better ones, for twenty years now.

Simon Amstell for your ayahuasca drenched insights and new tenderness.

Matt Morgan for oscillating between lumpen cynicism and crackpot theories that would get us all killed but always making everything funnier.

Roberta for helping me to remain connected with limitless realms of unknowable positivity through stretching.

Sharon Smith for remaining young and powerfully mercurial.

Dean Chalkley for the delightful image on the cover.

Adam Venit for continuing to be a compassionate and wise voice.

Noreen Oliver for being the Boadicea of British abstinence based recovery, for being a fearless leader of the trembling and the clucking.

Chip Somers for almost twelve years of twelve steps, thank you.

John Noel for dragging me out of the gutter and pinning me to the wall, thanks.

David Lynch, Bobby Roth, Deirdre, Lynn and John Hagelin for bringing transcendence to so many of my friends.

Meredith and Wainwright for using ancient China and

modern Muswell Hill to elevate me with old pins and new powders.

Usama Hasan, Tariq Ramadan, Dave Boyle and Laurence Easeman for your unused but greatly appreciated contributions – it was only deadlines that stymied us.

And Dave Graeber, Daniel Pinchbeck, Dave DeGraw, Naomi Klein, Noam Chomsky, Matt Stoller, Helena Norberg-Hodge, Peter Tatchell, Edward Slingerland and Thomas Piketty for making this book more than the intuitive ranting of a madman.

And Jemima, you incomparable editor of all reality, somewhere between a muse and a mandala. Thank you for all you did.

CONTENTS

*Where this asterisk appears I am obliged to add clarification so that this book can be published. Ben the editor gives me notes, with which I then argue, then Roger the lawyer who has to sign off gives me suggestions to make the book publishable.

You Say You Want A
Revolution

Jeremy Paxman is Britain's foremost political interviewer. He is fierce, not in a pugnacious way, like a salivating pit-bull; no, like a somnolent croc, eyes above the surface, knowing you will make a false move, waiting. Then snap, thrash, roll, you're finished. He eats home secretaries for breakfast, shits chancellors and wipes his arse on prime ministers. In five minutes' time I will be interviewed by Jeremy, on our nation's foremost news analysis show, *Newsnight*.

That's why I'm on my knees now, in the toilet of the lobby of the Landmark hotel. Praying. 'God, please make me a channel of your peace.' The first line of the St Francis prayer, popularised by Mother Teresa, bastardised by Margaret Thatcher and cherished by those of us who have fallen through the cracks and floated ourselves back up with crack.

I just want to be a channel of the peace. The peace exists; I don't need, thank God, to create the peace. All I have to do is become open and the peace will come, the peace is already there. Mother Teresa, one could argue, is a testimony to the principles outlined in this prayer; through service she has conquered the lower, selfish drives that serve survival and the ego, and become a tool of a Higher Purpose, or God. Margaret

Thatcher's case is less clear. What God she was serving in her systematic destruction of the values of our country as she jived in the brilliantined shadow of Ronnie Reagan is a mystery. But as she stands, newly elected and spattered by foreboding rain outside Number 10, it is the St Francis prayer that Maggie recites:

Lord, make me a channel of thy peace;
That where there is hatred, I may bring love;
That where there is wrong, I may bring the spirit of forgive-
ness;
That where there is discord, I may bring harmony;
That where there is error, I may bring truth;
That where there is doubt, I may bring faith;
That where there is despair, I may bring hope;
That where there are shadows, I may bring light;
That where there is sadness, I may bring joy.
Lord, grant that I may seek rather to comfort than to be
comforted;
To understand, than to be understood;
To love, than to be loved.
For it is by self-forgetting that one finds.
It is by forgiving that one is forgiven.
It is by dying that one awakens to eternal life.
Amen.

Now, I don't think she belted out the whole thing there and then, but you don't need to be Jeremy Paxman to see that Margaret Thatcher somewhat strayed from the sentiments outlined in this prayer.

She didn't bring much love to the miners of northern England. She wasn't that forgiving to the Argentinian sailors on the *Belgrano*. There was very little harmony among the poll-tax rioters and the police. You get the idea. So I suppose the prayer is not infallible; in the wrong hands it can evidently become a mantra for self-centred nihilism. That isn't the prayer's fault, though. For me it is a code that attunes my mind to its natural state: union, connection, oneness. In the Creole ramblings that I offer up in the frantic lavatorial incantations that precede the interview – some Vedic chants, yogic murmurs and even some Eminem lyrics – what I am trying to do is to connect, transcend, get out of myself. That is what I've been trying to do my whole life – get out of myself; get out of my mind; get out of Grays; get out of the feeling that I'm not good enough, that I'm alone, that I'm never going to be happy or loved – and I've tried to do it in a multitude of ways, always with the same outcome.

I've greeted a cavalcade of gleaming false idols like a jam-jar native, prostrate before the great white master. As a little boy, chocolate and television were deities to me; I sat on my knees before that goggle-box in spellbound devotion, the Penguin sacrament ritualistically devoured (nibble chocolate coating first, scrape centre with teeth, then eat biscuit). As a teen with porn, I was locked up mute like a Trappist in that bathroom, flagellating with stifled wails. With drugs and alcohol I made the pilgrimage to any bridge or corner and made my donations in the penury my God demanded. Then came fame, where I studied like Augustine and voyaged like a Jesuit. I was a zealous devotee to every prophet of the panoply and none brought anything but pain and disillusion. Only when salvation was offered did I become circumspect; only when the solution became available did I examine with a skeptical eye.

When I necked five-quid bottles of vodka, I did not read the label. When I scored rocks and bags off tumbleweed hobos blowing through the no-man's-land of Hackney estates, I conducted no litmus tests. As I sought sanctuary in twilight cemeteries entombed in stranger's limbs, I barely even asked their names.

But when the true dawn came, when the light rose, when I felt the fusion, I had no faith – I had questions. How do I know this is real? What if it doesn't work? How can I, after everything, just trust and let go? I still have questions, and in the inquisitor's chair in the suite-cum-studio of the Landmark hotel, so does Jeremy Paxman.

'So . . .' he says in a voice so intoned with sarcasm I wonder whether it will come out of his nose, 'how, if you think people shouldn't vote, are we going to change the world?'

'Through Revolution,' I say.

'You want a Revolution?'

'Yeah.'

'You believe there's going to be a Revolution ?' He shunts the question at me like a billiard ball.

'Jeremy, I have no doubt,' I reply.

Jeremy has been round the block a few times and has sat across from every johnny-come-lately mug with a cause and a plug who has had the gall to crop up on his show in the last twenty years. He looks me up and down – the hair, the beard, the ridiculous scarf.

'And how, may I ask, is this Revolution going to come about?'

Now that is a very good question, it's a question that a far less skilled interviewer than Jeremy Paxman would lob at you. But this isn't a far less skilled one, it's Paxman. And not just Paxman; it's my headmaster, it's the arresting officer, it's the people at work, friends, relatives, well-wishers and bystanders. 'How will this Revolution work? How can we change the world? How can we change ourselves? Can we really overthrow the corrupt and the powerful, not just the corruption in society but in ourselves?'

4

Well, I know the answer's yes. And as for the more complicated aspects of that question, well, I may not be Margaret
Thatcher, and I'm certainly no Mother Teresa (except we agree
on condoms), but I've given it some thought, so here we go,
sit down and strap in.

CHAPTER 1

Heroes' Journey

The first betrayal is in the name. 'Lakeside', the giant shopping centre, mall to Americans, and *maul* is right, because these citadels of global brands are not tender lovers, it is not a consensual caress, it's a maul.

After a slow, seductive drum-roll of propaganda beaten out in already yellowing local rags, Lakeside shopping centre landed in the defunct chalk pits of Grays, where I grew up, like a UFO.

A magnificent cathedral of glass and steel, adjacent, as the name suggests, to a lake. There was as yet no lake. The lake was, of course, man-made. The name Lakeside, a humdrum tick-tock hymn to mundanity and nature, required the manufacture of the lake its name implied, just to make sense of itself.

For me though, as a teenager, this was no time for semantic pedantry but one of inexplicable rapture. I couldn't wait for Lakeside to descend, to make sense of the as-yet-empty lake, to fill my life as surely as they'd fill that lake, to occupy my mind as surely as they'd occupy that barren land. I couldn't wait to go to Lakeside. The fact that I had no money was no obstacle to my excitement at the oncoming Mardi Gras of consumerism. Lakeside seemed like the answer, that's for sure, but what was the question?

What kind of void can there be in the life of a thirteen-year-old boy that requires a shopping centre to fill it? Why would a lad growing up in Essex in the eighties have a yearning to shop that would be a more probable endowment of one the gals from *Sex in the City?*

Joseph Campbell, the cultural anthropologist who I'll be banging on about a lot in this book, said, 'If you want to understand what's most important to a society, don't examine its art or literature, simply look at its biggest buildings.' In medieval societies the biggest buildings were its churches and palaces; using Campbell's method we can assume these were feudal cultures that revered their leaders and worshipped God. In modern Western cities the biggest buildings are the banks – bloody great towers that dominate the docklands – and the shopping centres, which architecturally ape the cathedrals they've replaced: domes, spires, eerie, celestial calm, fountains for fonts, food-courts for pews. If you were to ask the developers of Lakeside or any shopping centre what they are offering consumers (formerly known as 'people'), they'd say, 'It's all under one roof' – great, a ceiling, and more importantly 'choice'. Choice is the key. Apparently then what excited me as a bulimic Smiths fan and onanist was the possibility of choice, and for anybody to be stimulated by the idea of choice the pre-condition must be a lack of choice. Which is a way of saying a lack of power, a lack of freedom.

I'm not inferring that we need to revert to a medieval culture, by the way, all bubonic and snaggle-toothed with shabbily bandaged hands, chewing on a turnip, genuflecting in a ditch as a baron sweeps by on horseback. If we've learned anything from *Blackadder* it's that history was a shit-hole.

What I believe is that we're only just beginning to understand the incredible capacity of human beings, that we can become something unrecognisable, that we can have true freedom, not some tantalising emblem forever out of reach. Not weary compromise and nagging fear.

I used to believe in the system that I was born into: aspire, acquire, consume, get famous and glamorous, get high and mighty, get paid and laid. I saw what was being offered in wipe-clean magazines and silver screens and I signed up. I wanted choice, freedom, power, sex and drugs, and I've used them and they've used me.

'Why would you be satisfied with the scraps of fame and fortune, of sex and distraction?' asked a fellow recovering drunk that I was chatting to in New Orleans. He was well tanned – in an overly literal way, the way leather is tanned – his skin coarse and lined, his beard gripping his face like a furry fist. His shirt had faded stains and rings like coffee-cup marks on an old map. He looked like a man who had lived, who'd had long nights and fistfights, but his eyes were as clear as his words.

'Money, fame – those are the crumbs,' he said, brushing the words away with his thick forearm, 'I want to be at the banquet.' At this last he looked up and smiled. Then he strolled off with brutish majesty to do voluntary work with the plentiful New Orleans homeless. In retrospect his departure was melodramatic, like a grass in a police drama swanning off after a midnight subterranean confab with his cop handler, maybe grinding out a fag, then leaving – why don't they ever say, 'Well, I better be off then, toodle-oo,' like normal people?

The most positive thing about being a drug addict is that it calcifies your disillusion; someone else, also a drunk – I'm starting to think I spend too much time listening to these lushes – said to me, 'Drugs and alcohol are not our problem, reality is our problem; drugs and alcohol are our solution to that problem.' That's a very smart way of putting it.

The same impulse that made Lakeside seem a good idea to me also made heroin seem like a good idea. That might seem like a radical corollary to offer, but it isn't. When I was a kid in Grays I was aware of an emptiness, a sadness, a nameless sense of disconnection, so when it was suggested by a local paper, a local politician, a mayor or whatever that Lakeside might be the answer, I suppose I thought, 'Yes, Lakeside might be the answer.' Given that I subsequently went on to become addicted to anything that could be cooked, snorted or swallowed, it seems Lakeside's palliative qualities were at best limited. Perhaps I'm an extreme case. But isn't that all addiction really is, 'an extreme case'?

Aren't we all, in one way or another, trying to find a solution to the problem of reality? If I get this job, this girl, this guy, these shoes. If I pass this exam, eat this pizza, drink this booze, go on this holiday. Learn karate, learn yoga. If West Ham stay up, if my dick stays up, if I get more likes on Facebook, more fancy cookbooks, a better kitchen, cure this itchin', if she stops bitching.

Isn't there always some kind of condition to contentment? Isn't it always placed in the future, wrapped up in some object, either physical or ideological? I know for me it is and as an addict that always leads me to excess and then to trouble.

Do you feel like that? Are you looking for something? It's not just me, is it? Do you sometimes feel afraid, self-conscious, lonely, not good enough? I mean, you're reading this, so you must want to change something.

Don't leave me out on a limb, all vulnerable and exposed. Are you reading this on a yacht, through your Ray-Bans with, I dunno, a pair of glistening Russian sisters and a gob oozing with lobster juice as the sun shines down on you and the sisters smile up at you? And even if you are, especially if you are, is it working, behind the salty tang and priapic pang, is it real, is it real, is it like God is holding your hand?

I mean, I've tried decadence too. I lived in a Hollywood mansion, I went to the Oscars, I hosted big dos.

In 2002, at two weeks clean in a Bury St Edmunds B&B on

Christmas Eve, watching TV, perched on a single bed with my mum, both of us with the glum cordiality of an A&E waiting room – shell-shocked smiles and no hope – if some twinkling superficial fairy had flown in and said, 'You'll be taking your mum to the Oscars in a few years, don't worry,' I'd obviously have been surprised (I mean, a fairy), but what would've been incomprehensible to me would've been the veracious addition from the ethereal intruder that 'Oh, by the way, you'll both find the Oscars fucking boring.'

Lakeside is a local parish; Hollywood is the Vatican. I wondered how the other parishioners had fared when I went back to Grays recently. I wondered whether Lakeside had delivered, for the people I grew up with, the people I left behind, the people I was running from; I wondered if they got their choice, freedom and opportunity.

I fare-dodged my way out of Grays on the Fenchurch Street train, which primarily transports commuting city workers from Essex to the City of London. Stopping at Chafford Hundred – the new estate they built opposite the street where I grew up – Purfleet, Lakeside, Rainham, Dagenham Dock, Barking and Limehouse. I'd hide in the toilet, under my gelled quiff, with my own 'Out of Order' sign on the door, a cross between Del Boy and Matt Goss, puffing skunk, counting stops.

Now I glide in the back of Mick's Mercedes. Mick would be 'my driver' if I employed possessive determiners before people and if he exhibited a modicum of professionalism. Instead he is my mate, who drives me. It is still of course, in reality, a long way from where I am from – child of a single mum, on benefits, drug addicted – as we journey down the A13 past the disused Ford factory where my nan's husband, Bert, worked, past the marshes where there was talk of building Euro-Disney. I was naturally devastated when they went for Paris instead – I mean, fucking Paris?! Walt must be spinning in his grave, or cryogenic chamber, or wherever the hell it is they keep his brilliant Nazi corpse.

The reason for this trip down memory lane – or memory pain as I tend to call it, because my past is soaked in misery and rejection; it rejected me, then I rejected it – is that my school-friend Sam asked me to open a Mind shop. Mind is the mental-health charity that he works for, and I, with my history of mental illness, plus the fact that he's a mate and the irresistible pun 'open your Mind (shop), man', feel it's worth risking a visit to the scene of the crime. The crime of being born, which is the manner in which I regarded my birth as a troubled and troubling adolescent.

Grays wasn't great when I grew up, but a lot of that might've been because I was looking at it from inside my head and I reckon I could've been reared in Tuscany and rendered it a tragedy the way my nut operated. I had a tendency for misery. What Grays is and was – and as the name suggests, aside from my self-aggrandising melancholy – is a normal town. You could say a normal, suburban, Essex town; you could say a normal British town, or a normal northern European town, or even a normal town in a secular, Western democracy.

When I was a kid, that meant the town centre, where I was due to open 'your Mind man', had a market, chain stores and local businesses. People did their shopping there hung out, you know, normal stuff. When I disembarked from my tinted capsule of privilege, I was shocked to see how much Grays has changed. I mean, we're not describing the sacking of Rome here, not the desecration of the sacred treasures of a glorious city-state, it was always a bit of a dump, but the chain stores were gone, the local businesses were gone and the market had shut down.

Now there were pound shops, betting shops, charity shops and off-licences. The people of the town I'd left twenty years ago were different: more of them were drunk, more of them were visibly undernourished – more than that, though, I could feel that there was a despondency among the fifty or so folk assembled with listless anticipation around the barrier outside the Mind shop.

The more callous among you might say that was as a result of my impending visit, you swines, but it wasn't that. Something had been taken from them, and I could feel its absence. More shocking though than this sad deterioration is that Grays, this lesser, depleted Grays, with its food banks, Wonga loans and escalating addiction problem, is still normal.

This is happening everywhere. The richest 1 per cent of British people have as much as the poorest 55 per cent. Some people like me were in the 55 per cent and are now in the 1 per cent, but mostly, normal people are getting poorer. Globally it's worse. Oxfam say a bus with the eighty-five richest people in the world on it would contain more wealth than the collective assets of half the earth's population – that's three-and-a-half billion people.

Though I can't imagine they'd be getting on a bus with that kind of money, or be hanging out together. I bet there'd be a lot of tension, jealousy and petty bickering on that bus:

'My corporation is bigger than your corporation.'

'Yeah? I've got my own media network!'

'YEAH!? I've got an elite organisation that controls global politics.'

'Stop this bus, I want to return to my subaquatic palace with my half-fish brides and sing a song about the supremacy of marine life.'

The last example might be from the Disney film *The Little Mermaid*. Walt's frozen noggin is definitely on that bus.

In America, a country that, let's face it, has really run with this whole capitalism thing, the six heirs to the Walmart fortune have more wealth than the poorest 30 per cent of Americans. There's six of them! They can't even form a football team, how are they going to stop a Revolution when we act on the unfairness of that statistic? Unless the entire system is rigged to manoeuvre wealth to an elite group of people, then ensure that it remains there.

What you just read is crazy. Insane. Unbelievable but true. As real as your hands that are holding this book (Kindle/tablet – intraneural-brain hologram, if it's really far in the future), that information is as real as the breath that you are inhaling.

Six people whose dad was 'good at supermarkets' have more money than hundreds of millions of struggling Americans. A bus full of plutocrats, royals and oligarchs have as much money as every refugee, war child and pot-bellied, rough-sleeping person on the planet.

You can hear that is crazy, you can see that it's wrong, you feel that this is beyond disturbing. We're told there's nothing we can do about it, that this is 'the way things are'. Naturally, of course, that verdict emanates from the elite institutions, organisations and individuals that benefit from things being 'the way they are'.

More important perhaps than this galling inequality is the fact that we have a limited amount of time to resolve it. The same interests that benefit from this – for brevity, I'm going to say 'system' – need, in order to maintain it, to deplete the earth's resources so rapidly, violently and irresponsibly that our planet's ability to support human life is being threatened. This is also pretty fucked up.

I mean, if someone said they had a socio-economic system that creates a hugely wealthy elite at the cost of everyone else but it was ecologically sound, we'd tell them to fuck off. What we've got is one that is systematically inflating the wealth of the elite, rapidly suffocating everybody else, and it's destroying the planet that we all live on. I know you already know this. I know. We all know. But it's so absurd – psychopathic, in fact – that we obviously need to reiterate it.

These elites, these loonies on the diamond-encrusted fun bus, they live on the planet with us, they're basically the same as us. So they're in trouble too – unless this bus is equipped for space travel and they plan to wait until the earth is a scorched husk then blast off to a moon-base.

As I perused the new shelves bearing second-hand goods in a charity shop in the run-down town where I'm from, I thought about this stuff. The hymen ribbon that I'm supposed to cut is slung unsliced across the door. The volunteers have half-empty glasses of supermarché champagne, collectively willing it to be a good day.

Two uncomfortable certainties, though, loiter like bailiffs manacling the bonhomie: 1) taking care of mentally ill people is not the job of a charity but the state; and 2) this charity shop isn't going to fucking work anyway. We already have charity shops. One of the few areas in which we are well catered for is charity shops; they're cropping up everywhere like zombies rising from the graves of the dead proper shops.

We keep our chins up as we plod through the ritual: scissors come out, applause, people bowl in, mill about, pick up a tragic jumper, weigh up a porcelain duchess in the palm of the hand. A councillor says something, a mentally ill person on the long road to sanity says something, I say something – I'm a few paces further down the road.

A church fete-type lady rosily thrusts a pair of women's jeans at me – 'These'll do for you, Russell' – I buy them and we laugh. Really, though, I'd like to scratch the record off, to rake the needle across the grooves and say, 'What the fuck are we all doing?' What gravity is this that holds us down, who installed this low suffocating sky? I get that feeling a lot, like I want to peer round the corner of reality, to scratch the record off, to say I know there's something else, I know it.

I know this isn't the best use of our time here. 'There is a crack in everything, that's how the light gets in,' sang Leonard Cohen. You can see it; just behind reality, there is a light, you can feel it. Just behind your thoughts there is a silence. He knew the answer was there, that's why he became a Buddhist and fucked off to live in them mountains. Either that or it was because his management nicked all his money.

I was particularly attuned to these ideas whilst frolicking in indigenous poverty because I was guest-editing a British political magazine called the *New Statesman*. They'd asked me what the theme of the issue would be, 'Revolution,' I said. So they pulled together a variety of journalists, philosophers and activists to contribute on aspects of the subject. Naomi Klein's article described an ecological conference where the requirement for radical action was spelled out.

Brad Werner, a complex systems researcher (which sounds like a job that would be hard to monitor for a supervisor – 'Oy, Werner, are you researching that complex system or are you dickin' around on your phone?') speaking at last year's American Geophysical Union (which must surely use pornography on the invitation to have any hope of luring trade), said that our planet is fucked. He researched our complex system – the earth, I suppose, is a complex system – and concluded that we, the people that live on it, are fucked. I'm not even joking: his lecture was titled 'Is Earth Fucked?' so the American Geophysical Union isn't as square as its name implies. They do swear words and everything.

What Brad Werner said, though, is that the capitalist system is so rapacious in its consumption of earth's resources, and the measures that have thus far been imposed so ineffectual, that the only hope we have of saving the planet is for action to come from outside of the system.

They are not going to do anything to prevent ecological meltdown; it contravenes their ideology, so change has to be imposed from the outside.

That means by us. All that Kyoto stuff – reduce carbon emissions by 'x' by year 'y' – is not worth a wank in a windsock. It's a bullshit gesture, the equivalent of the salad they sell in McDonald's. Too little, too late.

It's like giving Fred West a detention.

We know we can't trust these fuckers to behave properly. Look at the tobacco industry: they knew they were killing their customers for decades before they coughed up the carcinogenic truth; they'd be blagging us to this day if they thought they could get away with it.

You can bet we'll go on a similar journey with mobile phones. That hot tingle in your ear is not a sign that all is hunky-dory on the lughole front.

James Lovelock, the bloke who came up with Gaia theory, that the Earth is one symbiotic, interrelated organism where harmonious life forms support or regulate each other, says we shouldn't bother with recycling, wind turbines and priuses – it's all a lot of bollocks he says – not literally, though he might've if he'd been at that crazy, hang loose festival of cursing 'The American Geophysical Union'.

Now I don't reckon Lovelock is saying sit back and enjoy the apocalypse, I think he's saying we require radical action fast, and that radical action will not come from the very interests that created and benefit from things being the way they are. The one place we cannot look for change is to the occupants of the bejewelled bus. They are the problem, we are the solution, so we have to look inside ourselves.

*   *   *

I LEFT GRAYS in luxury this time, climbing back into the cradle of Mick's car. A Mercedes. The anaesthetic of privilege, the prison of comfort. People want departing photographs and

17

autographs, more scraps, more crumbs. A bloke around my age, clutching a baton of super-strength cider, puts his arm round me. I used to drink White Lightning. I am mugged by his breath as our eyes momentarily meet. I shut the door on my past and the present.

I was a little winded by what I'd seen. Going back to the place where you are from is always fraught, memories scattered like broken glass on every pavement, be careful where you tread. I meditated, feeling a little guilty that I have the space to.

A space for peace to which everyone is entitled.

'It's alright for you in the back of a car that Hitler used to ride in,' I imagined that drunk bloke saying. I'd have to point out that it wasn't literally Hitler's car, that would be a spooky heirloom, but it is alright for me. I do have a life where I can make time to meditate, eat well, do yoga, exercise, reflect, relax. That's what money buys you. Is it possible for everyone to have that life? Is it possible for anyone to be happy when such rudimentary things are exclusive?

They tell you that you ought eat five fruit and veg a day, then seven; I read somewhere once that you should eat as much as ten, face in a trough all day long, chowing on kale.

The way these conclusions are reached is that scientists look at a huge batch of data and observe the correlation between the consumption of fruit and veg and longevity.

They then conclude that you, as an individual, should eat more fruit and veg. The onus is on you; you are responsible for what you eat.

Of course other conclusions could be drawn from this data. The same people that live these long lives and eat all this fruit and veg are also, in the main, wealthy, they have good jobs, regular holidays, exercise and avoid the incessant stress of poverty. Another, more truthful, more frightening, conclusion we could reach then is that we should have a society where the resources enjoyed by the fruit-gobbling elite are shared around, and the privileges, including the fruit and veg, enjoyed by everybody.

With this conclusion the obligation is not on you as an individual to obediently skip down to Waitrose and buy more celery, it is on you as a member of society to fight for a fairer system where more people have access to resources.

A *Newsnight* producer calls. 'I think it's really interesting that you've never voted,' she says, 'you should talk about that tomorrow with Paxman.' I agree, bemused that it is regarded as unusual.

The idea that voting is pointless, democracy a façade and that no one is representing ordinary people is more resonant than ever as I leave my ordinary town behind. Amidst the guilt and anger I feel in the back of the Führer-mobile there is hope. Whilst it's clear that on an individual, communal and global level that radical change is necessary, I feel a powerful, transcendent optimism. I know change is possible, I know there is an alternative, because I live a completely different life to the one I was born with. I also know that the solution is not fame or money or any transient adornment of the individual. The only Revolution that can really change the world is the one in your own consciousness, and mine has already begun.

CHAPTER 2

Serenity Now

We have found ourselves in an insane situation; that is irrefutable. How is this unfair, exploitative system maintained? Quentin Crisp, the English fop, wit and subject of Sting's song 'An Englishman in New York', said, 'Charisma is the ability to influence without logic.' Well, David Cameron, Donald Rumsfeld and Rupert Murdoch must, in spite of their dish-face, dishrag, anodyne-plus appearances, be packing like Elvis Presley to hold this carnival of inequality together.

There is no logic in adhering to an unfair, destructive system unless it's at the sizzling behest of the inconceivably sexy. The most potent tool in maintaining the status quo is our belief that change is impossible. 'Democracy is the worst form of government except for all those other forms that have been tried from time to time.' Winston Churchill said this on being informed he'd been voted out of office in spite of Britain's victory in the Second World War.

Supposedly he said it in the bath, which is a tough environment to conjure up epigrams from, especially if you're also trying to keep a cigar dry. How convenient for the elites that thrive in this hegemony that there is no viable system but the one that places them in a tower of ineffable privilege.

How fortunate that there is no possibility of change. How extraordinary that any alternative that is offered is either studiously ignored or viciously discredited.

Coming to believe that my life could be different, that I could be restored to sanity, was an integral step in my recovery from addiction. I believe it is vital too on a social scale.

You've probably noticed by now that I keep alluding to God. Unless you're that bloke on the yacht and are only paying cursory attention to this book as the sisters begin to squabble and the bubbly begins to flatten. To be honest, oligarchs are not the intended readership of this book. If you are one, I'd like you to gently place the book on the deck, for posterity, and leap into the briny.

The reason I keep mentioning God is because I believe in God. A lot of people are surprised by that, what with it being 2014 and this being a technologically advanced secular culture.

God is primarily regarded as the preserve of thick white people and angry brown people. Since Friedrich Nietzsche (deceased) declared, 'God is dead,' we've been exploring the observation of British writer G. K. Chesterton, who said, 'The death of God doesn't mean man will believe in nothing but that he will believe in anything.'

I'm a good example of that: at thirteen a believer in Lakeside, at eight a believer in biscuits, at seventeen a devoted wanker, at nineteen a fanatical drug user, before winding up in the monastery of celebrity.

After the troubling Mind-shop epiphany I went back to my old school, to see if it was as bad as I remember it or if it had somehow managed to burrow downwards from the gutter. Whenever I'm in front of young people I sense the authority figures present prodding me to deliver a kind of 'Just Say No', 'If I can do it, you can!', 'Pull yer'self up by yer' bootstraps' monologue of individualistic triumph over adversity.

This is awkward for me because that is not my message. I don't like dispatching trite little diatribes on behalf of an establishment that I despise, and often have to wrench the pendulum of my extreme nature back to equanimity before I tell kids to riot, or torch their exam papers or their school.

I have it in me, this extremist, destructive impulse. When the pie-eyed teens in the school hall where I, decades before, had grasped the tendril with which I would swing out of Essex, like a tubby Tarzan, look to me full of *X Factor* ambition and Xbox distraction and tell me that they 'want to be famous too', I wince, but I want to tell them they've been swindled. That they are being horribly misled by the dominant cultural narratives.

In spite of the anguish my addiction to drugs and alcohol has caused me, I wouldn't relinquish its lessons and I certainly wouldn't tell other people, least of all young people, not to drink and take drugs.

The war against drugs, which is a war against drug addicts (about which Bill Hicks beautifully observed, 'If there's a war against drugs and we're losing, that means that the drug addicts are winning') is a good example of the system's disingenuity on an individual, legal and global level.

Drug addiction is an illness. Criminalising people that are ill is cruel, yes, but also insidious. It's also bloody futile: no self-respecting drug addict is remotely dissuaded from pursuing their habit by the legal status of the drug that they are taking. All criminalisation achieves is unsafe, unregulated drug use, the demonisation of users and the creation of an international criminal economy. You know this, I know this, and more worryingly the people that maintain this system know it, so why is it being maintained? Who benefits?

Well, on this I'm qualified to postulate. I may not have successfully overthrown a government or devised more productive, fairer and more enjoyable social systems before, so there will be some conjecture in this book; what I have done, though, with considerable assistance is navigated myself from one set of feelings where drinking and taking drugs were my only solution to a state where, one day at a time, I never drink or take drugs. What happened?

As a lost little boy in Essex, awaiting Lakeside, adoring the ambivalent beaming patriarch Ronald McDonald, I felt a discontentment. I loved my mother, was uncomfortable around my stepfather and adored my absent dad. I felt disconnected, though, and frustrated. My mum was ill a lot, I was uneasy at home, unsettled and insecure. This feeling of irritability and alienation meant I was malleable. Have you ever tried to argue with someone who doesn't want anything from you? It's hard. Have you ever noticed in a row with someone that no longer loves you that you have no recourse? No tools with which to bargain. If you stroll up to a stranger and tell them that unless they comply with your demands they'll never see you again, it's unlikely that they'll fling themselves at your feet and beg you not to go. They'll just wander off.

When people are content they are difficult to manoeuvre. We are perennially discontent and offered placebos as remedies. My intention in writing this book is to make you feel better, to offer you a solution to the way you feel.

I am confident that this is necessary. When do you ever meet people that are happy? Genuinely happy? Only children, the mentally ill and daytime television presenters.

My belief is that it is possible to feel happier, because I feel better than I used to. I am beginning to understand where the solution lies, primarily because of an exhausting process of trial, and mostly error. My qualification to write a book on how to change yourself and change the world is not that I'm better than you, it's that I'm worse. Not that I'm smarter, but that I'm dumber: I bought the lie hook, line and sinker.

My only quality has been an unwitting momentum, a willingness to wade through the static dissatisfaction that has been piped into my mind from the moment I learned language. What if that feeling, of inadequacy, isolation and anxiety isn't just me? What if it isn't internally engineered but the result of concerted effort, the product of a transmission? An ongoing broadcast from the powerful that has colonised my mind?

Who is it in here, inside your mind, reading these words, feeling that fear? Is there an awareness, an exempt presence, gleaming behind the waterfall of words that commentate on every event, label every object, judge everyone you come into contact with? And is there another way to feel? Is it possible to be in this world and feel another way? Can you conceive, even for a moment, of a species, similar to us but a little more evolved, that have transcended the idea that solutions to the way we feel can be externally acquired? What would that look like? How would that feel – to be liberated from the bureaucracy of managing your recalcitrant mind? Is it possible that there is a conspiracy to make us feel this way?

If we were cops right now, we'd look for a motive. If our peace of mind, our God-given right to live in harmony with our environment and one another, has been murdered, who are the prime suspects? Well, who has a motive?

CHAPTER 3

One Hand Clapping

By the time I was a junkie I needed drugs.

Lakeside had been a letdown. Once you've walked round its three floors, clocked a few birds, mostly uninterested, maybe nicked a pen or a CD, or got threatened by some hard lads from Tilbury, what's left to do? There's stuff to look at on the other side of the glass; mostly you can't afford it. That opened up the possibility that the problem was an economic one. If I could buy that stuff, everything would be alright. A brighter bloke would've given more consideration to that equation, but not me. I devoted myself to acquiring the means to solving the problem as presented.

Get money. I got money, I got the stuff on the other side of the glass and it didn't work. There's a moment where a new pair of shoes or whatever can be a fetishised and satisfactory little trinket. Treading like a foot-bound geisha past perilous puddles. Keeping the Reebok pumps on indoors whilst watching telly, looking down at them during the commercial break. But before too long these tootsie totems lose their lustre. 'Obviously I need a new pair of shoes, this anaesthetic is wearing off.' Luckily there's a new, improved Reebok shoe coming to a sports shop near you soon, so the carousel continues. Up and down the escalator in Lakeside, brushing past the fake ferns, gobbing in the fountain, bunking off from school, wondering quietly in some antechamber of my occupied mind what the fuss had been about but never stopping to reflect, 'Why am I even going to Lakeside? This clearly isn't working.' Making enough money to become an effective consumer takes time, dedication, devotion. The wait is miserable. It never occurred that the objective was flawed and that the rules were skewed.

When in 2011 young people all over Britain seemingly spontaneously decided to break the glass and snatch the idols from the altar, it was condemned as nihilistic and antisocial. That may be the case, what is more antisocial and nihilistic is the imposition of such dubious idolatry.

The unrelenting bombardment of consumer imagery, the intoxicating message that you are not good enough. You are too fat, spotty and wan. You are not as fit as David Beckham or Beyoncé, escape your life into this PlayStation, mask the stench of your failure with this fragrance, run from your debts in these gleaming new shoes. Don't be you. Don't be you. If it had occurred to me, and if I'd had the guts, I'd've reduced that treacherous temple to shards. I'd've torched that shrine and scarred the sky with a smog like the fugue like they'd glued to my mind.

Luckily, I didn't: my auntie Janet worked in John Lewis.

Adam Curtis, in his revolutionary documentary series *The Century of the Self*, delineated expertly how the theories of Sigmund Freud were deployed by his nephew Edward Bernays to create the profession of PR and generate the consumer boom of the fifties. Prior to the inclusion of psychological principles in sales, products were sold on the basis of utility: 'Do you have feet? Why not try shoes?' Fair enough.

What they evidently realised was that once a consumer had a pair of shoes they were no longer a viable target, that they'd killed a customer – a bit like the tobacco industry. The small but seismic interjection that Bernays, the nepotistic little villain, enacted was this: 'Buy these shoes, they'll make you feel sexy.' Then it doesn't matter how many shoes you have, you can always purchase more; who doesn't want to be more sexy? It wasn't just sexiness, though that was a lot of it. What Bernays established was the connection between consuming a product and feeling better. Of course a shoe cannot make you feel sexy indefinitely, unless you fuck it. Even then I imagine there would be a subsequent period of guilt, and you'd get some askew glances in Foot Locker. No wonder they make people put that little pop sock on before they try 'em on.

A friend of mine, and yes, I know this sentence makes me sound like a weirdo – I am a weirdo and I'm a sucker for a swami: if you want me to pay attention to your opinion, put a curtain on before you tell me. I love a mystical costume. I once waited for about five hours with a Tibetan monk in LAX airport; his passport was yellow – not due to the passage of time, that's how they print them. Yellow passports: truly Tibet is another country.

He was having a hard time getting through customs: the post 9/11 policy was draconian and all encompassing. I mean, for a Buddhist monk to be suspected of terrorism requires a pretty radical misinterpretation of the nature of Buddhism. Given their doctrine prevents them eating sausages, it's unlikely they'd endorse a policy of hijacks and tower toppling. I always have a hard time getting into the US too, due to my ancient and somewhat trivial criminal record. That don't prevent me from marching into secondary immigration with the escorting official like a cross between Hannibal Lecter and Lil Wayne.

Once I was sent all the way back to England by US customs – that was mad. I'd done a whole transatlantic flight and was promptly turned round and sent straight back home, like the grand old Duke of York (who sounded like a general whose methods were in need of investigation: 'So you've been marching

29

the men up and down the hill, have you? For days now? And have you found any weapons of mass destruction?).

When they escorted me back to the plane – honestly, this sounds like a lie, but it isn't – they cuffed me between two guards and led me back to my seat. It was like *Con Air*; in my mind I pretended I was an international Mr Big who was an enemy of the system. Then I just got on the plane and watched films and got fussed over by hostesses. It's odd the way that, in spite of the exuberant appurtenances of fame, the undeniable and, let's face it, enjoyable tokens granted by success, I've always had one foot in the gutter. In secondary immigration, as I await processing, I sit with people for whom I imagine the experience is less of a novelty. To be blunt, non-white people.

Mexican and Arabian people, mostly – I assume, I don't look at their passports; they don't have them, they're behind the desks with the border police, equally trapped and obese, behind the counter, often the same colour as the people they're casually harassing. 'Who does this notion of nation most suit?' I wonder as I sit there, unable to use my phone. Proper rich people don't encounter these rooms, these borders, these problems. For them the world is as it is when seen from space, without boundary, without limitation, full of fluid possibility and whispering wonder. Often the principles that need to be employed for the majority are already enjoyed by the elites: they support one another; they sell state assets to the businesses their friends own; when their banks collapse because of irresponsibility or misfortune, they bail their pals out. They know it's the right thing to do, it's how they treat their friends and family; they just don't want it for the rest of us.

I'm aware that now, due to my good fortune, I am a member of the 1 per cent. That now I am a tourist in poverty, when on occasion I've found myself in cuffs or in cells or cowed by authority, I know I can afford lawyers, I know I am privileged now. I know too with each word I type I am building a bridge of words that leads me back to the poverty I've come from, that by decrying this inequality, I will have to relinquish the benefits that this system has given me. I'd be lying if I said that didn't frighten me.

Anyone who's been poor and gets rich is stalked by guilt and fear. Guilt because you know it isn't fair, that life hasn't changed for everyone, and fear because you feel like a fraud, that one day there'll be a knock on the door or a tap on the shoulder or a smack in the mouth and they'll take it back. It's not like I'm gonna pay voluntary tax to our corrupt government, as suggested by that honey-glazed chump Boris Johnson; donations aren't the answer, especially not to that cartel of Etonian skanks.

Systemic change on a global scale is what's required, and because I know that is happening, that it is inevitable, that we are awakening, I will, when I know how, sever the gilded chains. 'Oh yeah, mate? When?' you could crow with legitimate suspicion. Well, I suppose, like every aspect of this project, we'll work that out together.

Anyway. I'm in an airport with a monk, remember? I felt he was a powerful dude. Like he had a connection to a light far more powerful than the strip lights that bleach you into inhumane subservience in LAX. But again, that could be because he was dressed in a curtain. I admit I'm highly suggestible (isn't he the king of the Rastas? Sorry. Probably racist, as is the whole curtain thing). If Nigel Farage kept up all his xenophobic chumminess and gin-blossomed hate but did it dressed like Aladdin, I'd vote for him at the drop of a hat.

I wonder, with this monk, had he been done up in an Adidas tracksuit and a pair of Crocs, if I'd've been so keen to hang out in customs for an additional few hours after I'd been processed. I was carrying his bag and doing translations between him and the cops – even though I don't speak

Tibetan. He'd say something, then I'd just say what I reckoned he'd said while looking all holy. We got out eventually, I took him to his taxi. He didn't even seem that grateful. I think I was getting on his nerves: 'Who is this bloke that looks like Charles Manson who keeps bugging me? I'm pretty sure he's not a qualified interpreter.'

He looked relieved when he shut the cab door and left me behind. That's the problem with trying to be friends with Buddhists. They don't get attached.

I later found out he'd served loads of time in prison for refusing to renege on his holy vows after the Chinese nicked him, and he was in LA to attend the launch of a documentary about him. I got an invite but I didn't go, I was still smarting from the rejection.

I only mentioned this monk to let you know that I am vulnerable to mystical-looking people. I actually want to recount a maxim passed on to me by my friend Radhanath Swami, which I've mentioned frequently but is irresistible in the context of this book: 'All desires are the inappropriate substitute for the desire to be at one with God.' I like ruminating on that idea. To test its efficacy, let's start with desires that are a considerable distance from rapture, or enlightenment, or transcendence. Say, for example, you really want to smash a gateau down your gob while gyrating in a rum-fuelled frenzy through a bleak suburban orgy. That's your desire – to eat cake, get drunk and have loveless sex in an appalling flat in Croydon – where is God in that grey decadence?

Our survival impulses have gone awry. We no longer live in an environment where fat and sugar, the only bits of a gateau worth having, are scarce; they are abundant, but our daft ol' anachronistic brainbox doesn't know that. That wouldn't be a problem if you had a balanced life, as part of a supportive, if not loving, community, like our species was designed to live in.

The moderation and regulation of these impulses is a challenge but not impossible – unless you live in a culture that continually stimulates these lower, atavistic desires. The booze becomes a necessary anaesthetic in conditions like these. The natural desire for sex becomes distorted when we are abstracted from our social purpose, our reproductive function, our community values and our interconnectedness.

We are living in a zoo, or more accurately a farm, our collective consciousness, our individual consciousness, has been hijacked by a power structure that needs us to remain atomised and disconnected. We want union, we want connection, we need it the way we need other forms of nutrition, and denied it, we delve into the lower impulses for sanctuary.

We have been segregated and severed, from each other and even from ourselves. We have been told that freedom is the ability to pursue petty, trivial desires when true freedom is freedom from these petty, trivial desires.

When I was bulimic, I needed to fill myself up, there was a void to fill, I needed to purge, I felt poisoned. Why? I don't buy any modern psychoanalytic diagnosis. I don't buy ADHD or OCD; they have as much veracity as MTV and the WBC. I've heard that pharmaceutical companies lobby for conditions to be diagnosed for which they have the chemical solution.

I was disconnected, cut off from the source. When I was piping and chasing and fucking and faming, what I wanted was a connection, and with no map, no key, no code, I settled for sedation.

I want to tell that eager berk, toddling from Lakeside to the Westside, to check his compass, lost in naivety. I want to tell him to sit still and breathe and ask him, do you really think that the answer lies on the other side of Simon Cowell's smile? Or in the fairground ride of lacquered pride that won't change you inside? He wouldn't've listened, though: he was very determined. And very high on drugs.

33

If you can't escape the system, you've got to escape from yourself. If you're looking for God, for salvation, for a connection, for sanctuary from the cuckoo self incubating in you, and there's no map, no guide, no story, no folk memory of how to get there, sooner or later you'll pick up a bottle, a pipe or a brick.

In Maslow's pyramid of needs, Abraham Maslow demonstrates the hierarchy of human requirements, most basic at the bottom, in a diagram. If you ask me, putting people's most basic requirements in a pyramid is bloody exclusive in the first place: they're extremely difficult to build, only pharaohs are allowed in 'em, and Indiana Jones was very nearly killed trying to get the treasure out. If Maslow really wants people to have a better standard of living, he should've used a tree, or a Primark, or something a bit more affordable. If you look at the pyramid, you'll see our most basic needs are not being catered for. Housing is on the bottom tier, and there are plenty of people whose accommodation is insecure. By the time you reach the second tier – security of body, employment, resources and health – pretty much everyone is fucked. The remaining tiers outline important but less tangible requirements, like self-esteem and spiritual and familial connection. God knows who's getting access to the penthouse floor of Maslow's pyramid, probably just the Queen and the leaders of the illuminati – that's probably where the bejewelled fun bus of privilege is taking them.

The reason I became a drug addict was because it was too painful not to. What's more, I had no means to describe the pain and no way to access any kind of solution. In the absence of any alternative, self-medication was a smart thing to do. Even now, eleven years clean, I still feel the feelings that led me to drink and take drugs, but now I have access to an alternative way to change my feelings. The techniques are simple but not easy. I believe that by sharing these methods we can overcome

34

together, not only addiction to substances, but our addiction to a way of life that has been intoxicating us all.

Firstly I had to accept that there was a problem – that was blessedly evident with drink and drugs: I was miserable, becoming physically sick, getting hospitalised and arrested. The people that loved me were afraid that I was going to die; it was clear that something had to change, but I couldn't see an alternative. I was fortunate in that my problem was obvious and pronounced but didn't kill me. I know so many people that shuffle along with anxiety and pain like a stone in their shoe, but because they're coping, holding down a job, not being forcibly institutionalised, they shuffle on, unaware that there is an alternative.

Once I'd accepted there was a problem I was able to regard my situation differently. When I was in treatment it was explained to me that I couldn't use drugs or drink, one day at a time. This was anathema to me: my life, identity and ability to cope on the most fundamental level were all dependent on substance use. I could not countenance even the most trivial interaction without some kind of chemical wetsuit to protect me. When I was introduced to the concept of 'getting to bed that night without using' I was afraid and suspicious. The fear had become a prison whose walls I would not breach.

Without the compassion of others, the support and encouragement of people who had been through what I was going through, and learned to live a different life, I would never have been able to stop. Through them I saw a vision of how I could live differently. If people whose problems had been more severe than mine could stop, then perhaps I could. More importantly than that, the feelings they described were the same as the ones I was experiencing. This gave me something that my life had lacked until that point: community. Common unity.

CHAPTER 4

Top Right Corner

Joseph Campbell said all the problems that we are experiencing – economic disparity, ecological meltdown, crime, alienation, atomisation, war, starvation – are the result of us having no communal myth. A story that unites us, defines us, in relationship to ourselves, other people and nature. Campbell says the myths that we do have are antiquated and irrelevant 'desert myths'.

Christianity, Islam and Judaism, the dominant faiths in our culture, were devised to guide people living in very different circumstances to our own – put simply, deserts. How do the teachings of Christ or Abraham or Muhammad help us in the modern, post-industrial, secular world? Not to say these stories are totally obsolete; there's some terrific advice in all of them. Primarily, though, they have become tools for oppression, segregation and conflict. The aspects of these ideologies that testify against oppression, segregation and conflict, which would seem to be the most vital bits, are consistently ignored.

Stripped of these myths altogether, though, what do we become? Where do we go? Without codes that emphasise our unity and the presence of a sacred consciousness, it seems that we become dominated by materialism and individualism.

Campbell said, 'All religions are true in that the metaphor is true.' I think this means that religions are meant to be literary maps, not literal doctrines, a signpost to the unknowable, a hymn to the inconceivable.

Edward Slingerland is a professor of Ancient Chinese Philosophy from Stanford University. Stanford University is most famous for 'The Stanford Experiment', where in 1971, for a proposed two-week period, a group of male students were divided into prisoners and guards to perform a mocked-up prison experiment. The students took to their roles so passionately that after just six days the experiment had to be disbanded. Professor Zimbardo, who was in charge of the experiment and has a name that suggests he'd be better suited to a life as a circus ringmaster, made himself prison warden and totally lost his ability to observe proceedings neutrally and, like his guards, got totally wrapped up in running a tip-top prison. By the second day of the experiment, everyone involved had apparently forgotten they were at a top university and were carrying on like lunatics, administering psychological torture, going on hunger strikes and locking folk up in solitary confinement. It was only when one of the guards' girlfriends turned up to discover her previously affable fella had turned into a shades-wearing sadist, snarling like Lee Marvin, that the plug was pulled.

The experiment was supposed to demonstrate how quickly we accept the roles that are ascribed to us. It also demonstrated, however, that Professor Zimbardo was a bit of a loose cannon.

Edward Slingerland, then, is a professor at the same university, which from one perspective is respectable and credible but from another is a bizarre thunderdome for crazy mind games. So I decide, when chatting to Slingerland, to remain objective and if at any point he tries to put me in an orange jumpsuit or tie me up and wee on me, to leg it.

Slingerland explains that Chinese philosophers like Confucius, Lao Tse, Zhuangzi and a few others were concerned with accessing a state called Wu-Wei, pronounced 'ooh-way'. This is a state of spontaneous flow. The ancient Chinese would use rituals and meditations to reach this state, and it was something that people were well into and were willing to go to extraordinary lengths to achieve. The way I identified with Wu-Wei was through football. You often hear athletes talking about being 'in the zone' – a state of un-self-conscious concentration. In the World Cup, when England inevitably end up in a quarter-final penalty shoot-out, I believe it is their inability to access Wu-Wei that means the Germans win. (This was written prior to the 2014 World Cup, so my assumption that England would reach the quarter-final has been exposed as hopelessly optimistic, but, look, I correctly predicted a German victory.)

If you are in a stadium with 80,000 screaming supporters and the hopes of a nation resting on the outcome of a penalty kick, you need to be focused, you need at that moment to be in a state of mind which is the result of great preparation but has total fluidity. Kind of like a self-induced trance where the body is free to act upon its training without the encumbrance of a neurotic mind. Stood in front of the keeper, the ball on the spot, you need to have access to all the preparation that has gone into perfecting the kick that will place the ball in the top-right corner of the net. You cannot be thinking, 'Oh God, if I miss this they'll burn effigies of me in Essex', 'I think my wife is fucking another member of the team', 'My dad never loved me, I don't deserve to score' – those mental codes are an obstacle to success.

I once was a guest on *Match of the Day*, a British Premier League football analysis show; before it began I hung out with the host, ex-England hero Gary Lineker, and pundit, another ex-England hero, Alan Shearer. I chatted to the two men about their lives as top-level athletes and they both agreed that the most important component in their success had been mental strength, the ability to focus the mind, literally in their case, on the goal, excluding all irrelevant, negative or distracting information.

Both of those men have a quality that you can feel in their presence of focus and assuredness. Lineker is more superficially affable and Shearer more stern, but there is a shared certainty and connectedness to their physicality that is interesting. I am especially interested, as I have never had that kind of physical confidence. My father and stepfather were both strong footballers, and as a child I must've received the message that the territory of sporting prowess was not mine to encroach. Without mentoring, training or initiation, this remains unaddressed. The initiation of youth by elders is a vital social ritual which is widely neglected in secular culture. When Campbell says, 'We need relevant myths, guiding stories,' he is referring to structural apparatus like this.

I was a sensitive boy. Another word for sensitive is aware; this awareness requires structure, guidance and direction, otherwise we cannot be certain what this sensitivity will become. My sensitivity became a kind of uncertainty. I still have anxieties about sport which are part of this early programming; the difference is that I now believe I can alter it. When I expressed my awe to the two England aces at their ability to be proficient under pressure, they replied, 'What about you? You can go on stage in front of thousands of people and make them laugh – that's much harder.' Through that observation I could understand how skills in one area could be transferred.

Before I go on stage or even on to a TV show, I prepare my mind, my consciousness. I repeat prayers, which, really, are linguistic codes that attune consciousness: words, mantras, vibrations that initiate neurological procedures. I treat the experience of going on stage, performing, as sacred. The origin of theatre is in religion. There is a shamanism in performance. Don't get me wrong, there doesn't have to be, you can get up on stage in front of thousands of people and confirm things they already know, if you like, but it is an opportunity to bring down information from other realms, to induce a collective state.

'That's a bit fuckin' grandiose, ain't it? Are you bringing down information from other realms when you're talking about your willy at the Hammersmith Apollo? Were you trying to induce a state of transcendent consciousness when you left that message on Andrew Sachs's answerphone?' Good point. There are definitely flaws in my nature and mistakes have been made, but I have observed that the more I have engaged with the transcendent, the more I have explored practices that are designed to alleviate the burden of materialism and individualism, the greater access I have to a feeling of serenity and freedom, the more I enjoy my work, the more I feel free. I think these techniques will work for anyone. I believe the techniques I have been taught to live drug-free, the methods I have used to improve my work and relationships, will work for anyone who uses them and will release anyone from any behaviour or pattern that impedes happiness, not just obvious stuff like drug addiction, less obvious stuff like food addiction, spending addiction or caring-too-much-what-other-people-think-of-you addiction.

The stuff I learned in order to make me better at my job has taught me that my job doesn't matter, that no individual job matters when compared to our common good. When we as individuals collectively access this frequency, we will realise that we have a shared destiny and that we can design a fair and rational system that does what it's supposed to do: enhances the whole and respects the individual.

Wu-Wei, Slingerland explained, is usually accessed when in a state of relaxed concentration in pursuit of a higher purpose.

That doesn't have to mean building an orphanage; I think the focus required to succeed in a penalty shoot-out is still an applicable example: when attuned to the objectives of the team and the supporters, an objective that transcends self, unencumbered by meddlesome individualistic concerns, you can achieve flow. When reflecting on the power that can be accessed by getting beyond the self, in the moment, it becomes apparent how prohibitive the concept of self is.

We are subject to a mass hypnosis and believe that our individual needs are more important and in conflict with our collective needs.

My friend Gareth has just returned from the 2014 FA Cup Final; he is a fan of defeated finalists Hull City FC. In spite of the extra-time defeat, he talks excitedly of how fulfilling the experience was. What he is describing is how social codes and rituals can be used to create an identity that supersedes the concept of self with which we habitually connect.

Who are you really? Are you your name? The place you are from? The negative feelings you had as a child? The anxieties you have about your future? No, these are all conceptual. In this moment now, your name is not real, your relationships are irrelevant and most importantly your thoughts, all your thoughts, are secondary. In my mind, even as I type and adhere to the metaphorical codes of language, there is another awareness. A distinct awareness. An awareness beyond, behind and around those incessant thoughts. Whilst some other inaccessible aspect of my being keeps my heart pumping, produces digestive enzymes, makes the muscles in my fingers spasm according to the precise qwerty ballet, there is awareness. This awareness is often neglected in favour of fear and regret or projected need.

If you are in Wembley Stadium, though, and Hull have just gone 2–0 up against the favourites, Arsenal, and all about you are thousands of people dressed in yellow and black, the same as you, singing the same songs as you, craving the same outcome as you, there is a synchronicity that takes you out of the self. Where else do we get to cry and pray and laugh and sing in communion these days? Where else do we receive the affirmation that we are connected to one another, that we are not born alone to die alone? In front of our TVs? Staring obediently at the glare of a smartphone? Infuriated in traffic in an aluminium cell?

We are imprisoned within, hypnotised without, denying ourselves access to the internal peace and external harmony. Can we execute the perfect jailbreak when we have become our own jailers?

CHAPTER 5

Is Everybody In?

Once by chance whilst in a church basement with other members of an abstinence-based recovery community, I heard coming through the grate an almighty wail from the main church hall.

A sound beyond language both intriguing and disturbing.

I regularly keep the company of other recovering drunks and addicts, as I learn a lot from those with more time clean than me, and more still from those with less. People with more time tell me how they continue to cope with an external world that will not submit to their imagined demands and an ego that is defined by its insatiability, this restless demon that forever wants more, that lingers like a tapeworm at the gateway to the soul, devouring and rejecting according to its needs.

From those that stagger in with fumes on their breath, stains on their teeth and fear in their eyes, I learn the most important lesson, gratitude. Whatever I endure in recovery, I need never again suffer the indignity of active addiction. The despair and hopelessness. The inexhaustible cycle of incremental self-immolation. I am reminded of how far I've come, of the miracle that, with help and humility, I can, one day at a time, live free from drugs and alcohol.

Today, though, the racket from the vent enchants me. This perversely seductive din is in need of investigation so I quietly slip out the back, though I could've clanged out in metal wellies with this crescendoing hullaballoo unabating in the next room. There is no interior door that leads me to the source of the siren so I wander round the Kensal Green church, a typical church in West London, St Martin's or St something, a few hundred years old or whatever, on a corner in the early evening. As I circumnavigate the unremarkable perimeter the alien choir grows louder and I'm pretty certain I've found the right door, so I give it an assertive shove, but it's locked. I strain to reach, a tiptoed meerkat peer up to the window, high like an apple in a fable. I can't see nothing, so I do a first knock. The first knock always quiet; the split intention of getting attention without causing a disturbance; the second knock a little more committal; the third, almost an attempt to split the wood, is the one they hear, the only one they heard, the one I might as well've done in the first place; if you're going to knock, knock.

Within there is a sparse congregation. Surprisingly small, given the discordant requiem of caterwauling. Of the thirty parishioners, all eyes face the front but for a girl aged about nine at the back with a book, at a doll's house desk, all little like when you go back to your old school.

I try not to look meek, although I wouldn't mind inheriting the earth, when I walk in. I try to seem, in spite of appearances, like I should be there. At this point, though, it doesn't matter, because the only person looking is the little girl and she is super-friendly and smiles. The adults, the everybody else, are looking to the front – well, facing the front because, most of their eyes are closed or rolled back in their heads or facing down at their feet as they sway and incant.

At the front there are three men, I reckon African, I reckon everyone is African – in the room, I mean, not everyone, although if humans all came from Africa originally then I suppose we all are. If humanity, instead of an object, is an event, then we are. If you watched in fast-frame photography, like a fungus, or a flower opening and shutting, with the sped-up movement of the sun, if you removed the concept of time that applies only to our linear lives, then humanity just sprang up and spread and grew and conquered then turned in on itself, then what? I suppose that's where we are now.

Not this lot, though, in Kensal Green. This thirty or so humans are entranced in some dance. The main man is a shoe-less bearded bloke. His hair and beard are grey, so his face looks like it's pushing through a storm cloud or dirty bubble bath, or like when Lenny Henry used to do David Bellamy. He is speaking in tongues. Loudly. The fellas that are with him are too; up there at the front of this modest church hall, unadorned with wooden rows or pulpits or stained glass, much more a place where Scouts would meet up or scones would be sold than a spirit summonsed. There's another bloke at the side playing a keyboard but you can only hear it intermittently because of the other, far weightier tunes; unidentifiable lyrics except, once in a while, I hear 'Jesus' like a twig floating by in a stream of babble.

Everyone looks poor. The women are mostly seated, occasion-ally escorted to the front by the equivalent of an altar boy or a verger. Once there the main man, the bearded preacher, bridles and jabs, spasms and gurns like a pre-ejaculatory James Brown. The younger ones, a fella with a shaved head and an orange polo shirt, like a cashier at Halfords might wear, and a bloke who in my head has already been replaced by Carlton from *The Fresh Prince of Bel Air*, swoop round each new arrival to the stage area, though let me stress it is not a stage, not raised, distinguished only in that it is nominally the 'front'. Intermittently, when a space becomes vacant, the assistants stray into the congregation to recruit another participant. The candidates are seemingly selected on the basis of eye contact, then ushered to the front. There is a pull-down screen with a projection of, I assume, a biblical text, again in an unrecognisable language, again but for the appearance here and there of 'Jesus'.

It looks to me to be a patriarchy: the men are dominant. I stand at the back, not knowing quite where to put my hands. I try clasped at the back like a royal being shown round a former colonial village, then at the front like a footballer in a wall awaiting a free kick. The little girl, who seems to be the only person there taking any managerial responsibility, sweetly offers me a chair. I tell her I'm okay. Me and her are the only ones not in some degree of reverie.

Bellamy, Orange Shirt and Carlton are screaming their heads off. A tall, really tall, man with a shaved head in a long, really long, suit is having a wild time up there and has none of my self-doubt in where to position his hands: they are thrust heavenwards, taut like a Nazi for whom one 'Sieg Heil' is just not enough, a double-barrelled Nazi.

The women sway and jump and shriek. Whilst this is all almost entirely foreign, there is something familiar, like a place in your mouth where food always gets caught. Something I recognise. It is orgiastic. This Christianity with a voodoo twist is on the brink of Dionysian breakdown. Through this ritual I see the root of ritual. The exorcising of the primal, the men engorged, enraged, the women serpentine and lithe. Only the child excluded. I get on my knees, which a few other people are doing, out of respect but also because I'm beginning to sense that it's only a matter of time before I'm ushered to the front. I've not been taught how to be religious. Religious studies at school doesn't even begin to cover it. There the world's greatest faiths and the universe's swirling mysteries are recited like bus timetables.

No teacher of RE ever said to me, 'Beyond the limited realm of the senses, the shallow pool of the known, is a great untamable ocean and we don't have a fucking clue what goes on in there.' What we receive through sight, sound, smell, taste and touch is all we know. We have tools that can enhance that information; we have theories for things that we suspect lie beyond that information, filtered through apparatus limited once more to those senses. Those senses are limited: the light range we detect is within a narrow spectrum, between infrared light and ultraviolet light; other species see light that we can't see. In the auditory realm we hear but a fraction of the sound vibrations: we don't hear high-pitched frequencies, like dog whistles; we don't hear low frequencies, like whale song. The world is awash with colours unseen and abuzz with unheard frequencies. Undetected and disregarded. The wise have always known that these inaccessible realms, these dimensions that cannot be breached by our beautifully blunt senses, hold the very codes to our existence, the invisible, electromagnetic foundations upon which our gross reality clumsily rests.

Expressible only through symbol and story as it can never be known by the innocent mind. The stories are formulas, poems, tools for reflection through which we may access the realm behind the thinking mind, the consciousness beyond knowing and known, the awareness that is not connected to the haphazard data of biography. The awareness that is not prickled and tugged by capricious emotion. The awareness that is aware that it is aware.

In meditation I access it, in yoga I feel it, on drugs it hit me like a hammer. At sixteen, staring into a bathroom mirror on LSD, contrary to instruction ('Don't look in the mirror, Russ, it'll fuck your head up'; mental note: look in mirror), I saw that my face wasn't my face at all, but a face that I lived behind and was welded to by a billion nerves. I looked into my eyes and saw there was something looking back at me that was not me, not what I'd taken to be me. The unrefined ocean beyond the shallow pool was cascading through the mirror back at me.

Nature looking at nature. Not me, little ol' Russ, tossed about on turbulent seas; these distinctions were engineered. On acid these realisations are absolute. The disobedient brain is whipped into its basket like a yapping hound cowed by Cesar Millan.

When meditating it is, initially, more tenuous. Let me explain it this way. You know that bloke who tightrope-walks between skyscrapers? No? You want his name? Google it yerself. His great triumph was a walk between the Twin Towers of the World Trade Center – I don't know the exact date except it was some time before September 11th 2001. He walks across a thick metal cable strung between the two buildings. Obviously this requires great training and presence of mind and, might I suggest, a touch of Wu-Wei. The last thing you want when suspended a mile above Manhattan in little ballet slippers is some taunting, recorded voice from your childhood telling you you're a cunt. More than the incredible bravery of the man and his tenacity and focus, I was interested in how they attached the rope between the two buildings. A helicopter? An elevator? How do you get a metal cable that probably weighs a ton across a 200-foot gap a quarter of a mile in the sky?

What they did was attach a thin piece of very light fishing thread to an arrow, then they shot the arrow between the two buildings. The thin thread was attached and then wires, strings, ropes and cables of gradually increasing thickness were pulled across. It is with increments of this nature that mantra meditation induces a different state of consciousness.

At first when you close your eyes the mantra is like a thin thread, continually interrupted by other thoughts. A mantra is just a word, a thought vibration, repeated in the mind. At some point in the past the mind has, for some reason, taken on the duty of trying to solve every single problem you are having, have had or might have in the future, which makes it a frenetic and restless device.

There is always something for it to think, always something for it to solve, so whenever I first start to meditate the mantra is a tiny clear droplet lost in a deluge of sludge. I'm not a person who finds meditation a doddle or to whom yoga comes naturally. To tell you the truth, I find the whole business a bit poncey and contrary to the way I used to see myself. It's only the fact that I decimated my life by aggressively pursuing the models of living that were most immediately available – eating, wanking, drinking, consuming, getting famous – that I was forced to look at alternatives. Alternatives that you could call spiritual.

I'm not a total idiot. If taking drugs worked I'd still be doing it, if promiscuous sex was continually fulfilling I'd've carried on, if fame and money were the answer I'd hurl this laptop out of the window and get on with making movies. They don't work, in spite of what I was told, and there's a reason for that, we'll discover.

I don't see myself as a yoga person or a man who meditates and prays and eats well and says 'Namaste' or 'God bless you'. I became that because I exhausted all other options. There was a point, I'll admit, when I flung myself, full force, into an LA New Age lifestyle. I'd just got divorced and a movie I wanted to do well didn't meet my expectations. My response to this was to stop shaving and start wearing pyjamas outdoors.

This is relatively typical behaviour for any lunatic; we see them everywhere, twitching, twisting, hollering at their imagined foes. The difference is I was doing it in Hollywood and my pyjamas looked suitably ethnic, so I think I got away with it. Although my mates have subsequently told me they were worried, and thinking about it they did drop hints like 'Trim your beard, you look like a shoe-bomber' and 'Stop wearing them gap-year trousers, you fuckin' nut' but I was immune.

A friend of mine, himself no stranger to mental illness, and that's putting it lightly – he's a right fucking fruitcake, living at his mum's on disability benefits – said to me, 'In India if you have a mental breakdown they don't build you back up again, they leave you in communion with God.' He then looked up, mimicking, I supposed, an Indian yogi, and raised his hands and eyes skywards as if he were playing a tiny accordion just in front of his hairline. 'They say, "Ah, he's in conversation with Brahman now" and they revere you. In this country they just give you a bus pass.' He carried on waving his hands and flickering his eyes.

'You've demonstrated that for too long now, mate,' I said; we were in company.

'I'm not demonstrating it,' he said, 'I'm doing it.'

He does have a free bus pass.

In a way I suppose what he meant was that when you redact the conventional behaviours and beliefs of your culture you're regarded as a nutter. But who are you, stripped of those things that tell you who you are? Your job, your car, your husband, your kids, your favourite TV show, that pasta dish you do that's just so mmm? All these things that will one day go with death if not before. With death if not before.

Good to find out who you are with nothing, because nothing is really what we have. During this pyjama time I was doing a lot of meditation and a lot of yoga, kundalini yoga. Kundalini yoga is the crack-cocaine of yoga; if hatha is a mild weed high, Iyenger is a deep hash glow and ashtanga is amphetamine, kundalini blows the fucking doors off.

Technically it is distinctive because of its use of 'breath of fire' – this is a rapid, rhythmic, usually nasal inhalation/exhalation that you motivate from the abdomen. This is accompanied by mantras and movements and definitely changes the way you feel. A cynical person might call this change wooziness brought on by hyperventilation, but I think that's reductive. What is the alteration in consciousness that occurs during inadvertent hyperventilation? There are several yoga positions that induce in me (in me? Is there a me?) a state of awareness that is cracked open with sudden abundance. Like the filters and commentary are suddenly flipped off. I don't in these scarce and beautiful moments have a conventional sense of self, I don't know my name, I don't know what I want or what I'm afraid of, all that data is wiped. And I fucking like it.

An hour of these kundalini exercises in the correct sequence can induce some interesting states of consciousness. Most yogas relax or invigorate. If you do hatha yoga your mental focus on breath and movement reduces the torrent of egoic thinking and designates the mind in the present, which, let's face it, is where it belongs; no point leaving the mind loitering around last Tuesday, especially if something bad happened.

Ashtanga is more aerobic and through the repeated move-ment and the strict relationship between breath and 'asana', or position, a vital elation can be experienced. My understanding of most yoga is that the exercises connect mind, body and spirit and in so doing alleviate the suffering of incessant thinking. When relieved of this thinking peace can come; like it says in the St Francis prayer, you become 'a channel of the peace', an instrument of a state that exists and wants to be expressed but is blocked by the kinks in the pipe, typically angst, fear, pride, whatever.

Interestingly, Ganesh the elephant-headed Hindu deity is known as the remover of obstacles. When I first heard that I thought it meant obstacles like a boss who irritates you or a boyfriend of a girl you like. Now I think it means the obstacles within the self that prevent you from being in harmony with 'God'. If you can be free from pride, self-pity, self-centredness, selfishness, jealousy, envy, intolerance, impatience, greed, glut-tony, lust, sloth, arrogance and dishonesty, then there is a state of serenity and connectedness within. Like Jesus said, 'The kingdom of heaven is within,' which seems, once and for all, to bust wide open the daft, afterlife view of heaven as some kind of Llando Calrissian cloud kingdom that you can get into, like Alton Towers, if you acquire enough good-boy tokens.

Kundalini in my view is more boldly transcendent, more euphoric, than other yoga that I've done, so I obviously got totally addicted to it and started doing it all the time. The experience wasn't entirely free from ego either as I was quite prolific in my physical engagement with female members of the class and eventually nominated myself as leader and took over the entire shebang like Hitler in a sari. In my hands, or, more importantly, my head, even a tranquil canvas like a yoga class can end up spattered with the neon splurge of my avaricious ego.

The need for personal vigilance is well demonstrated by my conduct around the kundalini yoga experience. I have no doubt that kundalini yoga as a technology for improving consciousness is valid and that doing it in communities is beneficial, but there is no context in which my ego, if not fastidiously monitored, won't run amok. It is extremely difficult to put aside a lifetime's conditioning. The only way I can stay drug-free is one day at a time, with vigilance, humility and support. My tendency is still, after eleven years, to drift towards oblivion. My appetite for attention too can only be positively directed with great care.

Look out your window, turn on your TV, see which values are being promoted, which aspects of humanity are being celebrated. The alarm bells of fear and desire are everywhere; these powerful, primal tools designed to aid survival in a world unrecognisable to modern, civilised humans are relentlessly jangled.

A facet of our unevolved nature, comparable to that which still craves sugar and fat, a relic from the days when it was scarce, is being pricked and jabbed and buzzed every time we see a billboard bikini or a Coca-Cola floozy. Our sabre-toothed terrors and mammoth anxieties are being dragged up and strung out by shrill transmissions about immigrants, junkies, pit-bulls and cancer. Once I sat in that kundalini class, in white robes, cross-legged, with pan-piped serenity caressing the congregation as we meditated as one, and all I was really thinking about was if I should buy a gun.

I was in America after all and you are allowed a gun. Have you ever held a 38 Glock? It feels so cool in your hand. Even the word makes you feel tough. Glock. Tupac had one, Eminem loves them – I want one. Never mind all this hippie-dippie, yin-yang, Ramadan, green-juice bullshit; I want a gat, like Tupac. Of course I think things like that: the messages that are broadcast on that frequency move fast and stick hard. Look at the state of the world. I didn't buy one, though; my mum had to remind me that I'm a peace-loving lad and that if I had a gun in the house, the person most at risk would be me. The kundalini techniques worked, they advanced my mind, they tuned me in; how much more powerful these techniques would be if supported by a culture of spiritual evolution, not one of self-fortification.

Perhaps if my religious education had constituted more than glum, Calvinist witterings and brass rubbings of church doors I'd be better equipped in the midst of the numinous howl in the Kensal Green church hall. Here a sentiment like 'Thine is the Kingdom, the power and the glory' is not a bureaucratic proposal stencilled on to a municipal sign – 'No diving, no heavy petting, glory in the blazing light of the Lord' – but a dance, a stomp, a chant.

I've been hunched at the back for a little while now, a static Rodin of disingenuous genuflection, when I think, 'Would it really matter if I got taken to the front?' I'm the only member of the congregation aside from the little girl who has as yet been spared the backslapping, prodding and spinning that occurs when you're summonsed to the front. I consider leaving – it'd be easy enough, just a nod to the tweenie-administrator and then a purposeful sidle. But, I think, how bad can it be? I'll just be hauled up the front before this spellbound assembly. I mean, it might be embarrassing, but no one ever died of embarrassment, even if shame is the number one cause of suicide. These paddocks we inhabit, these mind-made manacles that hold us back from the exhilarating naked chase of freedom. I should stay to prove to myself, other me, negative, fearful me, that we can do it, me and him, the pair of us, both 'me's': confident, strident, connected me and fearful, clenched, small-town, small-minded me, together.

I decide to stay, knowing too that anecdotes are the product of decisions like these. And as I kneel in negotiation with aspects of myself, along comes Carlton.

He seems slightly self-conscious too, like he is not too enraptured to notice that I'm conflicted. He gives me a 'Shall we do this?' nod and I give him a 'We shall' one back.

On the short walk to the front, past the others, either bowing or kneeling or whirling or howling, I feel glad that my life is this way; so full of jarring experience. Sometimes you feel that life is full and beautiful, all these worlds, all these people, all these experiences, all this wonder. You never know when you will encounter magic. Some solitary moment in a park can suddenly burst open with a spray of pre-school children in high-vis vests, hand in hand; maybe the teacher will ask you for directions and the children will look at you curious and open and you'll see that they are perfect. In the half-morning, half-grey glint, the cobwebs on bushes are gleaming with such radiant insistence, you can feel the playful unknown beckoning. Behind impassive stares in booths, behind the indifferent gum chew, behind the car horns, there is connection.

Now I'm up the front and Tall Bloke, Long Suit, is still Sieg-Heiling, women are still jiggling and beseeching. There is an unspoken acknowledgement that I am an interloper, that I am unlike everybody else there, neither Eritrean nor Ethiopian, and that there is a risk therefore that I am there to mock or judge or disrupt, and I'm capable of all those things. The three main men, Bellamy, Orange Shirt and Carlton close in and it's a bit like a scene from *The Lion King* – you know, one of the scary bits. Then there are hands on me and a kind of revolving. It's a bit like being the blindfolded one in 'pin the tail on the donkey'.

I don't know about you, but I'm a bit too self-conscious – well, 'selves-conscious', because there's more than one of me in here – to just leap into full-force abandonment. I've got a too finely attuned sense of humour; I'm too English to blaze out on to a dance floor or altar and start flinging my limbs around. The second voice, the fearful me, is not going to stand for that. He's in there, perched on an ottoman, waiting for me to relax, and then with an intonation like Terry Thomas, 'What on earth do you think you're doing? I suggest you sit back down.' It's hard to commit or join in with him in there. Bellamy has clearly overcome any doubt he has in his self, if not in me, as he is now insistently enquiring, 'Do you accept Jesus Christ?' He says it in English, so he definitely knows I'm not Eritrean; the jig is up. 'Do you accept Jesus Christ?' he says again, like Jesus is a credit card and I'm an unhelpful waiter.

The conditions of the enquiry do not suggest that there is time for me to go into my honest answer, 'Yes, but there are caveats.'

Jesus Christ, the Son of God, sent to earth to redeem us all. Jesus Christ, the Jewish, nationalist radical. Jesus Christ, the metaphor for the divine within the corporeal. Jesus Christ, the human being superimposed, literally, placed on the cross:

the pagan, geometric emblem that represents on the vertical plane the relationship between the earth and the divine, and on the other, horizontal plane the lateral relationships between individual humans.

Christ as the end of paganism, the beginning of individualism, of idolatry. Of the acceptance that some humans are more equal than others. Christ as a reminder that we must all constantly die and be born again, moment to moment, to live forever in the now, as Wittgenstein says 'if eternity is taken not to be an infinite temporal duration but the quality of timelessness, then are we not all eternal if we live in the present.'

Christ as the symbol that the flesh human, that the carnal human ape, has expired and that we can achieve no more, until we transcend, until we ascend into new conscious realms and manifest the divine, 'on earth as it is in heaven'?

'Do you accept Jesus Christ?' he says again, and this time gives me a bit of a prod, which he tries to pass off as shamanic but I think is actually frustration. The answer, as I have outlined above, is conditionally 'yes'; the most expedient answer is a totally unconditional 'yes', so that is the answer I give.

'Yes.'

Bellamy wants more.

'Demon out!' he hollers, and grabs at my gut in a manner that in any, literally any, other context would be totally unacceptable. I mean, he grabs a handful of my belly – I'm not fat, so he's probably got some actual intestine an' all – then he sort of twists it like an apple stalk. I'm torn between the respectful compliance required of a tourist, shock, and also curiosity, as the place he grabs is where, if asked to point, I would consistently locate my anxiety. Anxiety that is exacerbated by being grabbed in the guts in a church hall in Kensal Green.

When, at the umpteenth time of asking, I admit in a voice as loud as I can muster that yes, I do accept Jesus, everyone cheers. They are well chuffed that I accept Jesus. I then shuffle back and take a seat, now less self-conscious and a little more entitled.

When the worship is at its peak, its wild, emphatic, orgiastic, juddering, shrieking, spasming peak, I wonder how will they ever climb down from this summit of selflessness? How will this animalistic holy frenzy segue into people shaking hands and stacking chairs?

At some Anglican sermon in Surrey, the 'file down the aisle, handshake, smile' ending is the energetic climax of proceedings. After a polite rendition of 'Jerusalem' (in which Blake was apparently being sarcastic) or 'All Things Bright and Beautiful' (which Stewart Lee breaks down beautifully) there isn't a moment of post-coital awkwardness where everyone thinks, 'Fuck me, we really let ourselves go there'; the hymns, the prayers, the sermon and the departure never interrupt the frequency of neat obedience. That is of course the problem. I mean, what's the point? If there is some omnipotent force behind all phenomena and we are trying to access it through our consciousness, then surely that can't be done without breaking a sweat or ruffling some hair?

The lady I sit next to explains that the language is Amharic, that this is a community of Ethiopian and Eritrean people, that they are Christian. I'm invited to stand up and introduce myself; from the pulpit, before I stand to speak, though, it is announced by the pastor that I am famous.

Another bloke, it transpires, is also there for the first time and feels compelled to admit apologetically that he isn't famous, which makes me feel a bit sad.

The problem I anticipated of re-entering a more normal tone of social interaction does not manifest. No one seems remotely bothered. I suppose to them it's normal and their ritual can withstand various pitches. A few people want photos or whatever: the little girl, Carlton, Tall Bloke, who is called Julian and is when he switches from Amharic to English actually bloody charming. As I leave I feel the value of shared ritual, community, common unity and a forum in which to express energy and sensations that don't have any safe context in secular society. We are paying a price for that. Where do we see this sense of abandon? Where do we participate in mass rituals of unity and transcendence? Where is it safe to put aside ego and self-consciousness? Anfield? Old Trafford? Upton Park?

Here in these aluminium coliseums there is licence to vent. For me, football is fused with fear and manhood and violence but also with craving, belonging and hope. It usually takes until about half time before I am even half relaxed. At first I am self-conscious, too aware of myself and my boundaries, real and imagined, to submerge. By staring into the lawn portal, by yielding to the rhythm of the chant, the drama of the game, the acceptance of the temporary order of the rules and the end-to-end chaos within it, I become hypnotised.

Where are we relieved from the bean counting, box ticking, horizonless mute-horror of our technological gulags? Leicester town centre, midnight, midwinter, drink some cider, get inside her. Two for one, in the *Sun*, Eng-ger-land. Do a gram, drop a pill, download an app, eat some crap, get a slap, mind the gap, do a line, Instagram, little grope in a cab.

CHAPTER 6

Tiny Problems in Infinite Space

When I still used, I was once working in Ibiza, hedonism capital of the nineties and turn of the millennium. People swayed in sweaty swathes and stayed, pilled-up for days. I couldn't participate, because I was too shy or broken, caught on some taut barbed wire in my mind. Me and my mate Matt, high one night, lost ourselves, found ourselves in a wood and pretended to be animals. It was just us, and we prowled and circled around. We locked eyes and growled and danced. 'Let's pretend we're animals' was forgotten and we *were* animals.

We are animals. We are free animals with a divine spark, we're not in a farm or a zoo or a theme park, we're free. We've forgotten that we're free. There's so much to do, so much on TV, that we've forgotten that we're free.

No rituals or myths that remind us that we have a shared destiny and shared needs, even if our shared destiny is death and our shared need is life. We have downloaded a program with a virus in it. We've been boxed off and ripped off.

Terence McKenna, the philosopher shaman fella, said the all-encompassing stance of conventional science is 'Give us one free miracle and we'll explain the rest.'

That one miracle is the spontaneous appearance of all matter, energy, phenomena, consciousness and rules in a single instant, which was preceded by and is surrounded by nothingness. This is the theory of the Big Bang.

My belief is that we do not currently operate on a frequency of consciousness that is capable of interpreting the information required to understand the great mystery.

I believe that the mechanical model for understanding nature is a metaphor that science has got stuck on: this prevailing idea that humans are machines, biological robots with computer-like brains. This belief will, to the advanced species that we are evolving into, seem as absurd as the flat-earth theories that we scoff at now.

Those flat-earth folk weren't just pretending they thought the earth was flat, they genuinely believed it; they looked down at the flat ground and its flat appearance and took that as empirical evidence of its flatness. They could not conceive of another way of seeing it.

Left to me the flat-earth theory would still be dominant. I've never been to space and seen the earth's curvature; I've seen pictures of the spherical earth placed in the context of our solar system or spinning like a misty marble in the blackness, but I can't say for sure what it looks like from space because I'm standing on it. It took a new emergent strain of understanding that challenged the dogma of the time to recontextualise the way we see our planet.

The time we live in now is similar because the mechanistic, reductive dogma of 'scientism' – the belief that everything in the world can be explained using the scientific method – is about to be similarly overthrown. There are just too many questions unanswered and unanswerable. Consciousness, the consciousness that is now experiencing these words, has no explanation in science. Scientists believe that matter has no consciousness and that consciousness comes from matter; that 70 per cent of the universe is made from dark matter, although they don't know what that is, what it does or anything. Just that it's there.

Science requires faith the way religion does. Science requires acceptance of metaphor, just the way religion does. 'Does science cause wars the way religion does?' you might ask. I would say those conflicts are actually about territory, either ideological or physical, and that those ideas are materialistic in the same way science is – and the weapons with which those wars are fought, who creates those?

I'm not condemning the process of gathering and testing information to advance our understanding of our environment – that is plainly a useful human tool. What I query is this pragmatic system of research being allowed to invade territories for which it was not designed to cater.

An astronomer once explained to me that the galaxy we live in, the Milky Way, is vast, too vast to be understood without metaphor, so he gave me one. He said if you picture the Milky Way as being the size of mainland Europe, our solar system – that's Mars, Venus, Saturn, us, here on Earth (you remember from school) – in a Milky Way the size of Europe our solar system would fit inside a single teacup somewhere in Belgium. He paused for my amazement, which I duly offered.

But really what can you say?

'Ooh, a teacup.'

'Blimey, Belgium.'

'Cor, it makes you think, doesn't it?'

Then he added, clearly sensing I was at a bit of a loss for words, having just been reduced to a dot on a speck in a teacup in a continent, 'Russell, there are 400 million *known* galaxies in our universe.'

I'd been looking through a telescope at Jupiter (or what we call Jupiter; it can't possibly know it's called that any more than a newborn baby can know whether it's a Christian or a Muslim), Jupiter is orbited by four moons. What struck me as I looked at Jupiter, 370 million miles away, in perfect suspension, with the moons visibly revolving, was not the might of this planet, which the Romans took to be the king of their gods, but its elegant fragility. The awe. Whatever you are doing, Jupiter and its moons are up there, silent or roaring, observing or ignoring, connected through time and light and an unbreakable chain of subatomic threads.

We receive data through five portals, five windows; the house of human consciousness has but five windows. Do you imagine that we will ever perceive all through these five windows? Do you imagine that that which is most important can ever be seen? How do you describe the most important things that have ever happened to you? The moment you knew you loved her: can you reassemble that magnetic pull with the Lego of light and language? The moment you heard he'd died: can you define it, calcify it, crystalise it, make it live again, or is it at best a kind of taxidermy that language can provide? A stuffed dead effigy with cold unseeing eyes.

And Jupiter revolves. And the moon watches, the moon you saw as a child, the moon that hung in the sky when Christ was crucified, the crescent moon, like a tear in heaven as the Prophet heard Allah. All human history, every poem, every lie, all here on this sphere.

> What am I, a small creature measuring seven spans of my own hand? I am enclosed in a potlike universe composed of material nature, the total material energy, false ego, ether, air, water and earth. And what is Your glory? Unlimited universes pass through the pores of Your body just as particles of dust pass through the openings of a screened window. (*Bhagavata Purana*, 10.14.11)

It is perhaps because of passages like the one above that Joseph Campbell favoured Hindu and pre-Hindu mythology as an efficient tool to convey important stories. Clearly this passage is poetic, philosophical and attempting to explain a mystery which now has been colonised by materialistic thinking. I also wonder whether 'seven hand spans' is a normal height. I've been trying to measure myself using this technique but am always hijacked at the groin. The American poet and feminist Muriel Rukeyser said, 'The world is not made of atoms, it's made of stories.' I suppose what that implies is that atoms are themselves a metaphor, a symbol, a tool for telling a story. They were only temporarily the zenith of our understanding; they have already been surpassed in the spiralling journey down into the microcosmic by quarks.

What mayhem too lives in that tiny world where electrons appear simultaneously in the same place – not different electrons, the same electron. Where electrons will behave as either particles or waves, depending on whether or not they are being observed. I don't want to seem ungrateful to science – science, after all, is what has provided me with this story – but now is the time to render unto Caesar what is Caesar's.

The ideological battle that needed to be fought against repressive orthodoxy, bigoted institutions and repressive religions can now be won. For it not to be futile we must overcome similar dogma now in the field of science.

A person experiences life as something separated from the rest – a kind of optical delusion of consciousness. Our task must be to free ourselves from this self-imposed prison, and through compassion, to find the reality of Oneness. (Albert Einstein.)

That bed-headed genius was on to something: we need to focus on relevant truths, the truths that will aid our survival.

Not the temporary truth that we are dislocated, mechanical blobs motivated by our cocks and our guts.

We must promote the pertinent truths, the way that bigoted Republicans have Frankensteined the perfect Christ for their cause. Their Jesus has pulled off one miracle further to those documented, by becoming some sort of gun-toting, homophobic, Rasputined-up Donald Trump.*

Bible Jesus, who, let's face it, has probably been through several prejudicial edits to reach the King James, whitewashed version, is still a considerable theological distance from the vicious prick that them lot are so into.

For a kick-off he doesn't give a toss about sex or pushing misogyny or homophobia. He in fact seems much more interested in the corruptive power of money. 'Give to the poor and receive treasure in heaven.'

Jesus is pretty committed to sharing. Also, as we know, it's the moneylenders that Jesus kicks out of the temple: 'This is my Father's house and you have turned it into a den of thieves.' It's the only time Jesus got really wound up. Even when he was being unjustly nailed to a cross he stayed mellow; when the crowd, given the chance to pardon one of the convicts up for crucifixion, chose Barabbas, a known crook, Jesus took it on the chin. The only time he ever let himself go and knocked over tables was when the financial industry was prioritised over normal people.

It wasn't the gays he kicked out of the temple: 'This is my Father's house and you have turned it into a gay bar.' The gays were fine; Jesus had no policy on sex.

---

* The idealized Christ of the right would be like Donald Trump, but with these additional qualities – the adjectives indicate that the qualities are an enhancement, exaggeration or supplement to Donald as is – that's why I didn't just write "Donald Trump" without adjectives. So I'm not saying Donald Trump is comparable to the Russian mystic Rasputin, who, incidentally, I adore or, I am legally obliged to say, homophobic.

I met some members of the Westboro Baptist Church once and they were alright. It was like they knew they were being silly. I had them on a chat show I was doing in America. I felt like I could've gone, 'Come on, lads, you don't really believe that God hates fags, do you?' and they'd've gone, 'Of course not, don't be daft, we're just having a bit of fun.'

The promotion of homophobia to priority status on the Lord's behalf takes some doing. The scriptural evidence that he gave a toss is scant. It seems to me that a lot of people are using religious arguments to advance their own prejudices. I don't think these preachers of hate and mad mullahs and whatnot were one day reading their doctrine of choice in a sanguine mood, aglow with joy and tolerance, when they happened upon a verse of bigoted scripture. 'Bloody hell! I was inclined to quite like the gays – my cousin is one – but look! Here in Leviticus it quite clearly states, 'Don't lie down with another man.' Well, that's that.'

Clearly prejudice is a permutation of some psychological fear, later mandated by convenient evidence from the book. If God appeared tomorrow and said he'd changed his mind, would homophobia disappear? You'd think if God was that bothered about homosexuality he'd've mentioned it in his top ten dos and don'ts. The Ten Commandments – it's not in there.

From a biblical perspective homosexuality is not considered as transgressive as the tenth commandment, 'Thou shalt not covet thy neighbour's oxen.'

If he'd considered it that important, he could've added a commandment – I mean, he is God, he doesn't have to stick to decimal neatness. He could just go, 'Oh yeah, number eleven is "Don't be gay."' Or let the whole oxen thing fall by the wayside.

From a balanced reading of the Ten Commandments we can only assume that God would prefer you to have gay sex than to covet your neighbour's oxen. If you'd had a terrible day at work, and had to do some sinning, just to unwind, the Commandments are clear about which sin is considered more unholy.

'God, I've had a terrible day at work, I've got to let off some steam. Either I'm going to have sex with Terry or I'm going to covet my neighbour's oxen.'

'What?! No, you mustn't do that, you better go hang out with Terry.'

'Thank you, Lord. I'm going to slide my erect penis right up Terry's anus . . .'

'Fair enough, my son, I don't really have a policy on that. I will ask, though, that you don't look over next door's fence at them grazing oxen, then imagine, in your mind, "What would it be like if those oxen were my oxen?" Don't do that, will you?'

'I won't. I'm going to empty myself into Terry, then put my mouth over his rect . . .'

'Okay! Do what you've gotta do! Just remember: those are not your oxen!'

Anyone who claims to be operating on a model designed to fulfil the will of Jesus, or Allah, or Krishna, or anyone, who isn't first and foremost dedicated to the union of all humankind and service of the needy is on a massive blag. Whether that's hillbilly situationists like the WBC, self-serving neo-liberalists or Taliban gangsters.

Any American politician who says they're Christian must have as their uppermost priority the removal of the money-lenders from the temple, the undue, corrupt and disgusting influence of the financial industry on public life. Any British politician, like Prime Minister David Cameron, who claims to be a Christian, which means 'to practise the teachings of Jesus Christ', has to, like Jesus, heal the sick, not, like a cunt, sell off the NHS.

'Which bit of Christianity do you believe in?'

'Ooh, I'd have to say the bit where you turn up at a church in a suit at Christmas or Easter and stand around looking a bit solemn.'

Yes, that's clearly what he was driving at.

The only meaningful interpretation of any religious teaching is to honour the divine within ourselves and love the divine in one another.

To disavow the individualistic, materialistic evangelism of our age and serve that which transcends these lowly impulses.

Any version of any theology that manifests as dazzling costumes and palaces for the bloke at the front is bollocks.

Most religion is wrapped round the bellicose enforcement of a metaphor, but that doesn't mean we should dismiss the mystery. Science has donned the haughty robes of the pedagogues it displaced, but we can be grateful for the new lexicon and the contemporary understanding of ancient truths.

When I was an atheist it was because I rejected authority, and why not reject the supreme authority of God, particularly that boring fucker on *Songs of Praise*. I could reject him with the unsentimental dispatch of a squeezed blackhead. When I got clean from drugs and alcohol I saw that the way I'd always seen the world was limited. It will always be limited. By yielding authority to a benign power I found a key to transcend previous limitations. Modest limitations, like being unable to survive without the use of drugs and alcohol. Until the time when I got clean I'd had little experience of loving, powerful authority. Authority had only been corrupt or inefficient in my experience.

My nan, who I never much loved (I had a 50 per cent success rate with nans: loved one, was cool about the other), and I were once ambulating down an Essex street. I believe it was Brentwood, now famed as the setting for the opera to idiocy that is *The Only Way Is Essex*.

My indifference to this nan need not have been her fault; she may simply have been an outer emblem of my inner discomfort. How did it feel in there to you when you were a child, in the aquarium of your head? I was lonely in mine as the world swam by in immaculately choreographed schools, like an inaccessible gang of Nemos. I was only really at ease with my mum and animals, and I treated them pretty badly.

If you feel how I felt, I have been taught a few techniques that might help you. Here's one for a kick-off: you have to forgive everyone for everything. You can't cling on to any blame that you may be using to make sense of the story of your life. Even me, with my story of one nan that I love and another that I don't – that story is being used to maintain a certain perspective of mine, a perspective that justifies the way I am, and by justifying the way I am I ensure that I stay the same. I'm no longer interested in staying the same, I'm interested in Revolution, that means I have to go back and change the story of my childhood.

You might think of yourself as some kind of umpire of veracity and righteousness: 'You can't change truth, you can't forgive people who've done wrong.' What helped me to overcome those outmoded concepts was the understanding that there is no such thing as right or wrong, merely an interrelated system of beliefs. I was taught that my reality, including the whole concept of 'a self', is a construct and that I can alter it if it isn't conducive to my well-being.

This perhaps undeservedly, unloved nan and I were walking along, likely only flung together as my mum was away in hospital, and she was explaining to me her religious beliefs. I now know that these beliefs were typical Protestant doctrine, and she was a relatively typical woman of her time and background. I recently researched my family tree and quite quickly labels of class are smudged into nonsense. For a couple of generations back, it's all very proletariat in every direction: Bethnal Green bottle-makers and jobs that belong in Dickens. But with the generational doubling that occurs, before too long it's a muddle of all manner of colliding types: scullery maids and sculptors, officers and gentlemen; there's no clear upstairs downstairs, as our ancestors were all resolutely fucking each other on the landing. The filthy dead perverts.

Then, of course, through the umbilical link we all tumble backwards down the spiraling DNA staircase to one common ancestor in Africa, and before that some bunch of curious monkeys. Down and down we go unto the sea, unto the dust, the single cellular dust. What impulse drove one cell to become two? What yearning pulled the fish on to the land? What caused apes to walk upright? Some invisible magnetic pull. Is there a difference between attraction and intention? Where is evolution taking us?

The early Christians favoured the fish as the symbol of their burgeoning cult, the cross perhaps still regarded as being too recent to be apt. The fish symbol that they deployed was appropriated in fact from a pre-existing pagan order that believed an oceanic goddess had given birth to humanity. Isn't that just a different way of saying we came from the sea?

Water too, in emblems both inner and outer, in the world of dreams, in the world of myth, symbolises the unconscious. 'Dreams are private myths, myths are public dreams,' said ol' Joe Campbell. I'm getting overly familiar now as I ransack his legacy.

The unconscious, the aspect of ourselves we by definition do not know, is difficult to describe. Carl Jung believed that we had a collective unconscious, that we were all sharing it like a bunch of unwitting communists.

Jung the mystical Sundance Kid, to Sigmund Freud's staunch Butch Cassidy, observed that common motifs cropped up in people's dreams, and that there was a corollary to symbols and even structure that could be found in various folk tales and myths. So Jung offered up the idea that consciousness could exist outside the mind and that we all have access to it.

This is implicit too in Campbell's work. In his global studies of the stories humans tell each other to make sense of the world, he found astonishing consistencies in the formula. Folk in Africa, Iceland, Nairobi and Wisconsin are all telling each other similar stories. How the fuck is that happening if we're a bunch of dislocated individuals living in a bunch of dislocated tribes?

A way of understanding it might be that the unconscious mind is up to all sorts of stuff all day long that I'm not taking responsibility for: blinking, peristalsis, digestion, fighting bacteria, fashioning perfect little stools that could be sold at a village fete with a flag stuck in them saying 'Russell's unconscious mind made this'.

Everybody's anatomical unconscious is doing more or less the same thing, unless they are 'deficient' or 'mutated'. David Eagleman said, 'Thinking that you are in charge of your totality of being, with all its complex facilities, is like a stowaway on an ocean steamliner thinking he's the captain of the ship.'

Conventional, mechanical, materialistic science will tell you that's because there's proteins stored in the genes telling them to do that. This isn't strictly true though. If you took an arm and a leg and ground them into a powder (and I'm not suggesting you do: it'd likely land you in the clink), you would discover that there is no particular genetic data that determines that a leg must be a leg and an arm, an arm. There is some untraceable component that does that defining work. Some people think that there is a magnetic memory, outside of the material, that guides the direction of the manifestation.

Once you accept the concept of data being held beyond the physical, new worlds open up. In a way, if my unconscious 'mind' and yours are doing the same job, more or less, of generating cells and movements and procedures, the imposition of anatomic individualisation is redundant.

We're all doing the same thing, dreaming the same dream, in the words of Belinda Carlisle, who also said, 'Heaven is a place on earth,' by which she might've meant that the concept of a divine realm is not in the hereafter but present now as a realm of being, achieved when we look beyond our material parameters and individualistic desires. I'm going to listen to that track again; in fact the whole album warrants further scrutiny in the light of these revelations.

Again, I'm not advocating the abandonment of science like a modern-day Ned Ludd (a concept he would've especially hated), smashing up the microscopes and telescopes and particle accelerators, merely that we accept that we have allowed it to stray beyond its rightful dominion. When you get Richard Dawkins yapping menopausally at some poor hamstrung old archbishop, while we dismantle our environment due to the materialistic, pessimistic principles that the atheistic tyranny of the day is tacitly sponsoring, it is time to look for a new story.

If all there is is only that which we can prove, then we live as disconnected, condemned animals. We need faith now more than ever because our ideologies are obscuring the fact that we have more important things in common than in conflict.

My nan walks purposefully with me at her side. We are definitely not *flâneurs*, who wandered with no specific intent, mostly through the Parisian streets of a century ago, knowing that abundant wonder will be uncovered if you trust the day to be glorious. Of course they were bowling about in Paris, likely off their nuts on absinthe, not shuffling up Brentwood High Street in Clarks sandals with a fist full of dolly mixtures and a nan they don't much like, because the narrative of themselves they've constructed requires adversity.

73

'I believe in God,' says my nan in a way that makes the idea of an omnipotent, unifying frequency of energy manifesting matter from pure consciousness sound like a chore. An unnecessary chore at that, like cleaning under the fridge.

I tell her, plucky little seven-year-old that I was, that I don't. This pisses her off. Her faith in God is not robust enough to withstand the casual blasphemy of an agnostic tot. 'Who do you think made the world then?' I remember her demanding as fiercely as Jeremy Paxman would later insist I provide an instant global infrastructure for a post-revolutionary utopia.

'Builders,' I said, thinking on my feet. This flummoxed her and put her in a bad mood for the rest of the walk. If she'd hit back with 'What about construction at a planetary or galactic level?' she'd've had me on the ropes. At that age I wouldn't't've been able to riposte with 'an advanced species of extraterrestrials who we have been mistakenly ascribing divine attributes to due to our own technological limitations' or 'a spontaneous cosmic combustion that contained at its genesis the code for all subsequent astronomical, chemical and biological evolution'. I probably would've just cried.

Anyway, I'm supposed to be explaining the power of forgiveness, not gloating about a conflict in the early eighties in which I fared well against an old lady.

Since getting clean from drugs and alcohol I have been taught that I played a part in the manufacture of all the negative beliefs and experiences from my past and I certainly play a part in their maintenance. I now look at my nan in another way.

As a human being just like me, trying to cope with her own flaws and challenges. Fearful of what would become of her sick daughter, confused by the grandchild born of a match that she was adverse to. Alone and approaching the end of her life with regret, and lacking a functioning system of guidance and comfort. Trying her best. Taking on the responsibility of an unusual little boy with glib, atheistic tendencies, she still behaved dutifully. Perhaps this very conversation sparked in me the spirit of metaphysical enquiry that has led to the faith in God I now have.

CHAPTER 7

A Few Rotten Apples

Whilst I write this, Britain, the concept of a country I live in, as the result of a European election, has advanced this odd political outfit called Ukip.

It's six months since I did the interview with Jeremy Paxman that inspired this book, and British media today is awash with half-hearted condemnations of my observation that voting is pointless and my admission that I have never voted.

My assertion that other people oughtn't vote either was born of the same instinctive rejection of the mantle of appointed social prefect that prevents me from telling teenagers to 'Just Say No' to drugs. I cannot confine my patronage to the circuitry of their minuscule wisdom.

'People died so you'd have the right to vote.' No they did not, they died for freedom. In the case where freedom was explicitly attached to the symbol of democratic rights, like female suffrage, I don't imagine they'd've been so willing if they'd known how tokenistic voting was to become.

Note too these martyrs did not achieve their ends by participating in a hollow, predefined ritual, the infertile dry-hump of gestural democracy; they did it by direct action.

Emily Davison, the hero of women's suffrage, hurled herself in front of the king's horses; she defied the tyranny that oppressed her and broke the boundaries that contained her. I imagine too that this woman would have had the rebellious perspicacity to understand that the system she was opposing would adjust to incorporate the female vote and deftly render it irrelevant. This woman, who left her job as a teacher to dedicate her life to activism, was imprisoned nine times. She used methods as severe and diverse as arson and hunger-striking to protest and at the time of her death would have been regarded as a terrorist.

Today her legacy has been so thoroughly douched that an anodyne brass plaque can be placed in the halls of Westminster, a trite, bland tribute to her heroism. Emily Davison would not be urging the disempowered people of today to vote, she'd be urging them to riot. Has the once gleaming sword of democracy, this weapon of power for the masses, been so blunted that it is now seen merely as a quilted draught excluder upon which extremists might stumble? To stop Ukip getting more seats in Thurrock council or in Brussels, this is democracy's endgame? It's like using Excalibur to put a new plug on a toaster.

It hadn't occurred to me, coming from where I'm from, that people considered parliamentary politics as anything other than a distraction. I only mentioned not voting in my *New Statesman* article that led to the Paxman furore because I was informed it was noteworthy.

For me, it's standard. I don't feel irresponsible for telling kids not to vote, I feel like I deserve a Blue Peter badge for not telling them to riot. For not telling them that they are entitled to destroy the cathedrals of tyranny, erected to mock them in the heart of their community. That they should rise up and destroy the system that imprisons them, ignores them, condemns and maligns them. By any means necessary. I might also note that I think it unlikely that people aren't voting because I told them not to; it is more likely that they're not voting because they are subject to the same conditions that led me not to vote. The realisation that it's totally bloody pointless.

That the crime of occupying an Apple Store and redistributing its contents is nothing, nothing compared to the larceny*
that took place to get those goods on the shelves. That torching
a Nike Town is no crime at all compared to the incessant
immolation of the rights of the workers that made the goods
within, the burning of the codes that means those that profit
from the store do not give back to the society in which they
flourish.

I don't feel inclined to rally youth to put an *x* in a box on
a little ballot ticket but on the doors of those who will be spared
when the plague descends. For we are at a turning point: the
exploitation has now reached a pitch where the disenfranchised
and exploited can look to a culpable minority with vengeful
eyes. This minority, though, cannot be defined by the colour
of their skin but by the colour of their god. Green. These
worshippers of Mammon have with their ascendance into privilege marked themselves out from among us. To tell the multi-
tudinous dispossessed to take the rage of the terraces and the
streets, mendaciously aimed by Wapping propaganda and
Rothermere smears at society's most vulnerable and poorest,
and take aim at this most deserving target.

The system that exploits us cannot function without us –
without our labour, without our compliance, without our
consent. If we want a society in which people with insufficient
resources are given what they are owed, where are we to look
for recompense? To other people who also have nothing? The
weak? The dispossessed? People who have arrived here more

---

* I am not suggesting that Apple literally pilfer and steal like a big, giant,
glossy artful dodger, more that the corporate world in its entirety is a kind of
thief of more wholesome values, such as sharing. Through the dominance
of organisations like Apple, whose products I continually use, we are all robbed
of something more valuable than the trinkets they provide. Furthermore their
exploitation of tax loopholes and policies of maximizing tax avoidance opportunities, like most big firms, is a kind of social robbery.

recently than we have? Or ought we be looking to organisations that have abundance? Excess. Wealth. There is no great mystery to unravel, the solution is quite simple. We must spontaneously cooperate, we must immediately overcome our superficial differences of accent and lexicon and come together to organise society effectively.

The capitalist system is not the result of our collective greed; it is the manifestation of the greed of a few and the manipulation of the many. A global superstructure has been established to ensure the continuation of the current hegemony. There are some ideas worth voting for, no party in any civilised nation will propose them, because they are not there to represent us and to ensure that the necessary change to protect us and our planet but to simply maintain the current system.

Here are some ideas. I got them from a diverse group of activists, ecologists and economists, many of whom struck me as eccentric, but these ideas are more fair than the ones that currently govern our reality and are neatly guiding us to Armageddon.

Obviously our ultimate aim is to live in self-governing, fully autonomous, ecologically responsible, egalitarian communities. Where like-minded people, or people with compatible cultures (because all our minds are ultimately alike), can live together without fucking around with what other people are up to. The organs, both ideological and practical, are already in place: we have accommodation, hospitals, transportation and communication networks. All we have to do is disband the corruption that skews them for the advancement of an elite.

The global treaties and economic infrastructure that has benefited the eighty-five occupants of the bejewelled bus of privilege can be subverted for the benefit of us all. It's easy: all we have to do is agree that that is our intention.

I asked lifelong anti-globalisation campaigner Helena Norberg-Hodge what to do to change the world.

Helena is mostly concerned with 'counter-development' – this means providing practical opposition and alternatives to governments' and big businesses' continuing promotion of globalisation and the consolidation of corporate power. Helena is interested in people that are resisting those policies, demanding a re-regulation of trade and finance and establishing models of agriculture and distribution which don't contravene obvious ecological laws. In response to my plea for solutions she promptly sent this list:

1. **Rein in the power of big business** by renegotiating trade treaties to insist that multinational corporations be place-based and accountable to nation states; revoking the charters of any corporation with revenues larger than the smallest national GNP; scrapping the WTO and creating a WEO (World Environment Organisation); controlling the private funding of political campaigns.

Now, you might've got a bit bored while reading that, you may have felt a feeling in your tummy of anxiety and a bit of psychological insecurity. 'I'm not allowed to read stuff about charters,' your second, critical voice may've said, 'I was rubbish at school.' My brain did all that stuff and I ploughed on.

All Helena's suggesting is that global trading institutions and regulations have been set up in partnership with massive companies, probably like those snidey bastards Monsanto, and as long as the rules or 'system' remain as they are, rich organisations will get richer and poor people will get poorer.

The last sentence talks about 'controlling the private funding of political campaigns'. If you are an American, and why wouldn't you be, you have never been governed by a party that wasn't the most well funded during the electoral campaign that placed it in power. Whether you voted for the red one or the blue one, the donkey or the elephant, the brown bloke or the pink bloke, what you got was the richest party in that election. Every. Single. Time.

Now, I don't want to come over all cynical, but doesn't that imply that you could dispense with the entire democratic process and simply award power to the party with the most money in its campaign fund? Yes. It does. Maybe not always, just every, single time in history so far.

Given that power is granted to the party with the most money, do you think it is likely that the parties in power feel an obligation to represent the desires and needs of the organisations that give them that money? Yes, so do I.

I'll give you an example of how I saw this unfold in real time recently. About a week ago I was reading the *Sun*, a British tabloid newspaper that stimulates lower, primal energy centres like fear, sexual desire, jealousy and mindless tribalism, when I encountered an inexplicably upbeat story about 'fracking', the process of extracting gas from deep in the earth to sell back to people as fuel.

The process is controversial and there are several brilliant documentaries that expertly demonstrate the numerous dangerous effects. Poisoning, flammable water, cancer, the sort of negative consequences a child might guess at if you told them you were planning to explode your way into the earth's core, extricate gas and sell it. How can you even begin to claim to own that? On what basis can an energy corporation claim to own gas at the earth's core? What's next? Are they going to claim they own our earwax and our uncried tears and start burrowing into our heads for a few sheckles?

Out of nowhere one morning, probably a Thursday, or a Wednesday, one of the days, the *Sun*, apropos of nothing, announced with twitching enthusiasm that fracking is great.

A double-page spread extolling its virtues, with a table-thumping condemnation of those who oppose it – there are massive demonstrations at a pilot site in Balcombe, West Sussex.

They even had *Sun* staff dressed up in comedic Batman and Robin outfits joyously trivialising the issue to anyone who'd listen. That's odd, I thought, why does the *Sun*, part of an international media conglomerate, support fracking? Is it just a general buccaneering fraternity of capitalists all helping each other out, or is there a more obvious correlation?

I once visited WikiLeaks founder Julian Assange in the Ecuadorian embassy in London, where he is forced to live for reasons I've never fully understood; in fact the whole concept of embassies and treaties and conceptual distinctions of that nature seem barmy to me.

That you can just say, 'This building is in Ecuador' and everyone has to go, 'Oh, okay' and pretend they're not standing in the middle of London.

Or that truce in the middle of the First World War, where on Christmas Day when the English and Germans stopped and played football. Surely the realisation that it was a possibility made the war on Boxing Day particularly dispiriting. Unless, I suppose, you'd been fouled or had a goal disallowed. Then you might think, 'I'm glad I get the chance to spray you with machine-gun fire, Jurgen. There's no way that was a penalty.'

If we can imagine there's a bit of Ecuador in London or a bit of peace in the middle of a war, then surely we can imagine a fairer world and decide to live in that.

I asked Assange if he believed in conspiracies, or more pertinently, 'The Conspiracy' that global politics is governed by a shady cabal who meet in a smoky, dim-lit room and cacklingly manipulate our destiny. He doesn't, which is remarkable given that he was answering me from internment in a pretend bit of Ecuador as the result of Swedish sexual assault charges that arose after he exposed war crimes in a Middle Eastern conflict.

He said that he saw the status quo more as a marauding

83

Mongol horde of capitalists with shared interests charging fero-
ciously in the same direction. The direction of 'make as much
money as possible' with no other considerations.

I disagree with Julian, but the point is moot: the result is the
same. Also all his opinions are somewhat stymied and robbed
of efficacy as he's banged up in a dislocated lump of Latin
America. It was a bizarre experience, visiting him in there. Not
least because I, as was the custom at the time, went to the
pow-wow armed with a yoga teacher. I was hanging out with
her a lot. I took her along to the MTV Movie Awards which
I was hosting, where at one point, perhaps the summit of my
own personal Everest of Hollywood kookiness, she vetoed a
joke from my opening monologue. It wasn't unspiritual or mean;
I think it was about Jennifer Aniston. It was cut 'for time', like
the monologue was saggy. I don't know if that makes it less
weird.

Tej, her name was, and she was a bloody good kundalini yoga
teacher and the lessons and techniques definitely induced interesting states of mind. Most people would've left it at that, but
with my tendency for extremism, I first became teacher's pet
and then, in a macabre switcheroo, made the teacher into my
pet.

I've already told you I'm a sucker for a mystic costume. I'm
like a wartime gal with a thing for uniforms, swooning at a GI,
and Tej's get-up was world class. Kundalini practitioners dress
entirely in white – why not? They also wear a turban as the
yogic practice they follow is derived from the Sikh faith.

Tej was a lovely woman and we became good friends, I learned
a lot and had a good laugh. A fair amount of that fun may have
been derived, I realise in retrospect, from the novel thrill of
turning up at unexpected places with a yogi. Like the MTV
Movie Awards, or the Ecuadorian embassy.

During the production of my, let's call it experimental –

with the emphasis on the 'mental' – TV show *Brand X* (surely the last punning derivation my surname can provide), the whole of Tej's yoga class, which consisted of about one hundred people, was uprooted and placed, each morning, at the studio where the show was recorded. That's pretty mad, isn't it? We left the comfort, tranquillity, sweet smells and fine foods of the purpose-built yoga centre to practise yoga in the functioning canteen of a TV production facility. Sometimes when you're famous you can get away with being a lunatic. Especially if you're like me and think the system is corrupt and rules have to be broken and conformity challenged. Before too long you have a scenario where the teamsters who do all the heavy lifting on a TV show are confronted with the daily spectacle of a hundred yoga devotees descending on their canteen.

Anyway, whichever of us is right, me or Assange, doesn't matter, but it transpired after I joked about the *Sun's* fracking story on my online (badly named) news analysis show *The Trews* and asked viewers if they could help me understand why this extraneous display of mindless propaganda was printed, I received some interesting responses. Rupert Murdoch, who owns News UK, of which the *Sun* is a subsidiary, sits on the board of US energy giant Genie Oil and Gas, which specialises in shale gas. That is another, nicer word for fracking. Shale gas sounds nice and natural, like a sea breeze, a gale made from shells. Who could object to that? Certainly not a regular reader of Murdoch's *New York Post* title, which has run twenty positive fracking stories since 2011. The relationship between the *Sun* newspaper and UK government is well documented and criminal.

The second of Helena's suggestions concerns our relationship with food production.

2. **Re-localise food and farming** by taxing food miles; removing
   subsidies and research for large-scale, capital- and energy-
   intensive agriculture; giving support to small, diversified
   organic production and to the growing number of young
   people who want to take up farming.

This second suggestion is a bit easier for us to read and reiterates the difficulties we face when capitalism and its mechanics
are inserted into the most fundamental and necessary aspects
of our lives. Like food. Helena explained to me that most
countries import and export a worryingly similar quantity of
the same commodity.

America, for example, exports the same amount of beef as it
imports each year. If you must have beef, and I would suggest
we're eating too much of it, at least eat the beef that's near you
rather than sending that off to Japan or whatever while simultaneously getting some far-flung beef chopped up and whizzed
over on a jumbo jet like Freddie Mercury prolonging a holiday
romance.

Especially as we face several ecological crises that are being
exacerbated by this unnecessary bovine jet-setting. One, global
warming; and two, depletion of fossil fuels. Everyone knows
that, so why is a profligate and dangerous planet-wide trade
system being perpetuated? Because we are living under a fundamentalist dogma, the only relevant question is 'How do we
make the most money?' The answer to that is 'By abiding
superfluous trade tariffs.'

If that structure exists, it can be subverted or replaced. The
administrative structure that serves capitalism can be used to
serve a new, sustainable, nutritional system. A recent UN survey
concluded that the world's agricultural needs could be met by
localised, organic farming. Of course the organisations that
benefit from things being the way they are don't admit that.

They'll tell you that industrialised, genetically modified, patented farming is the only way to feed the world, half of who are starving anyway – another example of the floundering deceitful maintenance of the current order.

Remember when you were a kid and you thought that your diet had to constitute meat, eggs, cheese, bread and milk? The food groups? All that? The people that established that nutritional template were the people that sold, wait for it, meat, eggs, cheese, bread and milk. They discovered which commodities were easiest to produce and transport on an industrial scale and then told us that those commodities were the commodities that we should be consuming. In a way this Revolution will be a doddle because it isn't so much about creating new systems, it's more about disregarding obsolete ones.

The food industry in its present form is obsolete. A food industry is necessary, but we have to remove from the system all components that are superfluous. Flying beef around the world, like a dead, carved-up rent boy, because it serves the agenda of big business to the detriment of the planet and its people doesn't require the contemplation of a sociological or economic genius, we just have to stop doing it.

The way to do that is by disempowering the organisations that benefit from things staying the way they are. If that can be done by democratic process, fine. If not, that's fine too. The only option that isn't fine is things remaining as they are.

Helena told me that there are apples that are grown in Britain, flown to South Africa to be cleaned and waxed and then flown back here to be sold and eaten. That would be indulgent for the fruit at Kim and Kanye's wedding. It's happening to the apple in your lunchbox. The suggestion of Revolution is not mad. That is mad. Imagine if we had locally supported, collectively organised agriculture, where our apples were grown in, I dunno, Kent, and if you lived in Kent you could buy and eat those apples. In Kent. Then someone turned up and said, 'I've got a better idea, let me take over your orchard and all orchards like it, fly their produce around the globe to be spruced up and then we'll give 'em back to you, sound like a plan?' We'd tell 'em to fuck off, wouldn't we? Well, it has happened and we didn't, because nobody explained it to us.

The reason they don't explain this to us is because they know that if we find out the extraordinary lengths that they're going to to fuck us over, we will overthrow the current system and replace it with something fair. That's why all this important stuff is made to seem inaccessible, boring and abstract. That is why our participation in politics has been sanded down into an impotent nub. Stick your x into this box and congratulate yourself on being free.

It pisses me off. It makes me want to get together a gang of Toxteth's finest, of Broadwater Farm's most deadly, Belfast's most up for it, raid Molotov's drinks cabinet and light up the Westminster sky.

I understand why people loot shops. I understand why people in Thurrock, where I'm from, vote for knee-jerk berks like Ukip. How the tendency to condemn the vulnerable outsiders flares up. Why should people be claiming benefits? Why should people be coming over here for work, welfare, health care?

Whilst behind this concentration of innocents marched out like a veil, lined up to be jeered at, in the shadow they cast the real criminals conduct their masquerade. The sneering puppeteers yank the strings and blind us.

Immigrants did not cause the financial crisis. Benefit cheats did not get multi-million-dollar bonuses. Disability claimants did not knowingly fracture the planet's stability.

The final point on Helena's list has broad ramifications and requires a huge change in the way institutions behave, but oddly it's already in line with the way most of us think.

3. **Prioritise life over profit** by rejecting GNP in favour of indicators that measure biodiversity, community coherence, personal well-being and other life-affirming criteria; radically reducing public spending on 'defence'; granting legal rights to ecosystems and non-human species; rewriting educational curricula to meet community and environmental needs rather than the needs of industry.

Right, there's quite a lot to think about in there. Prioritising life over profit is a good example of how the way our world is governed has moved out of alignment with our nature. That means our system has become aberrant. Edward Slingerland, the professor of Ancient Chinese Philosophy that explained the concept of Wu-Wei, told me the story of an artisan in the Zhuangzi.

This fella apparently carved bell-stands, for bells, obviously, that were vital in ancient ceremonial rituals. These bell-stands were evidentally top-drawer; everyone was crazy about them.

At this point in the story I had to make a bit of a psychological leap back to ancient China because where I'm from people don't get that excited about bell-stands. I was struggling to imagine a bell-stand of any description, let alone one that would really get me jazzed up. I mean, it's not even the bell, which would, for me, be the obvious star of the story – that's the thing that gets rung – but there you go. I am not a Stanford professor so I just kept my mouth shut.

Everyone was so enchanted by this bloke's bell-stands that someone eventually asked him how he made them – the equivalent of a local news item where the man who makes David Beckham's boots is patronised about his needlework skills.

Initially the craftsman is vague about his methods – coy, you might say – but after a probing he yields. 'I meditate,' he says, 'until I forget my intentions and attachments, until I forget the credit I will get for making a good bell-stand, the adulation, the money. Eventually I forget even myself. Then I go down to the forest in this focused, open state and I look at trees until I see a tree that already has the bell-stand in it. All I have to do then is remove the excess wood until all that remains is the bell-stand.'

It was around this point in Edward's recital that I realised the tale was allegorical, that he wasn't inexplicably giving me a highly specific and probably redundant lesson on ancient oriental carpentry but in fact describing how to materialise concepts from a higher realm.

First transcend the lower, basic requirements of the animal self: hungers, desires. I suppose that's why most religions have 'fasting' as a ritual, to see what lies on the other side of hunger, on the other side of these basic drives. Then look without prejudice at the nature of the challenge – in his case trees; in our case the machinery of global capitalism – wait until the solution reveals itself, then remove what is surfeit. In his case twigs, bark, leaves; in ours anything that isn't in the service of justly catering for our common requirements.

This story also reminds us of the need for this process to be peacefully undertaken.

Sometimes when we're incensed by the rancid tide of injustice the impulse is to attack. We must avoid this. We have learned that violence as a means is always unsuccessful.

CHAPTER 8

I Am An Anarchist-a

Gandhi, an extremely efficient revolutionary, is perhaps most admired for his excellent deployment of 'non-violent protest'. The ingenuity of non-violence is not immediately obvious to us, the inheritors of a world built upon martial means, but the principle is almost like mathematics. Authorities are trained to deal with a particular kind of conflict, violent conflict; by using violent means you are entering the territory that they are best qualified to control. Also by becoming violent you are tuning into the frequency that you are trying to overcome, the frequency of violation, violence FM.

'Be the change you wish to see in the world,' said Gandhi. If you want a non-violent world, you cannot use violence to achieve it. He also said, 'In the end the British will walk out because 100,000 British cannot control 350 million Indians if those Indians refuse to cooperate.' A small minority cannot control an uncooperative majority, so they must be distracted, divided, tyrannised or anaesthetised into compliance. Gandhi dealt with the colonisation of nations by nations; we deal now with the colonisation of consciousness by corporations.

I spoke to David Graeber, the anthropologist, economist, writer and Occupy movement member. Typically I would write 'Occupy movement leader' but they eschew such titles in the movement. David is an anarchist. I don't know much about anarchism; I only know about anarchy from graffiti, the Sex Pistols and as a kind of slur or reprimand from my mum, 'Is that what you want? It'd be anarchy!'

Well, according to David Graeber, there's more to anarchy than not tidying your bedroom, spitting and having a Mohican; in fact it isn't defiantly disorderly at all, it is a society that has no centralised power. David came round my house in east London during a torrential downpour to talk to me about Revolution.

It was properly raining. I stopped what I was doing to look out of the front door at the rain. One of those sudden outbursts of nature that serves as a deft reminder that even mighty structures like cities are temporary and nonsensical, it smashed its way down from the sky, all joyful and triumphant like 'ye faithful'. David turned up whilst I was marvelling at it and half planning an ark, with his jacket pulled up over his head like when you play Batman.

It was ridiculous, he was soaking. I had to get a towel and offer him clothes that he wouldn't take. I knew immediately that I'd like him, he just had one of those faces. I could see what he'd been like as a boy, probably always fenced off in the electronic penitentiary of a too-fast mind.

His eyes are narrow like a Japanese person or someone from the future in a film. He spoke, pertinently given the weather, like Rain Man, or like his voice was trying to become a synthesised burr like Stephen Hawkins's robot voice.

There was a salad on the table, still packaged, from a Thai takeaway. 'Can I have this?' said David, already unpacking it, like it was an energy coin in a computer game. Then he sat there eating, all wet and content with a towel round his head like ET on his way back to his spaceship. 'How's this bloke gonna dream up a new economic system?' I wondered.

David is most well known for his idea of debt cancellation.

Personal debt cancellation used to be a common policy in ancient civilisations; every seven years all debt was cancelled. The Bible refers to 'debt jubilees' where everyone's debt would be reset to zero. I think it's especially nice that it was called a 'jubilee', creating an even more euphoric sense of carnival.

In Islam too, usury, credit at extortionate rates – like Wonga or whatever offer – is forbidden. So this bizarre-sounding notion has strong historic precedent. It is a mark of how far into materialism we have descended that it seems unfeasible in our world.

David explained from beneath my towel that debt repayment has a powerful moral charge in our culture, that people feel ashamed about debt and guilty about non-payment. Seventy-five per cent of Americans are in debt, 40 per cent owing more than $50,000, whilst an estimated 9 million British people are in 'serious debt'.

What David Graeber, the anarchist, is suggesting is that all personal debt, debt for normal people, is cancelled.

Think about it.

That means you. All your debt cancelled.

When David said it I felt excited, like it was naughty, like it shouldn't be allowed. This is the feeling I still get when I start a car. 'I shouldn't be doing this,' I think, plunging down on the accelerator. The reality is, I shouldn't be – I'm a terrible driver. My conditioning kicked in when Dave Graeber (I say his name like 'Craig David') said that debt cancellation is a contemporary possibility. I nearly told him to shush and looked over my shoulder for a park keeper. Immediately, just by contemplating it, you feel like you're bunking off school. 'We can't cancel debt – we'll get the cane.'

I thought about the ramifications. Well, obviously, the majority of people would be thrilled. Tuesday night you go to bed with a credit card bill, mortgage and a bloody headache; Wednesday you wake up with a spring in your step and a pound note in your pocket. What a touch. Obviously this is not such good news for credit card companies and banks; overnight their entire operation has irrevocably altered.

Most of these companies are international too, so what would the impact be on global finances? I imagine a mainstream economist – and let me tell you off the bat, I've no fucking intention of asking one – would say this action would instigate financial meltdown.

What Graeber says in response to this is that $700 billion was written off and trillions were lent to banks as the result of the 2008 financial crash. That sounds like a lot but I can't get my head around economics – I'm not supposed to get my head around economics, none of us are, it's designed to be obtuse.

Look at those fucking NASDAQ, FTSE, Dow Jones things. Sometimes I accidentally press a button on my phone and the screen is filled with the numerical babblings of these unknowable entities and it's more baffling and mysterious than the Amharic cries that filled the Kensal Green church. They speak in numerical tongues as they worship their invisible God.

That instinctive feeling I had when I was a kid – I bet you had it too – when the financial report came on at the end of the News was 'This is bollocks!' That wasn't the result of innocence or ignorance, we were right. Since then there has been an attempt to inculcate and obfuscate and dress it up in conferences, rolling onscreen graphics and supercilious posturing, but we were right, it is bollocks.

How can we conceptualise a trillion dollars? Merrill Lynch, J. P. Morgan and Lehman Brothers were all lent in excess of a trillion dollars to get them through that crisis – that doesn't seem fair. Plus they all have names like Coronation Street baddies. 'Merrill Lynch and the Lehman brothers have burnt down the Rovers,' someone might say. 'It was probably an insurance job.'

At this point it's worth noting that the economy is not a real thing, it is a man-made system designed to serve us, an ideological machine.

It has gone wrong and is tyrannising us. We wouldn't tolerate that from a literal machine. If my vacuum cleaner went nuts and forced me to live in economic slavery, I wouldn't roll my eyes say 'Oh well' and humbly do its bidding. I'd turn it off and fuck it out the window.

When the reckless and greedy trading, lending and gambling of the financial industry led to the economic breakdown that if not resolved would've provoked social upheaval, possibly Revolution, the governments of affected nations got together (in a smoky dim-lit room?) and decided to press reset on the economy. Aside from a few people carrying plants out of their offices in cardboard boxes, I don't remember there being many consequences at all. Just some people with plants looking confused by a revolving door.

Oh, and 13.1 million American people had their homes foreclosed. Because their debt, it turns out, was real; it was only the debt within the financial sector that was imaginary. It was only the people who generated the crisis who got three magical wishes from an economic genie. There was no abracadabra for ordinary people, they just got abraca-fucked.

So we are not discussing whether or not debt cancellation is a possibility; we know it is, we've seen it, they've done it. All we are discussing is who it is possible for. Them or us.

I've just typed myself into a revolutionary fervour again. Every so often the fury at injustice rises up in me and makes me want to smash something or burn something, but nothing in my immediate environment belongs to me so I have to refrain.

Unless of course we consider that the concept of property is preposterous, like a Native American chief, Great Elk or one of them, who when us lot (by us I suppose I mean white

95

Europeans – you might not be one, I hope you're not actually, sorry for unconsciously addressing this book to imperialists) turned up in their country with contracts, were confounded.

'How can you "own" a river? The river is our brother . . .'

'Yeah, alright, mate. Sign this, will ya? Here're some blankets for yer trouble.'

We are so acclimatised to our metaphors that we no longer see them as imaginary, or symbolic. We forget that most things that define us are conceptual. Most things that we consider real are the material manifestation of an idea. The laptop upon which I type, once an idea in some boffin's noggin, the words that I type, a consensual code of Saxon and Latin, my merrily dancing fingers the result of an unrealised uteral form, tracking some invisible plan towards realisation.

Four o'clock on Wednesday: just a concept, an agreement, not actual, not real like an apple or a heartbeat. Karate: just a system of breath and movement.

My support of West Ham United FC is a totemic symbol. Since I started supporting them, when I was born, a hereditary legacy, like my eyebrows or my addiction, they had different players, different owners, a different kit. Soon they will move to a different stadium; they play now in a different league, in a different way under a different manager.

What then is the West Ham that I support? It is the West Ham that my dad supports, that everyone at my school supported, that everyone at Upton Park supports? Those men terrified me on my early visits, and still, if I'm honest, unnerve me a bit now, with their tribal roars and curses, with their tears and vows, with their beers and rows. The chanting, the defiance, each of them, each of us – us, there's the word – knowing that the game as we know it is dying, that the fraction of the club that belongs to us is being ever eroded.

The concept of belonging commodified like all else. Their

belief versus our belief. The songs so route-one evocative and plain: 'West Ham Till I Die', 'I'm Forever Blowing Bubbles', 'West Ham's Claret and Blue Army' – anthems of place and unity.

Folk codes of pride and togetherness, pride in both senses, honour and togetherness. Ring-fenced emotion permitted only at three o' clock for ninety minutes in the sanctuary of the stadium. Can we march that pride out of the gates and into the streets? Can we harness it? Direct it? Use it for something less stymied by white lines and whistles, that could pour from the terraces and into the oak and leather chambers, the steel and glass towers?

Money and the economy are just symbols, ideas, tools. If they don't serve us, if they don't serve the planet, then they have to change. They are not serving us, or the planet, so why are they not changing? Where is the resistance coming from? It must be benefiting somebody. It is probably the occupants of the bejewelled bus; they seem to be behind all this mayhem.

Of course, if we suggest alternatives that inconvenience them they'll say it's impossible, implausible, sixth-form, naive, Nazi; they'll say anything to prevent the realisation that change is necessary and inevitable.

David said that secretly, even those that benefit most from capitalism know its demise is imminent. What they are preparing for now is what follows it. Something fairer, or the militaristic maintenance of a comparable tyranny. I think, given the evidence of history, it's obvious they'll favour the latter.

Is there evidence that those in authority are preparing to confront mass uprising?

David as an anarchist is opposed to centralised power in any form. He believes that people should be entrusted and empowered, that given the opportunity, released from the chains of authority and the spell of a corrupting media, we will form fair and functioning systems; they may not be perfect, but remember, we're not competing with perfection, we're competing with corruption, inequality and destruction.

I asked him if we could formulate a centralised revolutionary movement to coordinate transition. He said this, the anarchist: 'Well, my own approach is to avoid constituting any sort of new authority, because in a revolutionary situation, there's crisis and conflict and therefore always an excuse for the provisional authorities, however well meaning, to amass more and more power.'

Which is a fair point. That Arab Spring we were all so excited about on Twitter turned out to be fuck-all. As usual. I suppose we could try to ensure that a military junta isn't placed in power at any point. Those guys with uniforms and medals and sunglasses are normally wrong 'uns.

I asked him what he envisaged then, whilst simultaneously stuffing my beret and mirrored shades down the side of the sofa.

'My dream is to create a thousand autonomous institutions that can gradually take over the business of organising everyday life, pretty much ignoring the authorities, until gradually the whole apparatus of state comes to seem silly, unnecessary, a bunch of buffoons useful for entertainment perhaps, but no one we have to take seriously. Obviously that only works if they don't have the means to shoot you. The tricky thing is that means that much as you hate the cops, or the army, you're only going to win if at some point those guys decide they're just not going to follow orders to shoot you.'

I like the idea of creating autonomous organisations to perform necessary social functions that are not motivated by profit. This along with the principles of equality, non-violence and ecological responsibility are necessary pillars of Revolution.

I disagree with David's antipathy towards the police and military. This could be for a couple of reasons. Maybe David, as an anarchist, is always in protests, like Occupy Wall Street or marches, or whatever, and gets himself into confrontations with authority.

I've done a bit of that myself, not in his league, but I was always getting nicked when I was a junkie, so I've had my fair share of skirmishes with the law. However, I am fortunate in that I have a very positive feeling towards the police and army. The police that have arrested me have usually been alright and they've always had a point. I happen to think all drugs should be legal and when I was a drug user I paid no heed to prohibition, but I understand the position of the officers arresting me.

Mostly these arrests, futile though they were, were conducted in a relatively bonhomous and professional manner. Once a copper who pinched me in Soho, before searching my marijuana-laden bag, announced whilst rolling up the arms of his shirt with a magician's flourish, 'Nothing up this sleeve, nothing up this sleeve.'

I recall too that the chat in the back of the van weren't too bad as they dispatched me to the nick. It'd be less antagonistic perhaps if the police didn't wear police uniforms. It's a crime when someone else does, impersonating a police officer; maybe the police oughtn't impersonate police officers either.

The uniform, a dehumanising device. I've encountered the police in domesticity, stripped of the thin blue line: my mate Rene Zagger's older brother was a copper, and I was struck by his normality. Once I house-sitted, with a mate, a copper's flat in south London and he had hash in his front room. And these days when I chat to the Met I see that they're not really any different from me. Normal people from around the estuary, supporting Spurs, or the Hammers, or Chelsea. An armed response vehicle pulled over in east London and the policeman driving it, younger than me, said he'd seen me on telly and that he agreed with me, politicians are 'full of shit', he said.

Cases where public disorder has been the offence have been less amicable. When arrested stealing porn in an all-night garage, or clambering nude across TV outside-broadcast vehicles in the midst of a riot, or even when picked up retrospectively, on-set, for affray and destruction of public property, there has been a more tangibly adversarial dynamic.

It is at an institutional level, when acting as the henchman of the establishment that the police become frightening. As individuals, as humans we find harmony. Ferguson, Orgreave, Hillsborough and the many unexplained deaths in custody are all manifestations of the dehumanisation that occurs when an institution that ought to serve the public glitches and becomes a tool for state oppression. The transference of $4.2 billion dollars of US military equipment to local police authorities across America is an indication of what the state regards the role of the police to be. Even Boris is buying up German water cannons to sluice down febrile Londoners. It's as if they know a change is coming.

CHAPTER 9

It's Big But It's Not Easy

The last time I was arrested was in New Orleans and wasn't that long ago. I was clean. It is worse getting arrested in recovery and it is worse getting arrested in America. This arrest came during my beard-and-pyjamas post-marital era.

I was making a film called *Paradise* (don't worry, no one has) with Diablo Cody, the writer of *Juno*. It was her directorial debut. She is a talented, y'know, Oscar-winning writer and a lovely person. I suppose I just wasn't up for making a film. The indicators were clear, with hindsight. For example, I was refusing to cut my hair for the part. Or beard. Hair is prissy but understandable; beard is inter-dimensional unreasonableness.

Diablo and I fashioned my beard together in my trailer, as cautiously as you'd sculpt a peace treaty between two nations that prefer war to peace. The reality was my identity outside of film-making had become more important to me, I was doing hours of yoga and meditation each day, I was going through a divorce and the result was a kind of hirsute intransigence.

I looked like the cliché of a terrorist and I behaved like one. Except the beard wasn't the symbol, it was the cause. I feel some guilt about my lack of enthusiasm for acting, like it's a bit ungrateful. Like I've let my teenage self down. Mind you, he let himself down a fair bit, the dirty little pervert. The dreams of my adolescent self were entangled with silvery screens and limousines, and I still feel that I need to offer up superficial sacrifices to his misguided alter. The fact is, though, I find film-making a boring process and its ends dubious. This could, of course, be due to the quality of the stuff I've done so far, as opposed to an essential rejection of an art form.

Maybe if I'd been 'R. P. McMurphy' or 'the Elephant Man' or 'Brian' I'd feel different.

It just wasn't what I thought it would be. It's not just the entertainment industry that has seemed like a mirage on arrival. What about clubs and parties? When I'm there I think, 'Is this it? Is this all there is? Is this what all the fuss is about?' This feeling of disillusionment perhaps climaxed around the time of my divorce and the making of this subsequent film. New Orleans, though, is not a city of lacklustre superficiality but one of unique vibrancy. Mark Twain, the thinking man's Colonel Saunders, said, 'America is New York, New Orleans and San Francisco. Everywhere else is Cleveland.'

The city is renowned for its spirit in every sense of the word, spirit, there is a Creole, Voodoo ambience, spirit, the people are plucky, vivacious and strong, spirit, everyone is pissed all the time. They are proud that there is an incessant festival, a rolling celebration. The architecture in the French Quarter – wrought-iron railings, low ceilings, narrow streets and vines – is perkily romantic and gently decadent, like a wink and a hand on your thigh. It must come from the swamp, the land itself unsure if it's a solid or a liquid, that could slip right back into the Mississippi and roll on by, so you might as well party.

I got arrested there. My mood was strange. Party towns are strange if you don't drink. If you're there working. If you're beginning to think that making films is not for you. If you're starting to consign easy promiscuity in the Big Easy to the ever-growing pile of defunct distractions. I don't let go without a struggle though. I didn't with booze or drugs and I won't with sex or

fame. The problem is that as access to spiritual data and practices of various kinds begin to make a difference it gets harder
to go back to sleep. So I was in New Orleans with a girl and
from the outside my life looks like it's supposed to look like.
She's a model, I'm in a movie, I rent a vintage sports car, of
course there's paparazzi, but in my teenage dream of me there
were paparazzi too.

They pursue the car through saxophone streets and I, like a
patient stirring mid-procedure as the anaesthetic fades, think
more than ever, 'This just won't do.' When you stop or move
they splat you with hostile chumminess – 'Hey Russ, who's the
girl?' They drive like jackals too, scavenging in your tracks, at
your heels. 'This looks how it's supposed to look but it doesn't
feel like it's supposed to feel', and then, several thwarted tricks
in, the idea kicks in that I am a man and that I can do whatever I want.

That I didn't sign a contract to be preyed upon or spied upon
or lied about, then sighed about, 'Oh I wonder why'd, it's
no-surprised' about. The car is bloody hard to drive. The lights
turn red and so do I. This brain I have sometimes just says to
me stuff like 'Russell, this is bullshit, these people have got no
right to chase you and harass you. Fuck 'em. Get out of the car
now and confront them.' Then another part of my brain, apparently distinct from the first bit, goes, 'Y'know what? You're right,
I'm in charge of the body, I'll take care of it.' Then whatever's
left of me that's not encompassed by those two, or three, gets
up and goes along with it.

The girl says something, the girl always says something. I'm
up and out the door, I'm in character, I think I've even got a
hat on. I'm committed to this now, whoever I am, this guy in
a hat, in a street by a car in New Orleans, this hirsute projection of a teenager's dreams. A languid mosaic of years of refusal,
and years of abuse all, and years of confusion.

At their car door now, iPhone hyenas. Window down, corners of mouth up. He says something from the capsule of his car that collides with how I see the world in that moment, that implies that me snatching his brandished phone out of his hand and throwing it is not a possibility. For me though it is, so I do. That smashes the pane of conviviality to smithereens. It also smashes the window of the building across the street. It sails through the air, his liberated phone, like a funereal dove, a symbol of my emancipation from press intrusion, and crashes presumptuously through the window of a law firm. The occupants will know their rights, I quickly deduce. The pap gets out of the car all confounded and flustered, like I'd tipped over the Monopoly board when he'd just secured Park Lane. There's the bit where we both pretend we're willing to have a fight, then the girl or his friend descend and it's broken up. Back in the car I'm buzzing, which doesn't help my driving. Pap car A and another pap-mobile are still following; I check them in my rear-view mirror, like a movie. In the end they chase us to a hotel. I didn't want to lead them back to where I was actually staying.

I didn't hear about it for a few days, then plain-clothed police come and arrest me at the casino where we are filming. Luckily the stereotype of bad-boy actor already exists so as I'm led off in cuffs there is an available reference. Such overt dramatic displays make me, in a compensatory demonstration, act all polite and genteel, like Alan Bennett getting pulled, or Prince Edward at Glastonbury.

I don't go in for a snarling, Wild-man performance in this instance, but virtually escort the arresting officers through the casino like Jeeves, bowing and tipping my hat.

In America when you're arrested they cuff your hands behind your back; usually in the UK they leave your hands in front. This makes me yearn for the comparative kindness of a British bobby as I'm helped into the back of the squad car, which has barely any leg-room.

With my American arrests, both of which followed paparazzi altercations – the first in LAX airport, where a spat with an intrusive pap who'd tried for a shot of my then wife's pants was humorously titled by my mate Matt as 'Liam Gallagher: The Musical' – there was a jarring record scratch from pre-arrest conviviality to the cuffing. It felt like I was famous right up to the moment my rights were read.

The mind is a machine that registers difference. I suppose we become inured to anything if subjected to it for long enough – poverty, or extreme privilege. Fame after a while seems ordinary. The accumulation of a million easy treats, a licence to speak your mind or sulk. It is possible to retreat into a cell of comfort, ceramic stillness. I am grateful for the disruptions that come and remind me of the shallow impermanence of fame as a condition. This is how I feel in retrospect when I reflect on my few hours in the New Orleans Police Department holding pen. It's not how I felt at the time though. I was freaked out.

That place was fucking scary; the process of industrialisation has given their justice system an inhuman hum. The strip lights and the strip searches, the efficiency, suffocates humanity.

I was marched in by the cops, formerly known as chatty, and routinely dropped on to the conveyer belt of the NOLA Police Department. There are a series of airlock doors, like in a spaceship, a fella behind a thick pane takes your name, someone else takes your belt and shoelaces, or anything you could hang yourself with – I'm a man who likes to accessorise, so it took a while. Splayed across the wall, you're patted down, more aggressively than in an airport and with less room for innuendo.

Across several airlocks in what I deemed to be the main area I could see a vast purgatory of inmates, divided by gender but in uniform, ubiquitous Guantánamo orange suits. I'm going to look awful in that, I thought. As a celebrity – how I loathe the word, but must be grateful for its perks here – I was placed on the other side of the wall-to-wall desk that divided the room, on the side of the police.

Whilst my 'man of the people' tag is one I cherish, I must confess to feeling somewhat relieved to be on the carpeted quarter of that room, not the linoleum ghetto, where here and there murmurs were exchanged regarding my arrival.

Arrests are like STD tests: you can never be 100 per cent confident of the outcome. Even though I knew I'd only been nicked for a trivial offence, the possibility of a damning conclusion seemed plausible given the awful situation I now found myself in.

Even though I knew that beyond the sedated, orange riot on one side and the podgy baton-wielding authority on the other there were an invisible army of lawyers, agents and producers making phone calls and pulling favours, I was a bit scared that due to a tantrum and a clerical error I was about to begin a life sentence among Louisiana's most dangerous and least fortunate.

Movies get made these days in cities that offer favourable economic conditions to film-makers, so at a governmental level there are relationships between studios and politicians which at this point were extremely convenient to me.

The other people there, being processed across the physical line of the long, chest-high barricade and the imperceptible but more imposing line of poverty, had none of my circumstantial advantages.

Most of them were black, all of them were poor, any material wealth necessarily accrued through illegal means as that is the only means available. I ended up sat next to the facilities overworked psychiatrist. He told me that everyone he saw had either addiction issues or mental-health issues or both.

Sitting quietly in this place you can feel the energy. There is a weary lack of hope. On either side of the bureau, people are weighed down by conditions. A pre-ploughed and unrewarding habitualised rut, like a destructive circuit in a broken brain. Neither side free. The captors as trapped and knackered as the people they're processing in this bloodless abattoir.

The poor enslaved by desperation, the rich imprisoned by luxury.

I'm not suggesting the New Orleans police are rich, I bet their salaries are shit, only that any system that requires such extremity to be maintained is detrimental to us all.

With my coterie of well-placed benefactors I was soon strolling out of jail and back on to set with a John Wayne walk and Lil Wayne grin, but for all my bravado and slapdash renditions of a new anecdote, that couple of hours had widened the crack. I'm lucky in that I've been able to be so gently awoken and reminded, a slap round the face rather than a five-year stretch.

CHAPTER 10

Ich Bin Ein Monarch

When travelling in impoverished regions in galling luxury, as I have done, you have to undergo some high-wire ethical arithmetic to legitimise your position. If you can't separate yourself from poverty geographically then you have to do it ideologically. You have to believe inequality is okay. You have to accept the ideas that segregate us from one another and nullify your human instinct for fairness.

Another thing Slingerland, the professor of Ancient Chinese Philosophy, mentioned was humankind's innate expectation of fairness. We have an instinct for it and instinctively we reject unfairness. He demonstrated this to me with the use of hazelnuts. As we spoke there were a bowl of them on the table. 'Russell,' he said, scooping up a handful, 'we humans have an inbuilt tendency towards fairness. If offered an unfair deal we will want to reject it. If I have a huge bowl of nuts and offer you just one or two, how do you feel?' The answer was actually quite complex. Firstly I dislike hazelnuts, considering them to be the verminous titbits of squirrels. Unless in a whole-nut chocolate bar – then I like them. Secondly they were my fucking hazelnuts anyway, we were in my house. Most pertinently though, I imagine, to the point that Slingerland was trying to make, I felt that it was an unfair offering when he had so many nuts. I told him so and he seemed pleased. Like when at school you see a teacher think,

'I'm really getting my point across here, I'm like Robin Williams in *Dead Poets Society*.'

Whilst I was thrilled to get a bit of tutorial approval, I was still reeling from the shoddy deal and told the glowing, nutty professor as much. He explained that human beings and even primates have an instinct for fairness even in situations where this instinct could be seen as detrimental. 'You still have more nuts now than before,' he chirped, failing to acknowledge that all nuts and indeed everything in the entire house belonged to me. We then watched an amazing clip on YouTube where monkeys in adjacent cages in a university laboratory perform the same task for food. Monkey A does the task and gets a grape, delicious. Monkey B who can see Monkey A performs the same task and is given cucumber, yuck.

Monkey B looks pissed off but eats his cucumber anyway. The experiment is immediately repeated and you can see that Monkey B is agitated when his uptown, up-alphabet neighbour is again given a grape. This time when he is presented with the cucumber, he is fucking furious; he throws it out the cage and rattles the bars. I got angry on his behalf and wanted to give the scientist a cucumber in a less amenable orifice. I also felt a bit pissed off with Monkey A, the grape-guzzling little bastard. I've not felt such antipathy towards a primate since that one in *Indiana Jones* that wore a little waistcoat betrayed Indy.

Professor Slingerland explained, between great frothing gobfulls of munched hazelnut, that this inherent sense of fairness we have is found in humans everywhere but studies show that it's less pronounced in environments where people are exposed to a lot of marketing. 'Capitalist, consumer culture inures us to unfairness,' he said. That made me angry.

When I was in India, a country where wealth and poverty share a disturbing proximity, I felt a discomfort in spite of being in the exalted position of Monkey A. Exclusive hotels require extensive, in fact military, security. Blokes with guns stand at the entrance. It has only just occurred to me that the word 'exclusive' specifically refers to the excluded, the people who aren't included, the majority who cannot attend. Like the exclusivity is a good thing.

'Sir, if that canapé was not delicious enough, let me assure you that but a mile from here there is a family in a shack eating food they found on the floor.'

'That's very reassuring but could you provide a photograph?'

As we entered the five-star splendour, through the metal detectors, past the armed guard, I realised that if this was what was required in order to preserve this degree of privilege it could not be indefinitely sustained. When you enter into the opulence of these places you check out of your humanity as you check in. Of course India is a land subject to much sectarian violence, religiously motivated. My belief is that all conflicts, though, are about resources or territory and the theological rhetoric merely a garnish to make it more palatable.

These devices that maintain division are what my friend Matt Stoller focused on when I asked him what ideas he had that would change the world. I first met Matt in Zuccotti Park, Manhattan, in the middle of the Occupy Wall Street protest in 2011.

This corporate square in the middle of the financial district had become a lurid and buoyant shanty town of placards and canvas. I was magnetised down from my Tribeca apartment by a curiosity that will not yield, that will not be sedated by my ego's ongoing acquisitive quest. Among the many stimulating encounters with cock-eyed optimists and hard-core anarchists my meeting with Matt stood out. Matt at that time worked for the government. He understands power: as a policy-wonk for a Democratic congressman his days were spent in the cogs of the lumbering Washington behemoth. He told me the Establishment was afraid of Occupy. They were afraid because typically protests are backed by non-profit organisations, themselves accountable to foundations who have boards, who have members who can be harassed and intimidated. Occupy doesn't work like that. It is a spontaneous, leaderless cooperative and that makes it harder to squash.

Any of you that saw *Brand X*, my US chat show, will recognise Matt, because I kidnapped him from that square and forced him into my life. I did this because I instantly identified him as a peculiar radical, good old me. I saw that beneath his cherubic, hay-coloured curls and proper job, he detested the system he was trapped in. I suppose as a man who was in Manhattan making a movie and had trotted down to the protest site dressed in jogger's Lycra, I identified with his quandary. Since then he has regularly prised apart the clenched and corrupt buttocks of American politics and allowed me to peer inside at its dirty workings. I asked Matt for ideas that would aid the Revolution; his response was, as usual, startling and almost proctologically insightful.

'No more private security for the wealthy and the powerful,' he said. I nervously demanded he explain himself. He did thusly:

'One economist argued in 2005 that roughly one in four Americans are employed to guard in various forms the wealth of the rich. So if you want to get rid of rich and poor, get rid of guard labour.'

This may be one of the many points in this book where you are shouting the word 'hypocrite' as you read. Don't think I'm unaware of the inevitability of such a charge. I know, I know. I'm rich, I'm famous, I have money, I'm being paid money for this book, I have had private security on and off for years.

There is no doubt that I as much as anyone have to change.

The only thing I can offer you in the face of this legitimate accusation is that change is something I'm good at. I know that change is a necessity. I have had to change to survive. I'd also like to add, by way of mitigation, that I could've just written 'Booky Wook 3', not mentioned global inequality, ecological meltdown, or the complicity of the entertainment industry in holding together a capitalist machine that exploits the vast majority of people, and collected my cheque.

When I was poor and complained about inequality they said I was bitter; now I'm rich and I complain about inequality they say I'm a hypocrite. I'm beginning to think they just don't want to talk about inequality.

Revolution is change, I believe in change, personal change most of all; at this time, however, we must coordinate a massive change, so please, shout hypocrite at an inanimate object if you must, but please don't dismiss the ideas in it.

Know, too, that I am prepared for change, that I have seen what fame and fortune have to offer and I know it's not the answer. That doesn't diminish these arguments, it enhances them. Of course I have to change as an individual and part of that will be sharing wealth, though without systemic change that will be a sweet, futile gesture.

Now let's get back to Matt Stoller, banning private security, ensuring that I'll have to have my own fist fights next time I'm leaving the Manchester Apollo.

'The definition of being rich means having more stuff than other people. In order to have more stuff, you need to protect that stuff with surveillance systems, guards, police, court systems, and so forth. All of those sombre-looking men in robes who call themselves judges are just sentinels whose job it is to convince you that this very silly system in which we give Paris Hilton as much as she wants while others go hungry is good and natural and right.'

This idea is extremely clever and highlights that there is exclusivity even around the use of violence. The state can legitimately use force to impose its will and increasingly so can the rich. Take away that facility and societies will begin to equalise. If that hotel in India that I went to was stripped of its security they'd have to address the complex issues that led to them requiring it.

'These systems can be very expensive. America employs more private security guards than high-school teachers. States and countries with high inequality tend to hire proportionally more guard labour. If you've ever spent time in a radically unequal city in South Africa, you'll see that both the rich and the poor live surrounded by private security contractors, barbed wire and electrified fencing. Some people have nice prison cages, and others have not so nice ones. But when there's inequality, there's got to be someone making sure, with force, that it stays that way.'

Matt here, metaphorically, broaches the notion that the rich too are impeded by inequality, imprisoned in their own way. Much like with my earlier plea for you to bypass the charge of hypocrisy, I now find myself in the unenviable position of urging you, like some weird, bizarro Jesus, to take pity on the rich.

It's not an easy concept to grasp, and I'm not suggesting it's a priority. Faced with a choice between empathising with 'the rich' and 'the homeless' by all means go with the homeless. It is reductive, though, not to acknowledge that all are encompassed by this system and none of us are free while it endures. I'm not saying it's worse to be one of Bernie Ecclestone's kids than Jason, the homeless bloke who lives under the bridge at the end of my street, I'm saying that the two are connected and everyone will benefit from change. I should also point out that empathy, sympathy and love are limitless resources, energies that never deplete, and at this time of dwindling fuels we should cherish and explore these inexhaustible inner resources more than ever.

'Companies spend a lot of money protecting their CEOs. Starbucks spent $1.4 million. Oracle spent $4.6 million. One casino empire – the Las Vegas Sands – spent $2.45 million. This money isn't security so much as it is designed to wall these people off from the society they rule so they never have to interact with normal people under circumstances they may not control. If you just got rid of this security, these people would be a lot less willing to ruthlessly prey on society.'

Prudently Matt here explains that at the pinnacle of our problem are those that benefit most from the current hegemony. The executors of these new empires that surpass nation. The logo is their flag, the dollar is their creed, we are all their unwitting subjects.

'People can argue about the right level of guard labour. You conceivably could still have public police, but their job should be to help protect everyone, not just a special class. If you got rid of all these private systems, or some of these systems of surveillance and coercive guarding of property, you'd have a lot less inequality. And powerful and wealthy people would spend a lot more time trying to make sure that society was harmonious, instead of just hiring their way out of the damage they can create.'

How clever of Matt to offer a policy that will require further change, that has built into it a kind of doomsday device that ensures further fairness. We get caught up in abstruse nomenclature but we're talking about pretty simple stuff here: fairness, sharing.

My mate Nik said if you were in a school playground with twenty kids in it and a couple of 'em took all the toys, you wouldn't just say, 'Oh well, that's life,' you'd explain to them that sharing is a basic human value and redistribute the toys. Let's overlook the fact that in this allegory we're hanging around a playground with unsupervised children; we might be teachers, or lollipop men, don't just assume we're paedos – that's not the point.

The point is with children you know that kids who don't share are in a way suffering as much as the kids who are deprived of Barbie, or Xboxes, or whatever the hell it is they have now. The minority that are hoarding resources are misguided in their belief that it can make them happy, and we have to be the adults and help them. By dismantling the machinery of capitalism, winning over the military with our flower-power clap-trap and redistributing all their wealth.

It's much easier in the allegory, where all you have to do is snatch a Rubik's Cube off a toddler and give it to some whimpering coward in a sandpit. Even with the paedo allegations.

Given that Matt's first suggestion has brought about a terrifying free-for-all and likely reignited the war between India and Pakistan, I was curious to see what else he had up the sleeve of his Harvard blazer. Yes, he did go to Harvard. The bloody hypocrite. His next idea to create a different world was equally cunning and revolutionary: get rid of all titles.

'Mr President. Ambassador. Admiral. Senator. The Honourable. Your Honour. Captain. Doctor. These are all titles that capitalism relies on to justify treating some people better than other people.'

Matt is an American, so when it comes to deferring to the entitled, let's face it, he's an amateur compared to the British. Look at me, simpering to Professor Slingerland whenever he's mentioned. I can't wait to prostrate myself before his sceptre of diplomas. I'm a right little lickspittle sneak down the doctor's an' all. 'Yes, Doctor; no, Doctor; please don't let me die, Doctor; charge what you must, Doctor; stick your finger where you fancy,

Doctor.' Plus we've got a bloody royal family. What's he going to say about that?

'One of the most remarkable things you learn when you work in a position of political influence is just how much titles separate the wealthy and the politicians from citizens. Ordinary people will use a title before addressing someone, and that immediately makes that ordinary person a supplicant, and the titled one a person of influence. Or if both have titles, then there's upper-class solidarity. Rank, hierarchy, these are designed to create a structure whereby power is shaped in the very act of greeting someone.'

I'm getting angry again. Matt's right! Titles are part of the invisible architecture of our social structure. I'm never using one again. If I ever see Professor Slingerland in the street, I shall alert him by hollering, 'Oy, fuck-face,' then throw a hazelnut at him.

What does Matt propose?

'One thing you can do to negate this power is to be firm but respectful, and address anyone and everyone by their last name. Mr, Ms or Mrs is all the title you should ever need. This allows you to treat everyone as your equal, and it shows everyone that they should treat you as their equal.'

Right. Fair enough, I went in a bit hard there on ol' Teddy Slingerland. Or just 'Mr' Slingerland according to Matt's polite Revolution. His suggestion of equal titles for all of us is provocative.

Particularly to those of us who live in monarchies.

I mean, in England we have a Queen for fuck's sake. A Queen! We have to call her things like 'Your Majesty'. YOUR MAJESTY! Like she's all majestic, like an eagle or a mountain. She's just a person. A little old lady in a shiny hat – that we paid for. Or 'Your Highness'! What the fuck is that?! What, she's high up, above us, at the top of a class pyramid on a shelf of money with her own face on it? We should be calling her Mrs Windsor. In fact that's not even her real name, they changed it in the war to distract us from the inconvenient fact that they were as German as the enemy that teenage boys were being encouraged, conscripted actually, to die fighting. Her actual name is Mrs Saxe-Coburg-Gotha.

'Mrs Saxe-Coburg-Gotha'!! No wonder they fucking changed it. It's the most German thing I've ever heard – she might as well've been called 'Mrs Bratwurst-Kraut-Nazi'.

Titles have got to go.

I'm not calling her 'Your Highness' or 'Your Majesty' just so we can pretend there isn't and hasn't always been an international cabal of rich landowners flitting merrily across the globe, getting us all to kill each other a couple of times a decade.

From now on she's Frau Saxe-Coburg-Gotha.

Come on Frau Saxe-Coburg-Gotha, it's time for you to have breakfast with Herr Saxe-Coburg-Gotha. And you can make it yerselves. And by the way, we're nicking this fucking great castle you've been dossing in and giving it to a hundred poor families. Actually you can stay if you want, they'll need a cleaner. You'll have to watch your lip, Herr Saxe-Coburg-Gotha some of 'em ain't white.'

We British have much to gain from Matt's title-less utopia. He continues:

'It is a small thing, seemingly inconsequential. But it's not.'

No, not to the Saxe-Coburg-Gothas, they're well fucked.

'If this became common, you'd shortly see sputtering rage from the powerful, and increased agitation from the erstwhile meek. People need to mark their dominance; that is the essence of highly unequal capitalism. If they can't do so, if they aren't allowed to be dominant, to be shown as being dominant, then the system cannot long be sustained.'

Matt's ideas are like the schemes of a cackling supervillain from a Bond movie: at first they seem innocuous but then they elegantly unravel the fabric of society. He suggests we start now:

'This is something that anyone and everyone can act on, a tiny act of rebellion that takes no money, influence or social status. You just need courage, and every human has that.'

CHAPTER 11

A Pair of Dames and a Double Slit

It was likely one of my early marches in which I noticed the police were actually normal blokes in unusual outfits. Trafalgar Square on a bright spring day, emerging from the Underground, bleary-eyed and tousled like the kids in *Peter Pan*, to the fairground mayhem of a protest on the brink. Horses galloping and paving slabs ripped up. Everything all different but the same, like my face on acid, or the last day of school, when you can bring games and not wear uniform. Or an ancient Roman carnival where the servants and the masters change roles. Carnivals and fairs are a break in the norm, to let off some steam. *Carne* means meat and refers in this context to celebrations that centre on a feast. The allotted reapportioning of meat so the people that got prime cuts get sausages and them that feast on bangers get steak, overseen by Hermes or Mercury or whatever trickster deity was germane to the culture. That's probably why we enjoy *I'm a Celebrity . . . Get Me Out of Here!* or when a politician gets egged, or scandalised.

These social valves prevent uprising and a permanent reordering of social hierarchies. In mass demonstrations I feel that trickster spirit surge. The people are sick of sausages and are

121

coming for your steak. Not me, I'm vegetarian. I prefer the playful spirit of Hermes in protest, regardless of how serious the objectives, as piety and solemnity are tyrants too, oppressing ludic joy.

When up against the wall of police shields, when you've been well kettled – that means herded – you're face to face with your oppressor. Or rather the guardians of order. The oppressors are miles away, at Whitehall, or Wall Street, or at a Bilderberg meeting; the men and women who hold the shields are people like us, same fears, desires, accents. They just have a costume and a few months' training at Hendon Police College under their belt.

Human beings who want the best for their families. David Cameron said, in a rare foray into compassion, 'Hug a hoodie.' He was right, we should. We should also cuddle a copper. Was that a bit 'Yeah, man', a bit reductive? It will be, the solution will not be rarefied, the Revolution will be televised, and it will be easy and based on simple things, like interconnectivity and union. Or love.

I'm still reeling from citing David Cameron, but actually he's a human too, isn't he? Strip away the Bullingdon balderdash and the Blairy gesticulations and he's a bloke, with kids and a wife, and a God, sporadically, and a day that he will die and people that will cry.

It's not that we want an old-style Revolution of guillotines and gulags and big fancy show-trials, it's actually a powerful but gentle process where we align to a new frequency. A social recalibration. We don't want to replace Cameron with another leader: the position of leader elevates a particular set of behaviours.

My mate Nik said the first act after a successful Revolution should be the execution of its leaders. Brutal, but smart. What he means is the type of people that lead revolutions have tendencies that could become corrosive in a position of power. We have to overthrow systems, inner and outer. We have to overthrow the David Cameron in our head. We can also over-throw the literal one – that will be more fun.

Sometimes when I'm casually condemning 'them', the poli-ticians, the Halliburtons, the media, the Bilderberg regulars, the presumed illuminati, I pause to consider my own conduct. Am I just a less efficient tyrant confined to the sphere of my own little life? The fact is I am sometimes a bit. I worry that my flaws, broadcast on a global stage, would bring about a tyranny not dissimilar to the one we're trying to replace.

My own defects of character, if not addressed by a spiritual programme, would make me as toxic as Rupert Murdoch or Hitler.* The Russian writer Aleksandr Solzhenitsyn said (and please don't be intimidated by the inclusion of such an esoteric reference, in fifteen seconds you'll have read as much of his work as I have), 'The dividing line between good and evil cuts through every human heart.'

We all have dualistic and duelling intentions. This is why systems are more important than individuals and the ideals we promote more important still. It's also why David Graeber – remember him, over there on the other side of that New Orleans anecdote that rolled by like the Mississippi – believes that we must be wary of concentrated power, even if the intention is to bring about a fair and self-governing society.

'I think one thing we've learned is that creating more

---

* I'm not saying that Rupert Murdoch is as bad as Hitler. Hitler's warmon-gering and genocide remain unchallenged as the greatest crimes of modern times. However a man in the position of power that Murdoch is in choosing to neglect the possibility to make the world a fairer, more loving place and instead electing to spread fear, suspicion and prejudice while obscuring facts about highly controversial but profitable practices like fracking could bring down all humanity. Legally though I'm obliged to say that Hitler and Murdoch are two distinct entities and that Hitler was a worse bloke.

centralised power to be able to start a process which is supposed to eventually lead to less centralised power always backfires,' he said.

I feel the manner in which we construct our social organisations is integral. Rather than just eradicating the systems, we could also consider adjusting them to authentically fulfil their stated roles.

A Member of Parliament or a congressman is supposed to represent us. That means they convey our collective will. That is not what is currently happening.

The police force in America pledge to 'protect and serve'. That would actually be dandy if it were happening. Bill Hicks used to joke that he'd like to hijack a typically unpunctual plane and force it to go to its scheduled destination on time.

David Graeber said the radical alternative that we should be aiming towards is 'democracy', because whatever it is that we're toiling under now, it is not democracy.

Democracy means if enough people want a fairer society, with more sharing, well-supported institutions and less exploitation by organisations that do not contribute, then their elected representatives will ensure that it is enacted. I suppose that corruption by definition is a deviation, a perversion from the intended path.

We know that's not what's happening, don't we? We know, for example, that the dismantling and privatisation of the National Health Service is not for the benefit of us, the people who use it.

It benefits the government that proposed it and the companies that are purchasing it. Nobody voted for that because nobody would be stupid enough to give us the option.

This troubles me, not intellectually, but spiritually. Spirituality ought not to be ethereal or insubstantial but pragmatic and active.

The reason I feel optimistic in such a superficially gloomy and apocalyptic climate is I know that there are wonderful possibilities for our species that we are only just beginning to reconsider.

When the physicist speaks of the expanding universe with atheistic wonder, he is feeling the same transcendent pull that Rumi describes:

> Do you know what you are?
> You are a manuscript of a divine letter.
> You are a mirror reflecting a noble face.
> This universe is not outside of you.
> Look inside yourself;
> everything that you want,
> you are already that.

Rumi was a Sufi mystic, though I imagine if you don't know who Rumi was the addition of the definition 'Sufi mystic' isn't tremendously helpful.

'Who is Alan Devonshire?'

'He had a great left peg but dodgy knees.'

'Oh. Thank you for clarifying.'

The manifest world is telling us what to do, with increasingly obvious signals; we need only look at our codes. Symptoms are signals. We are becoming through technology increasingly adept at reading and responding to signals; alas, due to the perverse prevailing ideology we are ignoring the most important messages.

The people that currently have power are tuned in on the wrong side of Solzhenitsyn's line, temporarily forgetting that they are divinely connected. Hence ecological meltdown. The obvious signals that we need to switch to different energy systems are being ignored because they're watching another channel where the moot, outdated signal of individualistic self-advancement is being bombastically broadcast. Now is the time to change channels.

Where now can we feel this connection in our pre-packed and prescriptive lives? When are we supposed to have time amidst the deadening thud of our futile duties.

'You'll find God among the poor,' they say. Is that true any more?

Is the connection between poverty and divinity simply a panacea for the world's destitute, an assurance that they'll be rewarded in the hereafter? Or does a material deficit provide space for God?

My love of God elevates the intention of this book beyond the dry and admirable establishment of collectivised communities.

I am enraptured by the magnetic pull of evolution: what is this energy that heals the body and escalates one cell to two, that repairs and creates and calculates in harmony with environment, outside of time? Where is evolution trying to go? Evolutionary psychologists would likely say the imposition of an anthropocentric concept like 'trying' or 'intending' is naive, but I'm not going to ask one, they get enough airtime, the killjoys.

I remain uncharmed by the incessant rationalisation that requires the spirit's capitulation.

The infusion of the scientific with the philosophical is materialism. The manifesto for our salvation is not in this sparse itinerary.

This all encompassing realm, this consciousness beyond mind, cannot be captured with language any more than you can appreciate Caravaggio by licking the canvas, or Mozart by sniffing the notes on a stave.

The Transcendental Meditation Foundation, which taught

me to meditate, conducted an experiment in Washington to evaluate the effects of concentrated meditation on that city's crime figures. They got a group of people, ranging between a few hundred to a thousand, to meditate in a hotel, to see if this would impact the behaviour of the wider community. From a cynical perspective it was a bold experiment to embark upon. Why would a bunch of . . . I'm going to assume hippies, sitting still in a room, thinking a word, change the way a criminal outside in Washington would behave? In fact who funded this madness? It makes no material sense. 'We are living in a material world and I am a material girl,' sang Madonna. And she's right, it is and she is.

Quantum physicist John Hagelin was one of the scientists behind this experiment. I've chatted to him about meditation and asked for neurological data that advances meditation beyond an esoteric practice for bearded wizards in the Himalayas. Transcendental Meditation, though, was actually brought to the West by a bearded wizard from the Himalayas. Known as the Maharishi, you might recognise him from the sixties, when he was at the epicentre of a countercultural explosion, perched cross-legged on a flower-strewn stage with the Beatles.

The technique of TM that the Maharishi taught them is the type of meditation that I use. Hagelin describes it as a tool to get 'beyond thought to the source of thought'. When scanned in a meditative state the brain behaves in a tangibly distinct electrophysical way, a fourth state of consciousness. Awake, asleep, dreaming and the meditative state.

There is some distance to traverse, according to conventional thinking, between meditation producing unusual brainwaves and crime falling in a major metropolis as a result of a group of people practising it.

Over the course of the two-month experiment crime fell by

23 per cent. What's more, the figure increased in tandem with the number of people practising. John Hagelin said through meditation we can access 'the unity beyond diversity'. That beyond the atomic, subatomic, nuclear, subnuclear, there is a unified field. The results of this experiment suggest that if a significant proportion of a population regularly meditate it will affect consciousness – beyond the people involved.

Burglaries, street crime and violence all fell as a result of the state of consciousness achieved by a group of people inwardly thinking a word until a state beyond thought was reached. That's weird.

It is irrefutable proof that beyond the world that we can currently measure with tools as yet inept for such an advanced task, there is a connection between the apparently separate consciousnesses of individuals.

Consciousness exists beyond your head, between our heads, and it can manifest harmony.

That is perilously close to affirmation of a Higher Power. My experiences of meditation began before bearded pyjama time, which a friend of mine is encouraging me to describe as a mental breakdown. I don't think it was as I would say that despair is a necessary ingredient of a breakdown. What did happen at the time of my divorce was that a lot of my beliefs and their outward manifestations fell away.

My marriage ended as a result of the kind of incompatibility recognisable to anyone who's been through a break-up. Where mine may have differed is that my wedding and accompanying move to Los Angeles represented to me the crescendo of a particular type of thinking.

I, like a lot of people who come from somewhere glum, was trying to be something spectacular, always though with the subtly unabating knowledge, like an unaddressed itch, that change comes from within.

The myth of the genie and his wishes or the stories of Midas or Faust are all, I suppose, telling the same story: that you cannot outwardly acquire solutions.

Anyone as indoctrinated by capitalism as me will miss the point in those tales.

The Midas touch is still thought of as a positive thing, as opposed to the gift to turn your wife into an inanimate lump of metal.

The three genie wishes always leads to the hapless recipient slumped, head on hands, lamenting, 'I wish I'd appreciated things the way they were.' Sorry! No more wishes. Usually in these stories people wish for fame and fortune and sex and power, the things kids today want (maybe not the sex), fed on *Closer* or *Us Weekly* or whatever. It's what I wanted.

These primary-coloured, neon-lit goals are what a lot of people want and serve as a kind of psychological signpost that bluntly indicates 'Away from Here'. The present isn't good enough; the people in these magazines seem happy, or at least heightened, their faces a papped mandala for the contemplation of the secular flock.

Transcendental Meditation practitioners have established a community in Fairfield, Iowa, where they can live in accordance with the Vedic principles behind TM. It is most recognisable for its two iconic meditation domes, which loom like tranquil boobs plopped on to the pastoral view. I just turned myself on then; that can't've been their intention.

The members of this community are attempting to inhabit a kind of utopia, to live now, in accordance with spiritual ideals, not to regard the ideal society as a tantalising pipe-dream forever out of reach, but as a daily reality.

I shall tell you now and for no extra charge that 'living in the present' seems to be the key component across every scripture, self-help book and religious group I've encountered. To harmonise with life in each moment, not to make happiness contingent on any prospective condition.

Not to be tormented by the past but to live in the reality of 'now', all else being a mental construct.

Osho, Eckhart Tolle, Jesus, Buddha, Oprah, anyone who's anyone who's ever grown a beard or shaved their head or dropped out and looked back at the material world with a sage shake of the head, a knowing wag of the finger and a beatific smile, are all saying 'Snap out of it', liberate yourself from the tyranny of egoic introspection.

This is the seam of the self that consumerism can continually mine, the unrelenting inner voice that wants and fears, that attaches and rejects. The people in robes and beards want us to learn to live beyond it, to calmly watch the chattering ego like clouds moving across a perfect sky, to identify with the stillness that is aware of the voice, that hears the voice, not the voice itself.

Well, that's easy for them to say, all relaxed in their flowing robes, like giant, hairy babies; it's extremely difficult, especially when that voice has such omnipresent external allies to rely on, whilst the very idea of a spiritual life has been marginalised and maligned.

Perhaps this state needn't be the product of strenuous esotericism; it's possible that calm presence of mind is our natural state, and our jittery materialism the result of constant indoctrination. Much as I love spirituality to be served up properly branded in a turban, dressed in curtains, the accoutrements are surely an aesthetic not a prerequisite.

Once, on holiday on the Pacific coast of Mexico, I met a man who possessed a stubborn spirituality that was more earth than air, more leather than muslin. I was on the kind of luxurious holiday that will be coldly ground out like a mink cigar when sanity is restored, set to stay in a resort called Cuiximala, which I will never be confident writing or pronouncing due to that 'x' in the middle of it.

I flew into Puerto Vallarta airport from Los Angeles, then had to get a prop plane from there to the resort. Me and my mate Nicola travelled there together, she in the role of an adult nanny to facilitate the extended infancy that fame affords. Fame is like a sequin-covered suit of armour that provides a holographic cover for actual me; most people, whether their opinion is positive or negative, are content to deal with the avatar, leaving me as tender as crabmeat within. Really it's an amplification of what happens if you're not famous. I don't imagine that we are often interacting on the pure frequency of essential nature; we usually have a pre-existing set of conditions and coordinates that we project on to people we meet or circumstances we encounter.

This is not just a psychological notion. Robert Lanza, in his concept-smashing book *Biocentrism*, explains that our perception of all physical external phenomena is in fact an internal reconstruction, elaborating on the results of experiments in quantum physics, that particles behave differently when under observation – itself a universe-shattering piece of information – so that, and forgive my inelegant comprehension of the quantum world, electrons fired out of a tiny little cannon, when unobserved, make a pattern that reveals they have behaved as 'a wave', and when observed, the kinky little bastards behave as 'particles'.

That's a bit fucking mad if you ask me. That's like finding out that when you go out your dog stands up on its hind legs, lights a fag and starts making phone calls. Or turns into a cloud.

Lanza describes how our conception of a candle as a yellow flame burning on a wick is a kind of mentally constructed illusion. He says an unobserved candle would have no intrinsic 'brightness' or 'yellowness', that these qualities require an interaction with consciousness. The bastard. A flame, he explains, is a hot gas. Like any light source it emits photons, which are tiny packets of electromagnetic energy. Which means electrical and magnetic impulses.

Lanza points out that we know from our simple, sexy everyday lives that electricity and magnetic energy have no visual properties. There is nothing inherently visual about a flame until the electromagnetic impulses, if measuring between 400 and 700 nanometres in length from crest to crest, hit the cells in our retinas, at the back of the eye. This makes a complex matrix of neurons fire in our brains and we subjectively perceive this as 'yellow brightness' occurring in the external world. Other creatures would see grey. At most we can conclude, says Lanza, that there is a stream of electromagnetic energy that if denied correlation with human consciousness is impossible to conceptualise. So when Elton John said Marilyn Monroe lived her life 'like a candle in the wind' he was probably bloody right, and if he wasn't we'll never know.

We apply reality from within. The world is our perception of the world. So what other people think of you, famous or not, is an independent construct taking place in their brain and we shouldn't worry too much about it.

On my trip to Mexico I encountered Ernesto, who clearly didn't give a toss about fame. Me and Nic were due to be met at Puerto Vallarta we knew not by whom. As soon as I saw Ernesto there, half-heartedly holding a sign with a pseudonym on it, and a fag a lot more committedly, I became curious. He wore a cloth baseball cap, like a mechanic in a movie, a red polo shirt and shorts. Everything he wore looked like it had at some point been used to polish an engine. He looked weathered; I suppose that means like he had been alive a while and spent a lot of time outside. As I approached I noticed that I couldn't easily imagine this man observing the usual custom in this circumstance and carrying my luggage. He didn't. I noticed I was disgruntled but left that unexpressed.

Brown he was, Ernesto, nicotine-stained fingers, good like wood compared to plastic, I observed, as he greeted us with a fraction of a smile, a few words in Spanish, and smoked his way from the main terminal to the smaller, adjacent terminal where the prop plane awaited.

It was a red and yellow plane, so comically small and vivid it might as well've been a cartoon. It in fact looked like 'Jimbo', an anthropomorphic aeroplane from children's BBC in the eighties. It was such a diminutive aviation device that boarding it was more akin to putting on a jacket than getting on a plane. It became clear, but was never explained, that Ernesto was the pilot when he got in the driving seat and started pressing buttons. Nicola is a nervous flyer, which is annoying because we all die in plane crashes, not just nervous people, but we, the fearless, are expected to console and coo and tell them it's okay and list statistics about air travel's relative safety, 'You're more likely to die in a road accident,' etc. Well, I'm sick of it.

They're getting short shrift from me now, these blubbering sky-nancies. Phobias are like fetishes if you ask me, nurtured little perversions that the sufferers secretly enjoy. The last time a nervous flyer tried it on with me I barked at her like she was talking in an exam, and threatened to sit on her.

Nicola sat in the back, which was like she was perched in a knapsack on my back, and nervously eyed Ernesto as he, with the slapdash dexterity of a bare-knuckle croupier, prodded and jabbed dials and switches. He indicated that we should put the seat belts on. They were those ones that have no spring-loaded recall, like in an old car; it was like draping a dressing-gown chord over your shoulder. We took off with the sense of excitement that accompanies the thrill of a fairground ride with none of the guaranteed safety.

When I meet a new person, I like to take them in, give them

a damn good staring at and check my files for references. I suppose that is the beginning of prejudice. Ernesto seemed to be softening, perhaps as a result of our excitement at taking off. He began to take on the role of guide, pointing out interesting bays and coves as we flew along the coastline. 'Here we will see sharks,' he said, lowering the altitude, and sure enough we could make out a dappled grey slither of wickedness shimmering in the azure.

I began to quiz Ernesto to see if he matched up to my prejudices. I assumed him to be a man who'd lived in close harmony with the land and with machines. A pragmatic man. He may never have left Mexico, I thought.

He continued to beguile with cavalier nods to jungle gaps where marijuana crops grew and, encouraged by our interest, as the resort drew near incorporated some aeronautical stunt work into his repertoire, swooping down till we were yards above the beach; swimming village kids waved like the opening credits of a travel programme. He dive-bombed a jeep on a dirt track, his former grease-monkey persona replaced by the debonair grace of a World War I flying ace. I felt great joy and safety and decided that I loved this man. Between stunts I'd looked at his eyes and they were blue like the sea, and like the sea they had sharks in them. Wild untamable nature and certainty. Connection and power, warmth. I immediately and unthinkingly made him a father figure. When Nicola, who was leaving the next day to fly to London, was taxied back by Ernesto, I went along for the ride.

This time a seasoned co-pilot with forty minutes' experience, I felt able to switch off a little and not be so self-consciously dazzled by the view. I took to my phone to make a few texts and whatnot. I must've stared mute and listless for longer than Ernesto deemed suitable, as he jerked the plane violently up, then down, taking my breath away and making me audibly yelp. He looked at me and smiled. 'In the moment,' he said.

I'm not often chided as an adult. I usually just do what I want, and drifting into a wet-lipped torpor agog at the screen of my self-administered i-tag is one of the ways I voluntarily squander the gift of life. Well, Ernesto weren't having it. He'd given himself the role of 'elder' and was belatedly initiating me into the present.

'Travel in the old ruts,' quotes my friend Meredith, some ancient Chinese maxim. The way lain down by elders. Pathways through the world, pathways through the mind; it's a shame that these days we so seldom have a guide. That our atomised world view, mimicking scientific doctrine, sees us as separate, distinct, alone, orbiting in space, touching only an infinite void.

My cognitive sleuthing about ol' Ernesto was quite wrong. He was well travelled and had resided in Paris and had lived all kinds of urbane adventures. He'd been flying since he was fifteen, though, and up there was so confident and connected it was hypnotic. It's helpful for me to have differing visions of what spirituality might be, that it can be expressed with dog-ends not dog collars, tattered caps not turbans. Infinite potential up there in the moment, in the clouds.

CHAPTER 12

Within You, and Without You

The Fairfield Transcendental Meditation community have attempted to create external conditions that support a higher cause. Of course the fear with such a community is that it might be a bit insipid and weird, or seem like a cult. I spent a few weeks there to see what it was like to be in an environment that nourished serenity and if I could live comfortably with serenity's immediate neighbours: earnestness and humourlessness.

Even if untroubled by these conceptual neighbours, the inhabitants of the meditation community in Fairfield have literal neighbours to contend with. They cohabit their town with the ordinary rural community of Fairfield, present long before a glorious set of transcendent knockers jiggled on to the horizon, generating a dissonant hum in the small town centre. Adjacent to the predictable pinewood-and-paperbacks vegan restaurant there's a bar selling Coors and shots with a stag-hunting arcade game in the corner. The indigenous labourers, I noted, eyed the newcomers the way any immigrant community can be viewed, as threatening and unwelcome, tranquil invaders from another dimension.

The problem with communities built around sitting still and doing nothing is that, yes, you guessed it, they're a bit fucking boring, particularly to people like me, brought up on shopping centres, porno mags and crack. When I'm in a TM-themed café, about to bite into something made of parsley, I might think, 'Fuck this, there's an arcade game next door where I can shoot a bambi in the bonce.'

This attitude of churlish indifference seems like nerdish deference contrasted with the belligerent antipathy of the indigenous farm folk, who regard the hippie-dippie interlopers, the denizens of the shimmering tit-temples, as one fey step away from transvestites. I shall tell you the one negative thing about the TM community I can think of, just to get it off my chest, then I can resume my primary purpose of encouraging you to incorporate spiritual practice of some kind into your life.

They do a thing called 'yogic flying'. Now, if someone says to me, 'Russell, would you like to partake in some yogic flying?' the image I have is of myself and a few hippies levitating like Aladdin, blissed out and superior, looking down on the world in every conceivable way. If the reality of the situation is a bunch of people with their legs crossed, hopping across crash mats, a hybrid of a sport's day sack race and the Paralympics, I shall feel short-changed.

I urge my brethren in the New Age realm, those of us who want to change the world, whether from a radical political perspective or a spiritual one, to be fastidious; Richard Dawkins is watching, like the librarian of all earth's knowledge, shushing and prodding and demanding over-due diligence.

If we tell Dickie Dawkins we at last have proof of the supernatural, that we are finally manifesting a glorious new dawn for humankind, that we are ready to join the angels, then invite him into a giant tit in Iowa and show him what looks like some highly motivated amputees clamouring for a top-shelf magazine, he is unlikely to be impressed. Not that impressing Dickie Dawkins is the aim of the game: he's made his mind up to be dour. I'd hate to go on holiday with him. 'These pyramids are inaccurate, fetch my spirit level. Actually just get me a normal level; I don't believe in spirits. No, I don't want to buy a fez!'

Whilst I stayed in Fairfield, Bobby Roth, a remarkable man, in essence a priest of the TM faith, taught me to meditate. Bob would eschew the priestly title as the TM movement is understandably keen to avoid any mantles that prevent its powerful technology being unappealing to secular people because it sounds 'out there' or religious people if it seems to conflict with their ideology. To me, though, Bob, who has become a dear friend, is a type of priest or swami. A devoted man.

I have recently begun to look for people's 'vicar nature'. It is a technique I happened upon quite by chance but I think it has a precedent in eastern mysticism. In Buddhism they talk of each of us having a 'Buddha nature', a divine self, the aspect of our total persona that is beyond our materialism and individualism. Well, that's all well and good. What I'm into is people's 'vicar nature' – what a person would be like if they were a vicar. You can do it on anyone; it doesn't have to be a vicar either if that isn't your bag, it could be a rabbi or an imam or whatever. Simply think of someone you know, like, I dunno, Hulk Hogan, and imagine them as a devotional being. When I do, it helps me to see where their material persona intersects with a well-meaning spiritual aspect. Reverend Hogan would be, I suspect, a real fire-and-brimstone guy, spasming and retching in the pulpit but easily moved to tears, perhaps by the plight of a childless couple in his parish. Anyway, let's not get carried away, it's just a tool to help me see where a person's essential self might dwell.

Oddly it's really easy to do with atheists. I can imagine Richard Dawkins as a vicar in an instant, Calvinist and insistent. Dogmatic and determined, having a stern hearthside chat with a seventeen-year-old boy on the cusp of coming out.

My point is that in spite of the lack of any theological title,

Bobby Roth is like a priest. We learned TM, Nik and I, over four days in one-hour sessions that were mostly technical, with minimal ritualism and mysticism. The only standout bit of hocus-pocus was in the final session when a rose and some rice were placed on an altar. The majority of the time was spent learning the technique.

The technique is this. You shut your eyes and inwardly, silently, think a mantra. A mantra is just a word or a series of words. In this case a word. You think the word the way you would think any thought, in a relaxed, unforced way. Not like an angry inner shout – that defeats the object. You calmly, silently repeat 'mantra'. Then again, 'mantra'. You continually think 'mantra'; if you notice another thought come, and it will, you don't get wound up like you're a Texan border guard and your own thoughts are Mexican fence hoppers, you just calmly return to thinking 'mantra'. Mantra is just an example by the way, your word is secret. It is given to you by your teacher and you mustn't tell anyone else.

That was one of the hardest aspects of the process; I nearly went mad not telling my mantra to anyone else. I was like the protagonist in an Edgar Allan Poe story, demented by my secret knowledge, a metal pellet of metronomic guilt pinging off the bars in my mind. Even writing about it now makes me want to type it in a gaudy font made of lime-green letters, but I won't because I'm so fucking spiritual. Apparently this desire to grass on your own mantra is common. I told a kid in the community school about it; she said she'd had it too when she'd first learned, and I felt relieved by the kinship. Then she went, 'Yeah, but I was only seven.'

After a while, sitting in silence, the repetition of the mantra becomes natural or hypnotic. Sometimes, even now, it takes ages, like my own brain is an over-entitled and caffeinated lodger, banging down cups and whistling TV jingles. It's fucking annoying. Honestly, sometimes I'm sitting, I'm sure looking double-Christ-like, but inwardly I'm thinking with the forensic specificity of a master forger an absolute facsimile of the Kylie Minogue song 'I Should Be So Lucky'. How does my brain do that? It is the exact song, perfectly recreated, every synthetic beat and squeak rendered as authentically as if Kylie was inside my skull.

Amazing as it is that the brain can conjure up these neuro-logical illusions, which on some subtle level are a physical reality, like they must be made of an electrical impulse which has a charge or a weight, it's a fucking drag when I can't volun-tarily stop it. There is no limit to what can be imagined either; we can now, in this moment, command the mind to play the Kylie track, then instead of her singing it, have the words emerge from the mouth of an elephant in dark glasses. Your mind is doing it now. It exists. Then you can put your school's hardest kid in there, mine was Jamie Dawkins (no relation), put him on the elephant's back, dressed as Bin Laden, singing the har-monies. We have created that now with conscious energy. It has a charge and a weight, it is real and distinct from nothingness; the absence of that thought object has a different weight and charge.

Given that we live in infinite space (I don't – I live in Shoreditch), the difference between that thought object as imagined and as reality, in our shared consensual material realm, is negligible.

I mean if space is limitless, LIMITLESS, then the difference in size between an electron, an atom, a golf ball, a football, the moon, the earth, Jupiter, is all irrelevant because the context has no limit.

If you put a golf ball and a football on a table in front of you the difference in size seems significant. If you go to the other side of the room, less so. If you go down the street the difference is even less significant. If you looked from the moon it would be hard to notice. That might seem like a big jump but it isn't because we are talking about a realm beyond contextualisation. This is what exists in consciousness. A potentially limitless realm in which we can engineer and then project new realities.

The astronaut Edgar D. Mitchell said of his experience of viewing Earth from the moon, 'You develop an instant global consciousness, a people orientation, an intense dissatisfaction with the state of the world and a compulsion to do something about it. From out there on the moon international politics looks so petty. You want to grab a politician by the scruff of the neck and drag him a quarter of a million miles and say "Look at that, you son of a bitch."'

I love this quote for many reasons. One, because it illustrates that all the well-meaning talk of oneness, such as you have found in this book, is built upon an empirical reality. We're all one, the human family; when you pull back to outer space or dive within to inner space, that becomes clear. I like that travelling to the moon was such an emotional and spiritual experience for Edgar, as I have always thought that astronauts would be tough military types that wouldn't be given to such profound pronouncements.

Mostly, though, I love his violent conclusion that he'd like to grab a politician by the scruff of the neck and take him to the moon. Firstly, because to grab anyone by the scruff of the neck is an animal and implausible thing to do. I just felt the back of my neck and there's barely any scruff to grab. Unless this politician had a particularly fat neck, Edgar would have to be content with an inch of skin between his thumb and forefinger, like he was holding a teacup; he might as well have his pinkie finger extended.

Then he'd have to kidnap the bloke, presumably from Washington, drag him all the way to Cape Canaveral, Florida, into the NASA HQ, presumably give him some basic space training, put him in a suit, a rocket, strap him in, spend a few days getting to the moon, then finally march him out and admonish him for his lack of perspective.

I don't think he could sustain his indignation for that long. I reckon he'd start to feel a connection to the terrified politician at some point during that journey, possibly in the training section, where they'd have to acclimatise to zero gravity in a swimming pool.

Also, surely once Edgar got back to the moon and he looked back to Earth, his love of all the members of the human family would kick back in and he might feel too guilty to lay into the sobbing and vertiginous undisclosed politician.

Among the small number of people who have seen our planet from space this sense of enlightenment is seemingly common. There are loads of comparable quotes that illustrate this strong sense of connection and fraternity. I chose Edgar D. Mitchell's one because he's the only astronaut who saw his epiphany as an impetus to snatch a senator and beat him up on the moon like an intergalactic Vito Corleone.

In meditation, through the repetition of your mantra, or in other techniques, with the focus of your attention on your breath, a candle or a riddle, eventually thought relents. What is consciousness when thought abates? What I have experienced when I'm able to get through the inner ticks and mental tricks that the ego uses to prevent transcendence is a warm relief. I had it today. At first when I closed my eyes I was uncomfortable and had to adjust myself, my back or legs or nuts can feel taut or trapped and I can't relax. I notice sometimes that I'm holding tension in my jaw or my shoulders, I consciously let it go; how can you be at peace if you are subtly exerting pressure, holding energy somewhere in your body? The first condition is quiet, the second is comfort, then I can start.

Today the Monty Python 'Lumberjack Song' was in residence in my head. I'd just watched it online and when I shut my eyes it vividly replayed. I didn't try to kick the jaunty ditty and grinning Michael Palin off the carousel of thoughts; I instead focused on letting go of the tension in my jaw and pulling a trapped bit of ballbag out from between my legs. It was my own ballbag.

This management of anatomical minutiae completed, I began thinking the mantra. The mantra vied with Palin and my jaw for mental supremacy. I stay relaxed and detached; I don't get aggressive about asserting the mantra. The temptation is to feel aggrieved that your own mind won't do your bidding. Like Dr Strangelove's hand saluting a disintegrated Reich of previous contemplation. The point is, though, the object of focus is not relevant. If I become attached to the idea of a perfect inward incantation, that is an egoic act. The aesthetics of thought activity are unimportant. In my experience the mystical qualities of the mantra, by which I mean, that which is not known, are secondary to the hypnotic effect of repetition. To me it seems that eventually the busy, chattering 'monkey-mind' eventually accepts that all that is happening is the repetition of a word and just sort of fucks off to sleep.

The Maharishi, and perhaps his version warrants more credence given it was he who brought this technique to the West, described it thusly: if the mantra is the word 'rose', every time the word 'rose' is repeated the conscious mind, in anticipation of the coming repetition, moves closer to the unconscious source of thought which generates all mental phenomena. With each repetition, deeper goes the awareness that hears it, in preemptive increments, until eventually that awareness is submerged within the source and thus unified.

The Maharishi's description is probably more scientific and prettier; go with whatever you want. The great American comedian Jerry Seinfeld, who has practised TM for over thirty years, puts it into typically succinct terms: 'It's like plugging your phone into a charger twice a day for twenty minutes.'

These two twenty-minute interludes – one in the morning, one in the evening – also serve to remind me that there is more to life than what I'm doing and thinking, what I fear and desire, what I think of other people and what they think of me. During those times I experience something beyond those concerns and it's a great relief.

My friend Meredith, who is archetypically a 'wise woman', who if we were in a fairy tale we'd meet in a wood – said to me, 'Enlightenment is already present, how could it be otherwise?' meaning that the state of enlightenment, union, Christ-consciousness or whatever must be present already in the mind, at least the capacity for it. It is not manufactured or engineered; it is by relinquishing other stimuli or factors that this state can emerge.

'The kingdom of heaven is within,' said Jesus, perhaps in reference to the euphoric relief from earthly burden achieved through alignment with a pre-existing but unutilised frequency of consciousness that carries you to the bliss that exists beyond self.

I experience that bliss when I meditate. It feels simultaneously relaxing and empowering. Actually, though, the awareness that it has been pleasant comes subsequently, because during a 'successful' meditative experience there really isn't a self to apply the labels of 'relaxing' or 'empowering'.

I wish I had it every time, but even after five years' practising, sometimes my scuttling mind will not yield, the jittery busybody of my inner museum cataloguing and caterwauling, applying adjectives and conditions to external phenomena that would be best left alone.

An unexpected benefit of this process is an increased compassion for others, a dawning recognition of the connection between us all. Since meditating I feel that the intuitive connection to others that I've always felt has been somehow enhanced.

I'm lucky in that I have a mother who is pathologically loving and gentle. Who unfussily loves animals and children and tries to see the good in everyone – thank God, because in my case it was pretty well hidden. This perhaps inherited positive trait, though, was redundant and unexpressed for much of my life as I was entangled in the sparkles and the spangles, mangled in the crackling drudge, addicted to attention and drugs.

Since I've been clean and have increasingly made spiritual pursuits my priority, these neglected traits have become more and more definite. Don't get me wrong, erring is for me a daily occurrence. Each evening when I reflect on the day's events, like a *Match of the Day* highlights show which is just about the stuff I've done, there's usually one or two clips where I wince at my selfishness or missed opportunities to move closer to the source.

*   *   *

FOR EXAMPLE, PART of the programme I follow is to each day, try to do something for someone else. If that seems gallingly obvious to you, you are likely not an addict. I can quite easily, if not guided by higher intention, spend the whole day just pursuing things for myself. Being nice to your cat or husband doesn't count: those immediate tribal alliances could be regarded as self-serving, in that it's like pruning the garden of your life. You live in these relationships as surely as you live in your house; maintenance is a necessity.

I mean general kindness to others in the spirit of service. This can include, for someone in my position, aiding, advising and supporting other recovering drug addicts and alcoholics. Taking time to help them with their, frankly incessant, problems and quandaries, knowing that some other poor recovering drunk will have to listen to mine. It can also mean helping strangers and people that circumstance has put in your way but are of no obvious benefit to you. What used to be called civility: carrying bags, opening doors, giving up seats – putting others before yourself.

I have begun to understand that in doing these things I ameliorate the invisible boundaries that imprison me in my head. If I prioritise the needs of others, even in small ways, above my own needs, the illusion of my material, individual self being supreme subtly begins to break down.

There is great relief in this as we were designed to live in communities and tribes but these systems have in our culture for various reasons broken down and we feel lonely as a result, because we are detached from nature – I don't mean nature as in a bunch of trees and rivers, although they're nice too; I mean nature as in our own nature, we are nature.

We are a part of the whole, connected to the whole, like old Edgar saw from the moon. We are all one, on a speck of dust in a shaft of light. When I live in the illusion of a separate self, the part of me that knows I am at one with all phenomena feels starved and bereft. These dopey little acts of kindness move me back towards the truth.

It actually gives me a little rush if I do a kind thing, like just phone someone up, someone who I want nothing from, and check if they're okay. After I've done it I get this little tingle and I think that is a small, synaptic reward for reconnecting with truth.

I saw once a depiction of the ol' brain in action; I saw the synapses, the nerves or tunnels or roads through which energy or information, travels. It wasn't a photo, this stuff is too microscopic to be observed in that way; it was probably some sort of scan or graphic. Energy travels from synapse to synapse across a tiny space.

A thought, or an impulse, crosses space to get to a related synapse. Consciousness, thoughts, are travelling through space in your head; we are travelling through space on this beautiful biosphere, Earth. If consciousness can traverse inner space, then perhaps it can traverse outer space. Perhaps we are as connected by consciousness as we are by the air that we all breathe. The air we inhale through the holes in our faces which tumbles into our lungs and blood, which travels through our hearts, which forms the words we speak, the air which we exhale, which is connected to all air, an unbroken entity, like all the water in all the rivers in the world, leading to the sea, touching one another.

John Lennon said when you look into the sky you think of it as far away but if you follow it down with your eyes you're standing in sky.

You can regard this as adorable tosh and bunkum if your conditioning demands it, but so much of the truth is neglected. These truths are more important than the beliefs that I was taught to make me a compliant subject instead of an active citizen.

West Ham's results, the Oscars, X *Factor*, even high cultural musings on Piketty or Roth or Bach or Beckett are not more important than the physical reality of our oneness. Anything that directs consciousness away from that truth instead of towards it is bollocks and it has to go.

Don't worry, I panicked myself there a bit. I'm not suggesting a year zero book-burning immolation of all culture. I'd really miss West Ham and, to be honest, there's nothing wrong with X *Factor*, in its place.

Given that the profound can be quite well hidden in the spritz, tits and glitz of the all-encompassing barmy mainstream culture, it is helpful to have stories, rituals and practices that attune us to less obvious but more important aspects of reality.

Prayer, meditation and simple altruistic acts are behavioural portals to a neglected dimension. My personal daily programme includes all three: I pray, meditate and try to be kind – not generally, particularly. If I feel sad or agitated, I check myself and think, 'Hang on, Russell, have you done anything for anyone but yourself today?' Shockingly the answer is sometimes 'No', then I immediately hurl myself into enforced altruism, inflicting my aid on anyone in the vicinity.

'Sir, let me carry that.'

'It's my walking stick, I need it.'

'Hogwash, hand it over.'

The super-Jedi level of advanced altruism is when you do a kindly act and don't get found out. Like no one is allowed to know about it. Now that is hard. God, I thought keeping my mantra secret was a challenge, try doing something generous and kind and not telling anyone – even your boyfriend or your mum. It's like knowing George Michael was gay in 1986 or that Kennedy was murdered by secret services in 1963 – you want to scream it from a grassy knoll outside the Club Tropicana.

If you tell anyone, it doesn't count. God, it's tough. The other practical measure you can take is to make amends when you inevitably do something wrong. If you're rude or if you hurt someone's feelings, you have to apologise. I often get impatient. Impatience means I think, or my ego thinks, that it knows how the world should be running and wants to impose its will.

My impatience can flare up in any situation. When I'm stuck in traffic I can quickly sever my connection to serenity and become a senselessly fuming impotent Hulk. The infuriating sense that my environment isn't behaving how it's supposed to is a kind of mental illness. The belief that my anger can influence the flow of cars up Shaftesbury Avenue is insanity. That is a very simple demonstration of how I voluntarily enter into a negative illusion. I become an impotent fury; the only people affected by my emotions are myself and the people with me, unless I allow it to contaminate the world further by winding down the window. To have the presence of mind to acknowledge that my only power in this situation is the power to make the situation worse.

I checked into a hotel the other day. I had a belief that the process of administering a key should happen more quickly than it was actually happening. I began to become hot and fast and flustered. I started to impose my will on the people working at the hotel. As this is happening, there is a silent presence in me that knows my conduct is not cool, that I have moved out of alignment with my principles, that I have become defective.

The presence also knows that it will be the one that has to come back downstairs to the hotel lobby later and apologise for being impolite and impatient. For now, though, this presence is tethered and very much a breathy backing vocal, drowned out by the bombastic lead singer who is saying stuff that is hard to own: 'Just use a skeleton key to get me to the room and then do the admin later and I'll sign when I next pass through.'

The backing vocal is in this moment just a passenger but knows this behaviour is arrogant, that this is not the man I have worked hard to become, that temporarily, arrogant Russell has seized control of the steering wheel and is trying to do as much damage as he can before he's pulled over. Even whilst I'm administering haughty admonishments, the secondary, recently acquired, more awakened aspect of my being is preparing to apologise. Of course the aim is to reach the point where I can fully contain the drama, where my defective conduct doesn't leak out into other people's lives. I reckon 80 per cent of my madness is caught at the gateway to the outside world, which I suppose is my mouth. Before, when I drank and used drugs, I had no ability to refine my madness and it would bleed, unfiltered, across the blank day. The drink and drugs are in effect tools to anaesthetise the impetus to act destructively and the pain caused as a consequence.

When drugs and alcohol and other compulsive behaviours are removed, you can address the problems that lead to their use. When you have an understanding of those behaviours and some techniques to help you when you inevitably err, it is possible to develop a different conscious experience through prayer and meditation.

Fairfield, Iowa, a community built round an ideal and a pair of tin boobs, provided me with sanctuary when I was writing *Booky Wook 2*. We stayed in one of the serene cottages that satellite out from the orbs. Bob Roth gave us daily meditation lessons and took us round the educational institutes which are central to the community. There was a university and several schools catering to kids of all ages and they seemed to me pretty typical, except twice daily the kids would break and meditate.

I meditated with the kids and it was lovely. I was surprised, though, when I chatted to a group of them that their ambitions for later life, which is one of the mandatory routes of enquiry open for an adult quizzing strange children, along with 'How's school?' and 'Are you courting?', were utterly in sync with those of any teenagers: they all wanted to be famous. The ambience of serenity and access to a realm of inner peace, a daily connection to the source of all phenomena, hadn't alleviated the yearning to strut about on stage in glittery leggings. Of course these kids were smart enough to dress it up in fancy notions of art and humanitarianism, we can all do that – 'I'm going on *Britain's Got Talent* to end the horror of landmines' – but it's difficult to avoid the conclusion that inner peace does not exempt you from the tractor beam of pop culture. Only one kid wanted to be a scientist and I'm pretty sure he was Japanese. Thinking about it, Lakeside had a sort of dome bit at the centre, like a mammary-gland conservatory, an augmented bust on an eroticised Statue of Liberty. Are humans really so geometrically rudimentary, like ducklings waddling along after our first nutritional kick?

I'm certainly not condemning Fairfield: it has a lot going for it, and an aspiration to place spirituality at the core of the human experience, more than all else, is integral to our survival.

Perhaps it's like communism in the traditionally understood sense: it must be absolute, it can't survive in an adversarial context, continually bombarded with oppositional consumer messaging. Those Fairfield kids with their stardust dreams are like pre-glasnost Moscow teens craving blue jeans and Big Macs.

One night a couple of college girls came to the house while me and Nik were sleeping, to flirt with us. We awoke to see them, youthful and hopeful, on the veranda. I was engaged at the time and had to turn them away due to a moral code. We watched them leave, dopily incensed by our angelic chastity, the way a dog watches distant sheep, doleful with swaddled instinct. We comprise the high ideals of the meditators and the earthly yearnings of the indigenous farm folk, for whom I noted (from posters about the town) a travelling cage-fighting contest was a forthcoming attraction.

CHAPTER 13

Spiderman on Line One

The oft-trotted-out Native American parable seems apposite here. It goes: 'Each of us has two dogs in us, a black one and a white one.' This is clearly metaphorical; don't get caught up in the old-lady-who-swallowed-a-fly anatomical improbability of the set-up, or the stock folk-tale assumption that black is negative and white positive, otherwise we'll be here all day and will never get to the point of the story.

If I was an Iroquois tribal witch doctor and you started quizzing me on the visual grammar of my fable, I'd slip you a herb to make you impotent or just whack you with my tomahawk.

'The two dogs are vying for dominance,' the tale continues.

'Which one wins?' asks the necessarily cooperative recipient of the lesson.

'The one I feed,' is the sage conclusion.

There are two Fairfields, as surely as we have multiple potential selves; the dominant ideology will likely be the one that's the focus of the most energy.

The subversion or coalescence with this corporeal, prior culture is the most obvious challenge we face in trying to bring about a truly different human experience. This is the nexus: do you want to learn how to unify your individual field of consciousness with a unified realm of bliss and tranquillity, or do you want to lie spread-eagled and drooling on crystal while Taylor Swift tickles your brain into a saccharine coma?

My only qualification for proselytising is my ardent pursuit of the latter option and eventual acceptance of the former. I suppose we must each ask of ourselves – or each other, have fun with it, it could be a quiz – two fundamental questions: 1) Are you happy with things the way they are? And 2) Do you believe that things could be better?

I know most people want change. I know most people can't be happy with the current regime, not least because in any electoral process worth having we might assume that the 3.5 billion people that have as much wealth collectively as the 85 people on the increasingly clammy, fast-moving, unsustainable fun bus would vote for a fairer system.

Surely the remaining 3.5 billion earthlings, minus the 85 fun bus-tards and their relatives, are up for some amendments an' all. I just used the calculator on my phone to subtract 85 from 3.5 billion and the answer had a letter in it. It did, it had a letter 'e' in it.

Even the calculator has gone berserk at this injustice.

That aside, I think a significant number of people are not happy with the way things are; I'm not and I've done alright out of this system – I've got a big house, a nice cat and when I write books, they're immediately put on the school curiculum. So this system has not been bad to me. I've been given everything that I wanted. The problem is, I didn't really want it, that desire was put there. Who put it there? And why?

And why doesn't it work? Do you remember when Haiti had that earthquake? You probably don't, you self-centred swine, and if you do I bet it's because of the star-spangled telethon that came in its wake.

The telethon is a near permanent fixture in our culture and

in a way the perfect concoction for a society that wants to release hot little farts of compassion, but without wanting to ever actually follow through.

I have done a fair bit of that stuff, like Comic Relief in the UK, and I was invited to participate in this grotesquely beautiful effort to provide aid for the victims of the 2010 disaster by George Clooney, and was instantly told by someone at the agency that attendance was mandatory as it was a good career opportunity. Which I'm sure, as much as the rice and antibiotics, soothed the displaced Haitians. 'I'm sorry you lost your house and leg and dog and daughter – here's some medicine that was purchased in the most glamorous way imaginable, in a format that's given some Hollywood newcomers a real chance to shine.' George Clooney obviously set up this event with the best of intentions, with incredible effort, using his visibility and luminance to draw attention to the vital need for humanitarian aid. Clearly no one would condemn him for this kindness. It is just unfortunate that when philanthropy meets the machinery of celebrity it acquires such an unpleasing hue.

The reason this event was spectacular in the crowded market place of televised benefits was because of the sheer density of stars. It was obscene. Like fame porn. As I nervously shuttled through security like a first-day intern into the CBS studios I was so overwhelmed by the frequency of famous faces in an enclosed space that I almost exploded. If I had've done it would have dramatically reconfigured the firmament of popular entertainment and been so newsworthy that it would've dwarfed the earthquake we were nominally there to redress. What is this tenuous equation between fame and tragedy?

What celestial matchmaker has slung together these mismatched phenomena? Fame to treat famine, fame to treat poverty, fame to take the boredom away. An implausible coupling that advances the benefactor more than the beneficiary.

A panacea for a sickness that we feed as we claim to treat it. A snake-oil cure for a reptilian nation. Still, I went anyway; as I say, it was a good opportunity.

I'm glad I went too, it was like Madam Tussauds after a visit from a wizard. I was instructed that under no circumstances was I to be late – this was a compassion party for the glitterati and lateness was not an option. At no point in the administrative process that preceded my attendance was there a whiff, hint or mention of the people of Haiti. It appalls me to confess that I don't recall having any actual connection with the reality of the situation: that a natural disaster had sent a nation spiralling into chaos, disarray and tragedy. In my head it was kind of like I was a last-minute replacement for the best man at George Clooney's wedding and had to get to the venue on time at all costs. Which sounds a bit like the plot of a film he'd be in.

I'm not pointing the finger at anyone else, by the way; they may all have been there with the noblest intent. I can't imagine Robert De Niro was there to hobnob and network. I'm prepared to accept sole responsibility for this hollowness and duplicity; perhaps it was just me that had no visceral, human connection to the suffering. Actually, though, isn't that was these telethons are for? Not to actualise the disaster, to make it real, feel it, process it and resolve it but to remove it, package it, give it a framework that is manageable somehow.

Yes, the tectonic plates are colliding and humanity is tumbling into the magma at the earth's core, but don't worry, we've got Leonardo DiCaprio on line 1.

If you're lucky, you get Leo or De Niro or Pacino or Daniel Day-Lewis or J-Lo or Brangelina.

In one little sweep of my eye across a distance of about twelve yards I was able to assemble the above constellation in some ghoulish, grafted menagerie of fame, the lot of them stacked up in phone banks like really well-groomed battery hens. It made me feel a bit sick and nervous and then laugh and do a bit of wee. But the density, the density of stars, too many to be a constellation, in such numbers they became more gas than solid; like the nebula of collapsing gas that incites the stellar inception. Like an episode of *Celebrity Squares* held at Diana's funeral.

Too much. Just too much, and as William Blake has always said, the road of excess leads to the palace of wisdom. The wisdom reached by excess of this nature is that it's all fucking bollocks, the celebrity equivalent of making a kid you catch smoking a fag do the whole packet. 'So it's fame you like, is it? Well, how about all the famous people in the world jammed into one, chilled airless, glass box? Hahahahahahaha!'

Not everyone who called in by phone to pledge their donation was lucky enough to get George or Jack or Al. Some of 'em got me and after about the third person had indignantly enquired 'Who?' and I had tired of explaining *Sarah Marshall* and Sachs-gate I just started saying 'Yeah, it's Spiderman here, how can I help you?' and hoping that Tobey Maguire couldn't hear me.

In my haste to arrive on time for this glistening festival of opulent first aid, me and my mates had driven like loonies the wrong way up the hard shoulder of a freeway. It's the only time I ever felt free on one.

I know George Clooney is probably a decent geezer an' all that and I'm no more condemning him for the vacuity of celebrity-driven humanitarianism than I am David Cameron for capitalism. I'm just saying, how long can you inhabit this sparkling candy palace without wanting to kick down the walls? If you're not on the inside trying to get out, are you outside trying to get in? Or are you indifferent to the whole charade? Were you never taken in?

Under what circumstances is continuing to live like this the best option? Only if you have no belief that any alternative is possible. Only then.

The celebrities feel better for taking part. The callers feel better for donating. The Haitians get a bit of aid that they should rightly have been given under the covenant of brotherhood that exists between us all, and we all just smile and pretend there's no alternative.

There is another way. There is the way. To live in accordance with truth, to accept we are on a planet that has resources and people on it. We have to respect the planet so we can use the resources to nourish the people. Somehow this simple equation has been allowed to become extremely confusing.

If I, so close to the peak, could glean no joy from that rarefied air, the air I was told, as soon as I'd acquired language, would absolve me, if in fact all I gleaned was the view from that peak, the vista true, that the whole climb had been a spellbound clamber up an edifice of foolishness, then what possible salvation can there be for those at the foothills or dying on the slopes or those for whom the climb is not even an option? What is their solution? Well, it's the same solution that's available to me, the only solution that will make any of us free. To detach the harness and fall within.

Now that's what I call an extended metaphor.

In Fairfield, Iowa, then, there could be the solution. But none of us want a boring solution. The Revolution cannot be boring.

CHAPTER 14

Get Money Out of Politics

Do we as human beings alive now, us, the sum total of humanity (I assume everyone is reading this book), do we have a vision? A shared vision towards which we can move in synchronicity?

As a man in recovery I must remain in serenity, clean and serene; I've spent enough time jazzed, wired, buzzing and gouching. Serenity is the first thing people with addiction issues are instructed to request:

> God, grant me the serenity,
> To accept the things I cannot change,
> Courage to change the things I can,
> And the wisdom to know the difference.

That's what junkies and alkies and bulimics and gamblers and sex addicts and love addicts and people who can't stop shopping, smoking, loving, fighting – whatever it is, there's someone out there who's doing too much of it – and for those people there's a solution and sanctuary, and in those places of sanctuary, this prayer is recited.

The first thing is serenity. The agitation has to end. The itchy irritability, the restlessness, the wanting. So do the lows, the self-loathing, wretched, heavy-hearted, lead-gutted, teary-eyed, dry-mouthed misery. The pain. So do the highs. The wide-eyed, bilious highs, the cheek-chewing, trouble-brewing highs, the never-stopping-till-I-touch-the-sky highs, the up-at-dawn, hitting-the-pipe highs, chasing, defacing, heart-racing highs, gagging, shagging, blagging highs. All the things we do to change the way we feel, the way the world looks and tastes: it's all got to go.

So courage is necessary. Courage to change yourself, the one thing you can change. Your attitude and actions. Neither the serenity nor the courage are available to you on your own; if they were, you would've found them by now – you've been pretty fastidious in your research.

God, however you conceptualise him, will have to grant them to you. And whatever you conceptualise God as, with your human mind, your individual brain, made up of instinctive responses, training and memories, however you conceptualise a power, that's beyond you and the decisions you've made so far, your conception will be extremely limited. Likely as limited as my cat's conception of the Internet.

The invisible network of interconnected portals that communicate data are beyond my cat's comprehension. My cat's inability to comprehend does not impede the Internet. The World Wide Web (which is incidentally quicker to say than double-you, double-you, double-you-dot) will continue to exist, regardless of my cat's awareness.

Pray then for wisdom, wisdom to know the difference between things we can change and things we can't. Likely this will be a lifetime's work undertaken one day at a time. Which for humans is the way time happens. I don't have to live the 25th of May 2022 yet. I might never have to. I only have to live in this moment. That's why meditation comes in handy and practising it as a community has benefits too. How are we to achieve real change, conditions in which practices that lead to a different type of consciousness can plausibly be pursued?

I spoke to my friend Dave DeGraw, a seasoned and let's say grizzled activist and member of the Occupy movement. Dave knows loads about global politics, protest, economics and so on, and uses words like 'metrics' and 'paradigm'. He also speaks a bit like a beatnik and seems forever on the verge of using antiquated Kerouacian slang like 'Cool it, daddio.' I wrote to him electronically and asked him how to change the world.

'If you're expecting political legislation to solve any of our problems, you're barking up the wrong dead ole tree. No matter what issue you care about most, no real lasting change will come from a rigged and corrupt system.'

I'd say his opening gambit there is a pretty good example of what I was saying. 'Dead ole tree' sounds like the way that Allen Ginsberg would describe a Republican's penis.

Dave's first observation is that to bring about real change we have to act outside the current political system, which chimes with what Naomi Klein said about advance on environmental issues: real change will not be delivered within the machinery of the current system – it's against their interests.

'Unless we get money out of politics – campaign finance, lobbying and the revolving door between governments and the most powerful global corporations – we are not going to create change within those old obsolete and decaying governmental systems.

Princeton University recently did a study revealing what those of us paying attention already know all too well: the United States is, in *scientifically proven fact, not a democracy*. They concluded that the US is controlled by economic elites.'

This is a prominent idea that is becoming popular. The structural reason that voting is redundant is that through the funding of political parties, lobbying and cronyism, corporations are able to ensure that their interests are prioritised above the needs of the electorate and that ideas that contravene their agenda don't even make it into the sphere of public debate. Whoever you vote for, you'll be voting for a party that represent a big-business agenda, not the will of the people.

'Here in the US, and in many countries around the world, these governments were created in a bygone era, in the time of the horse and wagon. It took days to get one handwritten message across state lines. You needed representatives for the government to function. Now, here we are, in 2014, with instantaneous worldwide communication. Now, we have access to unlimited information. A kid with a cell phone has access to more information than the president of the United States had only 25 years ago.'

*   *   *

TWENTY-FIVE YEARS AGO the president was Ronald Reagan, it's probably for the best. He didn't seem like he'd be that at ease with technology. I was quite anxious that he had the power to launch nuclear missiles, and rightly so, as we now know he was already suffering from dementia. It says a lot for our expectations of politicians that no one really noticed.

'The need to have a handful of "representatives" deciding our collective fate, to just have two or three dominant political parties, in this age of mass communication, is a sick and perverted joke.'

Dave is getting into his stride now, he's really moving into beatnik mode; he's probably on the precipice of taking a mighty puff on his 'doobie' and giving the bongos a real wallop.

'Once every two, four or six years we get to vote for Puppet A or Puppet B, oh please. Tommy Jefferson was an enlightened cat; he had a lot of brilliantly insightful riffs.'

Yep, thought so, he's called revered statesman Thomas Jefferson, 'Tommy', referred to him as 'an enlightened cat' and called his oratorical pronouncements 'riffs'. I bet he wrote this with no shoes and socks on, wearing them little round John Lennon sunglasses. He continues with a Jefferson quote:

'"Every generation needs a new Revolution." He said that over 200 years ago, not one Revolution in this nation since then.'

It's good to know that respectable, bewigged statesmen like Jefferson knew that to prevent an incremental drift towards hegemony and corruption each generation would need to re-assert a demand for fairness. One of the ways the current power structures are protected is through tradition: 'You can't meddle with the constitution, the economy, the monarchy – it's one of our proudest traditions.' A tradition is just an old idea, only of value if it remains relevant.

To remain relevant it must resonate with timeless principles, principles of unity and fairness. These institutions and statutes are riddled with language that fetishise unity and oneness: 'one nation under God', 'the monarch's duty to preserve peace'; when it comes to crunch time, the only time that's real, the only maxim these ideas protect, is elitist and hegemonic.

Dave DeGraw is right: traditions that do not help us are as valuable as excess fingernail and should be dispensed with in the same manner. I deplore those long, brown, curly-fingernail folk. I don't even especially like people who have one long thumbnail for guitar. My mate Karl has one and it scratched me the other day. I was sickened.

CHAPTER 15

Spectacular

How can modern technology aid democracy?

'From a technological standpoint, we are ready for "Liquid Democracy", with Liquid Democracy you can designate your vote on any issue to any person of your choice. For example, if there is an economic policy that is coming up for a vote, but you don't understand the policy that well, you can give your vote to someone you trust who does understand the policy. With the level of technology that we now have, that's a commonsense sensible political system that would provide a vibrant democracy and legitimately reflect the will of the people.'

Liquid Democracy then, a form of direct, electronic, participatory democracy that acknowledges that a lot of people won't vote on a tedious issue like planning permission for a new sewage system. Which inadvertently implies that the liquid in this liquid democracy is faecal. Nonetheless, in a devolved, collectivised, participatory democracy a small, self-determined constituency can nominate an accountable figure to act on their behalf. As we've said before in relation to Dave Graeber's input, democracy would be good, democracy ain't what we've got. An empowered, involved civil society who see their collective will delivered is now a possibility. Adam Curtis has insisted with a tenacity and fervour that truly only belongs in cage-fighting, that I point out that social media like Facebook and

Twitter are of no use when it comes to bringing about radical change, he regards these arriviste communicative tools as useful only for 'clicktivsm' and loose social ties, not the ardent bonds required to get people to risk their lives confronting authority. I think that as new ideologies are nurtured and deployed, new social tools like those mentioned will be as useful as anything else in connecting people and conveying information. As long as Facebook don't at the behest of the FBI stick up a load of moody info designed to put you on a massive downer.

Switzerland are already cracking on with direct democracy with results which are impeded, I think, by the context in which they occur. Switzerland, have you ever been there? It's peaceful, it's clean, the chocolate is delicious, but the Swiss people are dependant upon the same sources of information that everywhere else is, so their state of limited electronic referenda reflects that.

Anyone can get a bill voted on if they get 50,000 signatories. Some interesting referenda have been held:

1. Basic income: give everyone a basic income of twenty grand a year and get rid of all forms of welfare. Welfare carries stigmatisation – this policy could address that.

    They voted against it.

2. Maximum wage: CEOs of companies, head honchos and big cheeses are earning too much money. In America your average CEO (if you can conceive of such a being) earns 350 times the average worker's salary. There should be a cap for top earners, either a ratio, like ten times the lowest-paid member of the workforce, or a figure, say 500,000 euros, pounds or dollars. The Swiss held a referendum.

    They voted against it.

3. Restrictions on the construction of new places of worship, like mosques. A lot of folk, as you know, from the media are worried about the type of vocal and visual symbols people use when envisaging supreme energy fields from which all other energy fields are derived. The Swiss held a referendum on whether to ban the building of more mosques.

They voted for it.

Now, I am not about to claim, as we approach the midpoint of this book, to be a social scientist; there is too much dependence on anecdotal evidence, too much faith in the mystical and too much radicalism for that. Plus zero education in that field: you almost certainly require A levels, fuck that; my point is that the outcome of these referenda are suspiciously concordant with the will of the elites that typically exert their power through more easily manipulated dual-party democracy. Why is that?

'The first step toward evolution and freedom is to get a conscious understanding of the mental prison that we are all bred into. Our consciousness is conditioned from cradle to grave. As the ghost of Goethe whispers in the wind . . . "None are more hopelessly enslaved than those who falsely believe they are free."'

What the results of direct democracy in Switzerland indicate is that even measures that seem to put power directly into the hands of the people are redundant if we are not given access to reliable information. We need a media that isn't governed by the same ideology as the big businesses for whom our governments administrate. Dave uses this illustrative Guy Debord quote to help us understand the information we are fed through the media and the function of that information:

'"For what is communicated are orders . . . those who give them are also those who tell us what they think of them."'

Debord, who was a clever old stick and as French as adultery, was a 'situationist', this was a gang of avant-garde artists, political theorists and smart-arses who thought that Marxism was basically alright but a bit too strict – what with the gulags and murders and bullying.

That, though, didn't detract from the irrefutable fact that capitalism, in spite of providing us with lovely tellies and an apparently enhanced standard of living, was eroding the essential experience of being human. They thought that it led to social alienation – us lot feeling all lonely, detached from each other, our environment and our own nature, plus commodity fetishisation.

I like the word 'fetish' – you've probably noticed, I keep using it. Fetish was originally used to describe an object of religious devotion, like a relic sold by an archaeologist trickster: 'This is Saint Bernadette's finger – it's yours for a fiver.' You could then stare at the dubious digit and think a bunch of holy stuff, the object providing a visual focus for devotional mental activity.

These days when we hear the word – when I first heard the word – it was in regard to sexual fetish. 'Frank's got a foot fetish,' you might hear. This is where poor ol' Frank has got himself into such a palaver about how's yer father that he can no longer express himself through straightforward coital activity, which due to his childhood or whatever he regards as a dumb mechanical thrust of flesh pistons and clutching, mucus-covered valves.

His only way back to enjoyment of erotic activity is via a manageable deviation from the pure source, like a lovely well-pedicured tootsie, with violet-lacquered nails, like his Auntie Val used to have when she rocked him on her lap and he felt free from the clammy tyranny of Mummy's arms and the clattering exasperation of Daddy's tobacconated sigh. That's Frank for ya, the poor bugger.

Commodity fetishism is the application of fulfilment to an

object that can be acquired through the market. We know, don't we, in our little hearts, in our clearer, truer selves, that a Ferrari, whilst superficially, geometrically pleasing and aesthetically titillating with its curves and pulsating, scarlet haunches, is just a bloody dumb lump of potential travel. A swift little electronic cart.

We know, don't we, in the place in our hearts where we felt connected to our first friend, or first noticed that the grass in the garden was beautiful to touch or smell, that a pair of calf-high, Cuban-heeled, pointy-toed, zip-up, black Dior boots are just clods to plod the pavement with. We know, don't we – do we, Russell? – that they cannot, will not, shall not give us relief or sanctuary or love.

Do we really want to end our lives without discarding these lies? Do we want to hunker down into our earthly cradle, never having released from the grip of the anxious mind the ridiculous lie that material things can provide solutions, instead of the sublime?

Do you want those boots if the true cost is God? If the true cost is family? If the true cost is that most American of dreams, freedom?

Well, Guy Debord and his clever-clog chums thought it had to go. They cooked up this idea called 'the Spectacle' to help us understand what was going on, a philosophical tool that provided a story to deliver to our pickled brains the troubling truth that we were now experiencing a second-hand, approximate reality.

They demonstrated this by creating 'situations' that exposed the absurdity of our reality, the unquestioned reality which we all accept. The movement was inherently political and people still use it to make a point – like by nicking some valuable paintings from a museum and using them on barricades in a neighbourhood where there's a lot of argy-bargy – to demonstrate that the authorities when reclaiming the artworks are more concerned about the preservation of heirlooms than people.

Dom Joly, Sacha Baron Cohen and Jackass in a way do stuff derived from this tradition because their crazy public antics make us question the nature of customary, consensual behaviour. Mostly for a laugh, though. At its inception situationism was politically motivated.

These ideas were influential in the uprisings that took place all over the world in the sixties, particularly in Paris; as you know, the French are never truly happy unless chopping someone's head off or having it off with someone else's missus. I suppose the perfect scenario would be to have some petrified aristo genuflecting at the altar of the guillotine God while, just out of sight, Jacques (or whatever) carries on with his wife. But let's not get bogged down in senseless xenophobia, the point is that fetishism, whether religious, sexual or commercial, is a diversion from the source.

This idea is not dissimilar to Radhanath Swami's observation that 'All desire is the inappropriate substitute for the desire to be at one with God', or to live in harmony with the whole, in union with truth.

The truth. The truth is: there are on this frequency, from our human perspective, a planet, some beings, some resources; would it not be sensible to employ systems that benefit the planet, the beings and the resources?

Not needlessly revere artificial constructs that only benefit a few people? Dave now, the beatnik rabble-rouser that he is, explains some of the economic dimensions to our current absurd situation.

'Distribution and profits are at an all-time high. Instead of this dramatic increase in wealth creation delivering a healthier standard of living to everyone, it has been consolidated within a mere fraction of the global population.

'In the United States, 95 per cent of income gains since the recession began have gone to the top 0.01 per cent.'

Phew, I'm glad to find a statistic about extreme wealth that doesn't include me. As you know, one of the techniques to negate the ideas in this book, or the stuff I say, is to harp on about the fact that I've made a load of wedge. Well, I'm not in that problematic percentile, so that's good. Also I'm not averse to giving up wealth in circumstances determined by the collective will.

To contra-paraphrase New Labour architect and vandal of British socialism Peter Mandelson, I'm seriously comfortable with society getting extremely equal.

Now let's give Dave back the cudgel to browbeat us into supplicant acceptance of his version of contemporary finances.

'In the US, the 400 richest people have as much as 185 million people, over 60 per cent of the population. As absurd as that is, on a global scale, the richest 85 people have as much as 3.5 billion people, half of humanity!'

We are well aware of the fun-bus statistic but it's nice to hear it from a variety of sources; it's the sort of information that ought to be more prominent, promoted ahead of Kim and Kanye or even football. The more we think about this statistic, the more likely that we'll be moved to act on the peaceful establishment of a fair global alternative, some of the tenets of which are becoming apparent to us: self governance, decentralisation of power, cancellation of unfair debt, removal of corrupt global trade agreements, a return to local, responsible agriculture, the removal of the physical and psychological tools of the powerful, and portraits of me in every living room. I added the last one for a laugh.

Dave reckons, a bit like the economist Thomas Piketty (French of course) that this is not a glitch, a blip or a hiccup, this is the intended result of our economic system.

'This is not happening by mistake or inevitability. During the bailout of Wall Street, $30 trillion in support and subsidies went to the most powerful players on Wall Street. That was the greatest theft of wealth in history. Throughout the entire world, the Federal Reserve, IMF, World Bank, ECB and BIS carry out genocidal economic policies. Just because that sounds hyperbolic and incredibly harsh, doesn't mean it's not true.'

I don't recognise a lot of those acronyms. I know IMF – International Monetary Fund – but 'ECB' and 'BIS' are a mystery to me. 'Russell, you could google them in the time it took to write this sentence.' No I couldn't, I turn the Internet off when I write, otherwise I get distracted looking at pointless balderdash, trying to claim it's research.

Furthermore, it's bloody obvious that they're international financial institutions that were set up to deregulate trade conditions for global conglomerates and make it easier for marauding corporations to subjugate the rest of us into weary compliance.

Look it up yourself or ask a grown-up, I've got to write 100,000 words here and all so that at the end of it I get a ten-second warm consolatory glow – 'Ooh, I got shit GCSEs but look, I've done a book' – then a bunch of cunts telling me I'm a hypocrite, then probably someone'll go through this book with a fine-tooth comb, find an example of me being a bit sexist or something, and try and dismiss the broader argument. You look it up, we're all in this together and try-ing to get past the old ideas of exalted individuals solving problems.

Here's some more terrifying jargon from Dave.

'In the last year, the Federal Reserve handed out another trillion dollars through their "Quantitative Easing" (QE) program. Most all of that money, like the trillions during the bailout, went to the big six banks so they could dish out all-time record-breaking bonuses.

'Let's break this one minor Fed program down: with the trillion dollars they most recently handed out, you can give every unemployed person in America a $50k per year job.'

Quantitative Easing is a typically euphemistic piece of imperialistic lingo. It does, however, have the advantage of poetically inferring the application of a lubricant before a shafting.

Dave DeGraw here, like his Occupy cohort Dave Graeber, points out that resources are present, here in the abstract, symbolic form of dollars '$' this is a concept that refers to assumed wealth. Graeber said we could cancel the debts of everyone instead of an elite; DeGraw says we could use the money to create employment for loads of people and 'ease' life for ordinary people, not just an elite.

Both demonstrate that the system, its language, ideologies and practices, are volitional, not absolute. We are not discussing gravity here, a seemingly irrefutable law. It's just an idea that works well for the people who say it's the only idea there is. Like gravity for elites. If it was up to them the rest of us would be floating around or paying through the nose for lead booties.

This is not a worthy, humanitarian argument to aid the destitute, normal people; literally almost everyone is getting fucked.

'As bad as unemployment is, even among workers, almost half of the working population earns less today than people making minimum wage did in 1968. A stunning 76 per cent of the US population is living paycheck-to-paycheck. While US millionaires have $50 trillion in wealth, an all-time record number of people are toiling in poverty, hunger, prison and severe debt. When you fully grasp the situation, you realise that this is the greatest crime against humanity in the history of civilization.'

It's important to note that this is not a problem for radicals, or lefties, or hippies. If you are a person who breathes air and are not reading this on a bejewelled bus with eighty-four other plutocrats then this corrosive, outmoded doctrine is affecting you.

Even if you are a billionaire, a multi-billionaire, if you are Roman Abramovich or a Hinduja or Dick Cheney or George W. Bush (only joking, he wouldn't read a book, hahahahaha-hahahahahahaha), you are of course part of the whole of humanity, about to realise that individualism was an old, primitive idea, that materialism is a bric-a-brac concept for toddler brains, that we are at a moment of history where consciousness is going to coalesce, collectivise, return to the whole.

Where the business of being human is going to become something wonderfully, unrecognisable, so we must relegate the mundane to its rightful place; the practical, fair allocation of resources, the preservation of the planet, must naturally be prioritised so we can all get on with the exciting stuff: communing in unknown realms, summonsing new ideas into our reality.

The answers are all around us, cluttering up the culture like a magical amulet ignored in a junk shop.

CHAPTER 16

On Earth, As It Is In Heaven

If you grew up in a secular but previously Christian culture like I did, then these ideas were blandly recited in assembly, draped in antiquated code, like a verbal doily, making it seem like some tiresome ol' crud at a fete. The Lord's Prayer:

> Our Father, who art in heaven

The first word is 'our': we have a shared provenance; we come from the same place. We have one father. Clearly not biologically, but they didn't have words like 'biology' then; I wonder what words we lack now. What label-less realms evade us for want of a consensual symbol?

Right. So we all come from the same entity or 'father', now where is this guy? He's in 'heaven'.

Is that a place in the clouds, a place of silent reflection within all of us, a gay nightclub on Charing Cross Road in the nineties? The answer is 'Yes' to all three, but more importantly it implies a realm or dimension that is 'not here', not knowable, but from where we as children of this father emanate. Perhaps a subtler electromagnetic realm beyond our understanding from which all tangible phenomena is emitted.

In Sanskrit all characters are connected by a single line, the individual 'letters', 'words', 'sentences', 'concepts', therefore, demonstrably have the same genesis. They all come from the pure line, the total, unimpeded form.

'In the beginning there was the word' is how a very popular, relatively recent book commences. All came from the vibration, the vibration of unrealised infinite possibilities. Tap any physicist you like on the shoulder and they'll tell you that we are made of stardust, that the component elements of everything on our planet and in our bodies are made of nitrogen, hydrogen and carbon dioxide. So is the sun. So are all stars. In their 'give us one miracle and we'll describe the rest' version of events, there was a big bang, or a giant vibration, or a sound, or a word, then all things came into being. This to me still sounds divine.

So we all came from one place, an unknown dimension that is loving, or at least benevolent, like a father. Now, there's a bit of patriarchy thrown in there to subjugate the evident superior power of feminine creative energy. Anything that gives birth to something by our understanding is feminine, but let's give the people who wrote the prayer a break, they were probably men and were following orders. Also at some point it would be nice to get beyond dualistic concepts like masculine and feminine, because they're a bit old-fashioned.

The prayer, or 'thought code', continues:

hallowed be thy name

Hallowed is a word that really hasn't made the cut into the contemporary lexicon. It's probably the most antiquated word in the prayer. Who ever says 'hallowed' now? No one. It might be in the title of a Harry Potter film, is it? 'Deathly Hallows'? Is that one of 'em? I dunno.

Either way it just means worthy of reverence and a bit hard to grasp by the individualistic, repressed, unevolved, sense-bound consciousness. It's special and pure. Fine. Even the name of this father, in heaven, is radiant with some magical, ethereal, tricky-to-comprehend quality. Got it.

Thy kingdom come

This realm, where the creative force is, where we came from, that's all 'hallowed', is coming here.

Bloody hell, look alive, God's on his way. It might be an incantation, like we're inviting this realm to be realised in us, through us, through our bound consciousness. So don't panic.

Thy will be done,
On earth, as it is in heaven.

Yes, it was that, an incantation. Don't worry, God's not on his way in a fiery chariot of judgemental rage; we can manifest God, this divinity, this creative vibration, here in this dimension, and make it correlate with its subtler original frequency. We can download it. Really all that means is stop fucking about with things that don't have meaning, like money, Dior boots and blow-jobs, because it's stupid and detached from original intention. Not bad, just compartmentalised – do it if you want, you have free will, but if your intention is contentment you're wasting your time with all that.

Give us this day our daily bread

So we do need food – I mean, we have bodies, so some bread would be nice, or pasta or veg, anything really, I'm not fussy, but I will need some grub at some point. Interesting that it is 'us' – all of us. We are a community of people and we would like some bread. It's not 'Give me some bread and fuck the immigrants'; we ask on behalf of everyone.

177

Also we only need the bread today, in the moment, in the present. The future and the past are only relevant to the limited, animalistic, reductive view of reality that we indulge in to our detriment. We don't need ten years' worth of bread either, 'in case'; just our daily bread will do.

> And forgive us our trespasses

We will fuck up; we're just people, expressions of a higher consciousness, permutated through a physical dimension. I mean, we need bread and everything, we're flawed. Please be compassionate to us, divine creative power within us, without us. It reiterates 'us'.

> As we forgive those who trespass against us.

Ah, so there are conditions, we've got to be forgiving too; it's not a one-way street, this compassion, it's not perfect, we ourselves will have to let go of our perceived transgressions. Or trespasses, which I saw in incredibly literal terms as a kid and thought referred to scrumping or hijinks.

> And lead us not into temptation,
> But deliver us from evil.

This is a bit confusing. After everything that's preceded it, after all this righteousness, why would him 'leading us' into 'temptation' be likely?

Perhaps it is at this point that we acknowledge that it is not an external, abstract entity that we are addressing but our own nature. In the past I thought it a bit simplistic to consider hunger, lust and aggression as inferior to grace, love and service – by what barometer can we begin to measure? If all these qualities exist in our nature, how can we divide them up and apply tags like 'good' and 'bad' to them?

Aleister Crowley and all the pagan, devil-worshipping types extol a far less challenging 'Do what thou will shall be the whole of the law' philosophy. I gave it a whirl – hedonism, indulgence, animalism – and I believe there is an essential difference. Those impulses when acted upon create competitive and destructive conditions. Personally, too, I found that those impulses were deviations from the source.

Often I'd think, 'I must have some heroin' or 'I'd love an orgy' then I'd act on that and be surprised by the lack of fulfilment. I believe natural instincts 'go awry'; what was I really seeking when scoring and using heroin?

Heroin is an opiate; opiates are painkillers. I was in spiritual pain. I have come to believe that the reason I was using drugs was to treat a spiritual malady.

A flailing, disconnected tendril searching for connection and, failing to find it, I had to be sedated. When I began my life in abstinence-based recovery, living one day at a time without the use of drugs and alcohol, the impulse that drove me to seek out oblivion remained.

I believe it is the impulse for union that is denied by our atomised and secular culture. The flailing tendril then took on a somewhat obvious and visually apposite course of action to fulfil this longing for connection.

It's kind of transparent: the symptoms of addiction are like the behaviours of caged, pacing animals, a response to an unnatural condition.

Does it sound a bit phoney when I say that in my Grand Prix of priapic glee I was actually seeking salvation? Does that sound like something you might hear in a Southern Baptist church or a South London gospel gathering – or worse, a treatment centre for sexual addiction?

179

My research in this area has been quite thorough and I'd say my findings are quite conclusive. I've engaged in scenarios that from the outside, looking in, when I was an adolescent in Essex, would've been indistinguishable from Eden. Looking at a papped shot of myself emerging from a London nightclub at 2 a.m. with a blonde on each arm and shades on, I can still be deceived into thinking, 'Wow, I'd like to be him,' then I remember that I was him.

*   *   *

BROUGHT UP ON Frank McAvennie and Benny Hill and *Carry On* on the telly, it's easy to understand how a mental plan is formed. I can't unsee the truth behind the photograph, the reality behind the veil. That night with those two immaculate girls, delivered from Babestation,* via some club in Hanover Square, did not feel like it looked.

When I got back home to the house that I'd dutifully purchased and done up like a space-age Byron would've: flock, black wallpaper, shag-pile carpets, Jacuzzi – ah, the Jacuzzi, lowered in the garden by a crane, that gurgled like an oracle in my garden, murkier with each new sacrifice. A TV in every room, a yoga studio with a wipe-clean floor, but unless you do the yoga you don't get a wipe-clean mind.

The girls come in and drink wine. I don't drink wine, so I don't spill wine but they do. The humanity will not be silenced as we kiss; nagging angels burden me with their invitations. Glasses get broken like promises I was given, given then and given when I took these ideas on board.

Kisses are exchanged and lips get derivatively bitten and I

* They weren't delivered they came of their own volition. I just like the poetics of delivered, it sounds better. Those women aren't a corporate entity worthy of fearing, neither is Babestation. Silly business all round.

am unsmitten and unforgiven and when they leave I sit broken and longing on the chaise. The glass window above the door says No. 1 – number one Gardnor Road; it casts a shadow from a street lamp and on the wall it looks like 'No 1, no one', as my mate Matt observed, and I am alone but for the cat.

Even though, when it works, after I rip it up in front of 3,000 at the Brixton Academy and I head back with a netball team from Essex, all Fays and Tracys refracted from Grays, and 'Faces' after the mandatory Jacuzzi, I look up at them from the quilted mortuary slab of my chamber as they pick over me like thwarted but amused surgeons. I watch them through anaesthesia and pray amnesia will help me forget what I'm doomed to regret. Like perfumed and glossed vultures they peck my carcass and a petit mort is insufficient; I am like Frankenstein here, assembled from boneyard parts.

Other people's limbs and thoughts, stitched together and jerked to life.

Why is this not working? Was Sam Fox lying? Is Hugh Hefner lying? Is everybody lying? They look like broken toys to me, like an unlicensed Pitsea Market ET whose finger don't light up, given to me, sat on my knee.

I don't want to be led back to that, I want to be delivered from evil.

For thine is the Kingdom, the power and the glory, for ever and ever,

Amen.

CHAPTER 17

War! What Is It Good For?
Capitalism. Obviously.

If you can transcend the limits of the instinctual and anatomical self, you can become part of a kingdom of unified consciousness defined by power, glory and eternity. This is a journey I have made, but enlightenment is not like a summit that can be scaled then perched atop of like a jolly mountaineer with rosy cheeks eating a pork pie. It is a commitment to live in the moment.

When I consider myself to be a member of a community, living in the present, my agenda lifts, my agency returns and I am no longer a passive and redundant consumer but an awakened citizen. Dave DeGraw, who we left on the other side of the Lord's Prayer, explains the dilemma we face as an uninformed populace:

'Due to the mainstream media, the average person has no understanding of this unprecedented increase in wealth. Imagine if the average American understood that US millionaires now have $50 trillion in wealth.

'$1 trillion is 1,000 billion. For an estimated $30 billion you can end world hunger. You can wipe out the entire national debt of the US with just 25 per cent of that wealth.'

I always thought that classified information and top-secret

files mostly consisted of data that if known would cause people to rise up. Later in the book, Noam Chomsky will explain that to us in detail. We are creatures with an intuitive need for fairness. We are like the monkey in the cage fed cucumbers while our neighbours scoff grapes; we are in a position to look through the bars and see this injustice and to open the cage door.

Dave leaves us with another quote from Jefferson, 'Enlighten the people generally, and tyranny and oppressions of body and mind will vanish like evil spirits at the dawn of day.'

This is similar in intention to the Yogananda quote 'Darkness may reign in a cave for thousands of years, but bring in the light, and the darkness vanishes as though it had never been. Similarly, no matter what your defects, they are yours no longer when you bring in the light of goodness.'

*   *   *

THOMAS JEFFERSON, YOGANANDA and Dave are all saying the same thing: if people are informed, enlightened, awake, change will come. Well, that's easy enough, we just have to communicate with one another.

Having a Revolution will be easy. Maintaining the Revolution will be where we face challenges. The reason for this cockeyed optimism which has motored me this far through the book, and indeed life, is my certainty that we all want the same thing but are describing it differently and ascribing the solution to different structures.

Some people, like the Isis insurgents in Iraq, have an idealised view of Iraq and likely the world beyond, built upon, I suspect, a militant interpretation of Islam. Donald Rumsfeld and the US military industrial complex have a different ideal that they'd like to impose.

Out of sheer bloody diligence I have extensively researched

the meaning of the phrase 'military industrial complex' and as a result you are seconds away from knowing what it means and being able to dazzle your pals down the youth club or high-society banquet, depending on who the hell you think you are: 'an informal and changing coalition of groups with vested psychological, moral and material interests in the continuous development and maintenance of high levels of weaponry, in preservation of colonial markets and in military-strategic conceptions of internal affairs'.

Remember when that war with Iraq was on your telly? We were told it was absolutely necessary for our personal safety in, I dunno, Ohio or Plumstead, as Saddam Hussein was on the very precipice of developing weapons of mass destruction that would, in the wrong hands, which as far as I can work out means brown hands, ruin our experience of Argos and *Dancing on Ice*.

One million people took to the streets of London in protest under the banner of the Stop the War Coalition because they didn't believe there were any weapons; that Argos and *Dancing on Ice* were safe, and it was all an economically motivated, resource-driven trick.

It turned out they were right. There were no weapons that could do any serious damage. In fact when Saddam Hussein was found in a hole he was living in to stay out of trouble, Iraqi resources didn't stretch to full size Mars bars. He only had little fun-size ones down there, which to me is the sign of a nation on the brink of implosion.

Through the 20/20 vision of my retrospeculars we can now see that the primary beneficiaries of the most recent Middle Eastern conflict that Western nations got properly stuck into were not ordinary people in England, America or Iraq but big global companies that are above such quaint notions as nation.

Dick Cheney, a man whose name sounds like a prick encased

in armour, has strong ties to a company called Halliburton; they made $35 billion from post-war contracts. They do stuff to do with fuel refinery but have countless subsidiary affiliates, none of which, disappointingly, are Haribo, so nip that rumour in the bud.

Loads of British firms made tons from it too. In a way all this top-level corruption is just a manifestation of a particular aspect of understandable and ordinary human behaviour.

Like when I need plumbing done, I might get my mate Mick's cousin to do it, that I suppose is a form of cronyism. It would, I suppose, become more problematic if I lied and said next door were using their bathroom to make weapons, then went round and smashed it up, then gave Mick's cousin the job of repairing it and blamed my neighbours for the damage and made them liable. Especially if before the whole fiasco had taken place a million people had protested outside my house, saying it was a blag.

This is why people feel disaffected. Everyone knows, not just in their rational minds but in their guts, our collective folk knowledge, that we are being unduly shafted and grifted by the people at the top – whether it's Cameron and his mates cutting benefits or big financially motivated wars where poor people from this country go and kill poor people from Muslim countries so rich people from both countries can do their thing.

We've got more in common with the people we're bombing than the people we're bombing them for.

That is why it takes some pretty well drilled, old-fashioned optimism to get down the polling station on Election Day. The very system in which we are invited to ritualistically but irrelevantly participate is designed, *DESIGNED* to prevent significant change occurring.

The best arguments I've heard for voting since I admitted I don't do it have been to exhibit politeness for dead people.

Well, I believe in the Glory of God. I believe in the power of people to manifest, here on earth, a society that represents holy principles. This inoculates me from their bollocks.

Find out what the powerful want you to do, then don't do it.

What would most terrify the plutocrats and oligarchs that jerk the threads that twitch the flaccid marionettes?

An informed, engaged, collectivised, connected global population with no interest in petty prejudice, or tribal illusions sold to divide, whose energy is pragmatically directed at the creation of a justly organised society.

I met Alastair Campbell the other day and he's a lovely bloke who likes football, cares about people, tries to do the right thing and still justifies that inexcusable war. He told me he liked Tony Blair but didn't love him; thought social mobility could be reduced to people describing themselves as middle class; and was proud that less people than ever before describe themselves as working class.

Class is a daft system that we have to dismantle, even those of us who glory in glottal stops and hard-luck yarns. I've had a bit of a look round the aristocracy recently and they're not enjoying it; I think they'll be glad when it's over. To proceed we must accept each other, as we are not where we're from.

My mate Johann, who's been doing research for this book, thought I was too nice to Alastair Campbell – he surmised because I was enamoured of his chappish demeanour.

There may've been a bit of that, but I also know that as well as being a spin doctor extraordinaire, the power behind the throne, the ball-breaking, hard-talking, journo-smashing inspiration for The Thick of It's Malcolm Tucker, that he's got mental-health issues and I saw grace in him.

This business of seeing divine interconnected beauty in people has been happening more and more lately and I put it down to meditating too much. Liberated from the materialistic projections of anatomical distinction between humans, who I now see are a refracted projection of one supreme consciousness.

As Bill Hicks said, 'We are one consciousness experiencing itself subjectively, there's no such thing as death, life is only a dream and we are the imagination of ourselves.' Which ain't bad for a stand-up comedian from Texas. I felt for Campbell because I too have had the odd struggle with the brainbox, and I was fascinated with how he must cope with life after office.

'They tire of quiet, that have known the storm,' said Dorothy Parker. I told Campbell that quote and he went a bit wistful.

He's pretty good, as one of neo-liberalism's foremost propagandists, at getting his point across. I said to him, 'Alastair, what did you do that war for?'

He remarkably, and with a straight face, tied it into 9/11 (you remember, those towers; there were two of 'em, I think). He said that he and Tony, who has since gone on to become an adviser to a Kazakhstani dictator and a board member of a Middle Eastern oil company, were playing it by ear when the World Trade Center collapsed in a way that some people say looked like a controlled demolition.

He said, 'We had the same information as anyone else watching it on the TV when it happened,' which makes me question the value of international espionage, if all these James Bonds and Jason Bournes are getting their info off of Ceefax.

In the intervening period between the 9/11 attacks and the invasion of Iraq there was accrued considerable information that concluded that the only real link between Al-Qaeda and Iraq was the letter 'Q'. It was an alphabet war, which must be hard to stomach in Arabian countries, as they don't even use that alphabet.

The rationale for the war was reverse-engineered.* First the objective was decided upon – invade Iraq – then information was compiled that made that course of action plausible.

A bit like the homophobes I've mentioned who ransack the Bible for scriptural justification for their odd prejudices, which in truth can only really be strangled homosexual urges. Otherwise, why bother?

I'm sure there are other books that'll give you a much better account of why the war in Iraq was phoney and what the real reasons were; I fucking hope there are. Imagine there wasn't; imagine this was the most well-researched account of the political and economic motivations for the Iraq conflict available. Imagine that after this book came out I had to go on news shows with Colin Powell and Jack Straw and sternly talk them through what they'd done, while they looked down at their shoes, a bit red-eyed, and apologised. Then Obama had to have me at the White House and put his hands up and say I'd rumbled them. Then I was flown to Baghdad to meet with leaders of Isis to explain that there'd been a terrible mistake, that they were right to be angry and that their violence was distinct from that which had preceded it only in scale. Then they asked if I'd stay and be in charge of a unified Iraq and I agreed, but Obama said he'd step down and let me run America, so I do that an' all, and then I dissolved the Union into a federation of fully autonomous, interconnected collectives led by elected local jurors from the community that followed a central edict built on respecting the way

* Just so you know, Alastair Campbell didn't bowl into my front room and admit the war in Iraq was an unnecessary contrivance, he was as usual, world class at managing info. The reverse engineering is my summation and surely that of anyone who isn't either personally responsible for the war, or a total div.

of life of others and ecological responsibility, and then shut down Disneyland, saying it was 'childish'. That would be better than what's happening now and I've only had a few hours to research these ideas. Imagine what we could do together?

CHAPTER 18

U'KIP, If You Want, We're Awake

Like much of the stuff in this book – the economic ideas, the speculation on global trade treaties, the irregularities of the financial system – there are loads of books that will give you the score on Iraq far more adeptly.

I'm not Noam Chomsky, you've probably noticed; I'm happy to be Norman Wisdom. All I'd like to do is dispel the idea that there are no alternatives to the systems we are currently using to organise society. And that behind all the myriad corruption and injustice is one all-pervasive idea, and when it's overthrown, we'll all be better off.

Noam Chomsky is a linguist, political theorist and name you'd better start saying at gatherings if you want to be taken seriously. If you are one of the clever, educated people that is reading this book, you'll already know that he's a prominent dissident who has spoken out against US interventionism and the role of propaganda in sedating a population; if you're not clever and educated you now have a basic understanding and should stop putting yourself down.

Chomsky says that at this point in history alternative visions for society are vital and those based on cardinal human values of sharing and being ecologically minded deserve serious consideration.

The situationists, God love 'em, were on a quest for authentic life based on these cardinal values; authentic life with authentic relationships that embrace love, play, participation and creativity.

These are universal aspirations that are oddly neglected in our materialistic culture. One way to consolidate and unite the majority of humanity might be to focus on our similarities, not our differences. Sure, the Isis insurgents right now rampaging through Iraq, somewhat making a mockery of the initial impetus of the West's invasion, may be fuming and Muslim but beneath their militant goals we will find love. Of course Rumsfeld and Cheney and three generations of mercantile Bushes have got hopelessly entangled in cultural imperialism and greed, but beneath the lust for power is fear and beneath the fear is love.

As surely as the elemental ingredients that make up the temporary event of your face are carbon, hydrogen and oxygen, whether you're an antagonised Sunni mercenary or gout-infested neo-liberal tyrant, you are unified too by consciousness and love.

Consciousness and sentient awareness, which we're expected to believe has inexplicably flowered, with no physical, chemical or biological explanation, from the peculiarly perfect conditions of our planet.

With so much in common it's extremely primitive to fetishise and flap about difference. In certain anonymous, contingent fellowships that help communities of people to live free from addictions to substances and behaviours, one day at a time, there is a principle that each group is fully autonomous except in matters affecting other groups or these fellowships as a whole.

I think this is a beautiful principle. Any group, tribe, society, is free to live by any creed they choose, unless their conduct has a negative impact on other communities or our planet.

My friend Daniel Pinchbeck, who has spent the last ten years smashing his brain into a high-functioning mush with ayahuasca, has given us a brief account of what a global utopian vision could look like:

'We can create a peaceful planetary civilisation, entirely powered by renewable sources of energy, based on cradle-to-cradle practices, where everyone on earth enjoys a high quality of life.'

Daniel ain't playing, he's gone in hard there with an ecologically responsible peaceful planetary model. Unless you're some kind of ludicrous hippie you won't know what the hell 'cradle-to-cradle' refers to – well, I do. I looked it up. It's based on the idiom 'cradle to the grave'; by changing the grave bit to 'cradle', it implies that we have a responsibility beyond our own lifespan.

That is of course the type of idea that we must adopt. What 'cradle-to-cradle' means in practice are technologies, products and systems that don't produce waste, and implicit within these systems, as in the phrase itself, is a different attitude to ownership. I was given the example of a pair of cradle-to-cradle shoes, which sounds like something Jimmy Savile might've worn but is actually a pair of ecologically responsible trainers. Training shoes where the top part would be reused and the sole recycled, made from biological nutrients. Apparently these things already exist and I bet they're fuckin' rubbish. Which means I'd probably recycle 'em as soon as I got 'em and stick me Converse back on. I'm sure the aesthetics will improve and at some point I'm going to have to manage my priorities.

Daniel also mentions renewable energy, a subject about which we are being horribly misled. I recently saw a depiction of the area of solar panelling required to provide energy for the entire planet; it was titchy, about the size of Billericay. As usual the information we get on emergent ideas that can change the world is tightly controlled by people who want the world to stay the same.

Food and cigarettes are the best examples of industries where the genie has, after years of stifling, gotten out of the bottle. As I explained earlier, and as you knew anyway, these industries for years gave us information that suited their economic advance and, in conjunction with an ideologically and sometimes financially allied media, concealed information that hampered it.

This is why it is vital that we challenge the dominant ideological space.

'As part of this transition,' Daniel says, 'we can restore and replenish our planetary ecosystems. This shift can happen over the next decades.'

Daniel acknowledges that ecological reparation is a process that will take decades, but, optimist that he is, believes it is possible.

I've spent a fair bit of time with Daniel. He is what you might call a psychedelic shaman; he looks sort of like a live-action Shaggy from *Scooby-Doo*. Most notably I spent some time with him in an ashram-type thing in Utah, a temporary commune where free-thinking loonies congregated in yurts to discuss far-out ideas. I went because I've always been fascinated by this stuff. Like most people, I've always sensed there was more to 'heaven and earth, Horatio, than are dreamt of in your philosophy', as that misery guts Hamlet said to his pal before ballsing up court life in Elsinore.

My clumsy adolescent hallucinogenic experiments unravelled my limited conception of the sensory realm. I met an IVF physician once and he gave me a cool metaphor for contextualising knowledge, given additional credence by the fact that he spends his working life jamming recalcitrant spunk cells into dislocated eggs. This empiric knowledge of the micro had awoken him to fathomless tiny continents of impenetrable, invisible wilderness.

What is the process that accelerates cellular subdivision? Why do cells stop being indistinct and start to take on particular identities and agencies?

He's on the top of his game and has concluded that a convenient shorthand for this potent and purposeful entity is 'God'; the world as we understand it is limited, he explained. 'Imagine your sensory being as a finger,' he began. I often do, so for me it was a doddle. 'The conscious awareness in the sensorial and experiential world is like a finger in a glass of water: it can experience the parameters and depth of the glass, it can feel the edges. This is how our awareness interacts with the known. To comprehend the unknown we should imagine putting our finger into the ocean.'

What a lovely metaphor, easily envisaged and if necessary enacted. I might pop down the beach and plunge my dumb digit into the briny and inform the concerned onlookers I'm probing the unknown.

Where Pinchbeck and his tent-dwelling acolytes excel is in their willingness to bust the finger wide open with consciousness-expanding plants. Pinchbeck in particular has returned from his many voyages into inner space with all manner of useful social notions. Generally when I took acid I surfed along the treacherous coastline of impending mental breakdown; Pinchbeck meets a host of inter-dimensional beings that manifest in consciousness when the typical impediments of sensory inhibition are lifted.

I can't express to you how much I'd like to take ayahuasca, or the compound derived from it; accounts by those who've taken it read like hippy science fiction. Tiny bright beings of light offering giggly advice, the muddled narrative of your own life relayed with new clarity and meaning. It sounds brilliant.

As we sat huddled in a wigwam on a Utah ranch, the spilt Milky Way radiant above, I envied my cohorts. Wrapped in blankets with their unwrapped minds. Daniel and I then held an amplified discourse and took questions from the tripped-out assembly, me jealous like a diabetic at a bake-off, Daniel saying stuff like this:

'We can accomplish this Revolution through a collective movement of civil society that supersedes the current structure of nation-state governments and the corporate military industrial complex. The transition is from a paradigm of competition and domination to one of symbiosis and cooperation, from greed to altruism. It begins with the realisation of our shared responsibility for the future of the earth, and our inherent unity with each other and with all of life.'

In this short passage a new world is described. Big, powerful structures must be overcome to bring about this new, gentler, more free society where we work less and have more leisure. Where technology is used to liberate the many, not to engorge the few. Where positive human attributes like altruism and cooperation become the ideological pillars for society.

Our current system is the physical manifestation of will, but will, like everything, can change.

A recent demonstration of the power of activism and collective will is the change we have seen in attitudes and legislation with same-sex couples. I spoke to lifelong troublemaker Peter Tatchell. During his lifetime as a campaigner for equal rights for gay folk which must've at times seemed hopeless, like the time he was beaten up by Robert Mugabe's henchmen, or the hours he sat in a cell in Canterbury, having disrupted the archbishop's Easter Day address.

During the years that Tatchell has been campaigning, though, lesbian, gay, bisexual and transgender issues (LGBT) have undergone a transformation as radical as any endured by the 'T' in that acronym. People that argue against gay marriage now are peered at as if marvellous fossils emerging from a bigoted mist. When I was a kid homophobia was de rigueur, lads that played with girls de facto 'poofs', and a condemnatory 'Don't Die of Ignorance', 'HIV as Old Testament retribution' attitude was as unquestionably correct as 'Just Saying No' to drugs. It turns out both those ideas were half-arsed and unhelpful.

Kids come out as gay in their early teens now. Gay pride is attended by serving politicians, publicly, not sneakily in masks, and the legal rights denied same-sex couples for years are finally being granted.

This has been wrought by the tenacity of men and women like Tatchell who overcame years of abuse and frequent violence because they believed in their cause. A cause that affects us all because as long as there are maligned and persecuted groups it remains impossible, by definition, for anyone to inhabit a fair society.

Tatchell claims the changes we have seen in civil rights have come about due to internal lobbying (cheeky), activism and community self-empowerment. I said that with civil rights issues, is it true that the Establishment will ultimately concede because they pose no fundamental threat to the economic power and wealth of the Establishment? Tatchell agreed. He pointed out, though, that the concessions are still not easily granted.

I suppose that's because often the different groups that are campaigning for equality are often favoured targets for an Establishment keen to keep the majority of people divided and distracted. Gays, immigrants, disabled folk, different-coloured people: all crop up as accessible scapegoats when public tension reaches potentially threatening levels.

So it's expedient for the Establishment to mark them outsiders by pejorative legislation. When, though, as Tatchell says, the hearts and minds of the general population are won over, territory can be conceded.

Where I'm from, Grays, there's no love lost for the ol' gays and immigrants. In recent local elections Ukip did quite well by enforcing the erroneous belief that immigration was negatively impacting people's lives.

Ukip, like all far-right parties, offers a modest amplification of the prevailing political mentality. Nigel Farage said, for example, that elderly people are 'uncomfortable' with homosexuality. Well, Sir Ian McKellen seems alright with it. I met him on a chat show once and he very nearly charmed me into a new lifestyle in a cubicle.

If Farage's imaginary grandparents are abstractly uncomfortable with homosexuality, like all homophobes they don't have to do it. It's not like washing-up, an unpleasant but mandatory chore that if left undone will clutter up your kitchen. 'Well, I've watched *EastEnders*, I suppose I should be getting in the kitchen now and doing some gayness. That anus isn't going to felch itself.'

It's an abstract concept unless you voluntarily embrace it. Obviously outside of a tiny mad minority, no one thinks like that now. There will always be mileage, though, for those keen to distract us, in matters that have an atavistic, visceral attachment. Ideas that bypass our rational brains and inexplicably provoke fear or revulsion.

It is helpful, too, to continually stimulate that fear and nominate visible groups as receptacles for tenuous blame.

Tatchell said that over time the powerful will always acquiesce on civil rights issues if the opposition becomes voluminous; the real challenge comes, he observed, when you attack the economy. He described this as 'the fortress that must be protected at all costs'.

This fortress, though, is defended so vigorously precisely

because of its vulnerability. An economy that is designed to benefit the few to the detriment of the many obviously requires highly efficient structures in place around it.

Fawzi Ibrahim, who sees a powerful corollary between our current ecological crises and the deterioration of capitalism, said, 'Today humanity faces a stark choice: save the planet and ditch capitalism, or save capitalism and ditch the planet.'

The reason the occupants of the fun bus are so draconian in their defence of the economy is that they have decided to ditch the planet. You would think that Ibrahim's choice is a rhetorical one, to which the immediate and passionate response would be, 'We'll ditch capitalism, thanks, seeing as how it's gone nuts and isn't working anyway.'

The well-protected minority have the opposite intention, and that is why it is so integral for them to maintain that there are no alternatives. No alternatives except for a system that benefits them and destroys the planet. Does that sound right to you?

What about all the systems that preceded capitalism but now enhanced by a global communication network? Or the many new alternatives fleetingly précised in the pages of this book?

CHAPTER 19

Piketty, Licketty, Rollitty, Flicketty

It is a troubling indication of how low our expectations have sunk that even modest economic reform as proposed by Thomas Piketty is met with whoops of delirious rapture on one side and an international smear onslaught on the other.

He came round my house the other day, Thomas Piketty, French as kissing, with eyes that twinkled like petrol in a puddle. He had, though, the demeanour I know well: that of a man besieged by diagonal stabs of insidious judgement.

Dear ol' Thomassy Piketts, ol' Piketty, Licketty, Rollitty, Flicketty, has been given a right kicketty by the right wing for daring to suggest that we need transparency around the wealth and assets of the super-rich – the swines have been hiding their stuff, like hoarders on them programmes. Once we know what they have we can modestly tax them on their wealth instead of just their income.

The financial world has responded to this suggestion as if he'd just demanded they all diddle their sisters. The opposition to any kind of reform or redistribution is so pernicious and vociferous, Piketty agrees that we would require either cataclysm or a world-wide organised movement to implement it.

Capitalism is held together by will; it isn't, as we're constantly told, the result of some righteous, natural, tidal force. It is Machiavellian in construction and vulnerable if opposed. That is why the ideas of Piketty, who says he is a capitalist, just not a full-on evil one – may be like one of Darth Vadar's admirals that goes a bit whey-faced and reticent when the dark lord wants to blow up a moon or whatever – is met with a media death grip and strangled into silence. Death grip, by the way, is the literal translation of the word mortgage.

Imagine how the evil empire will respond when we start realising the full extent of our human potential and demand the kind of utopia that Daniel Pinchbeck is still in the middle of describing: 'Authoritarian structures of control can be replaced by mass volunteerism, orchestrated through social technologies that allow everyone to participate directly in a planetary democracy. We can realise society itself as a living, ever-changing work of art.'

Here again the possibility for a truly direct democracy is raised. Why are we pretending that we don't live in a culture where in spite of record-low voter turnouts in political elections, millions of people every Saturday night demonstrate their democratic right to vote for who they want to progress on X *Factor*. I've never voted in that either, but its success infers that the technology exists and an engaged populace will vote for something they care about. We can be all snooty if we like, but TV talent shows engage people emotionally in a way that politics doesn't.

People are affected by the stories and the songs and will dial in at a quid a time. Of course they'd do the same if we lived in an inclusive, truly democratic system where we all participated in the conversation to organise a fair and reflective society.

'We are already learning that science and mysticism are not opposites, but can be integrated. The study and exploration of the infinite dimensions of consciousness and mind-body states can be part of a post-materialist society. A new spiritual and religious impetus that embraces science and technology can become a unifying force.'

Daniel, the mushroom guzzling space-cowboy, shows his true psychedelic colours here by demanding the integration of science and mysticism.

I see that as a rational choice as we arrive at frontiers in the quantum world that seem to call into question even basic tenets of our understanding of the physical world: the nature of time, the nature of matter, the nature of space, the nature of nature.

The significance of consciousness itself as a participant in what we perceive as reality is increasingly negating what we understood to be objectivity. Our consciousness as observers at a subatomic level is influential, the quantum equivalent of 'a watched pot never boils'. An observed electron behaves as a particle; an un-watched one behaves as indeterminate waves of possibility.

There are many outcomes for even the smallest components of material; the interaction with consciousness affects outcome. These ideas that are emerging in quantum physics are outlined elsewhere in myth or religion. Your reality is the result of your attention and intention. We are through both science and mysticism on the precipice of a new understanding and have the potential to create new worlds. This is the time to align and discard old ideas that have fulfilled their function.

Christ's ascendance to heaven could be regarded as a symbol for the death of physical man, mortal man, carnal man, and the emergence of man that is one with God. Man that embraces the heavenly realm, the divine realm of quantum interconnection to be manifest on this material plane. To harmonise these superficially distinct but connected dimensions.

But how do we get there, Daniel, you fathomlessly insightful, inter-dimensional pothead?

'In the short term, global civilisation needs to make a rapid transition from fossil fuels to renewable sources of energy. This requires a new social contract, as a shift in energy paradigm is also a shift in political power.'

The priorities are reversing the current plan to 'ditch the planet to save capitalism' and ending the energy crisis. Once it is illegal for energy companies to profit by exploiting the planet, they'll stop doing it. Global consensus is impossible as long as people are separated from true power by nation states that act as intermediary administrators for psychopathic corporations that pursue their legal obligation for profit into the jaws of Armageddon.

'The next industrial Revolution is toward decentralised, autonomous and resilient systems where individuals and communities control their own destinies. This requires a transformation of our economic model from privatised control to cooperative models of ownership, which the social technologies of the Internet can facilitate.'

The agricultural Revolution took thousands of years, the industrial Revolution took hundreds, the technological tens. The spiritual Revolution, the Revolution we are about to realise, will be fast because the organisms are in place; all that needs to shift is consciousness, and that moves rapidly.

Visionaries like Daniel, inspired by mentors like Buckminster Fuller and Terence McKenna, can pull down new possibilities, conveniently in Daniel's case by loafing around the jungle, chomping up drugs. Human cultures have always had on their peripheries thinkers like these; the challenge for the rest of us is the realisation of these visions. Even this actually only requires us to act in union to achieve our mutual objectives.

CHAPTER 20

Submarine

In the next part of our book we are going to discuss how we bring corporations into line with common-sense thinking, how we the people can have authority and ownership of the organisations we work within, and how we can end corporatisation and homelessness for ever.

First, though, I'd like to boast about what I call my time in the US Marine Corps. I hope the gravitas of the tale will not be diminished by my admission that the period that 'my time' encompassed was about twenty-four hours.

I went to their San Diego training camp to learn how people behave when their individual identity is forcibly subsumed into a group identity. My whole life I have sought comfort in individualism. I escaped the banality of my background with the flamboyance of my haircut, the low expectations of my class with the grandiosity of my parlance, and the fear of being ordinary by becoming a professional weirdo. In a way my success in show business represents little more than the harvesting of my psychosis. I made my idiosyncrasies and flaws beneficial by exaggerating them.

That is not how they do things in the US Marine Corps. When we arrived at Camp Pendleton, me and my mates who were filming me – that's how I made life bearable in the past, by filming it – I had already, at the first sign of barbed wire and barbed remarks, done an about turn more deft than any military manoeuvre that I'd subsequently perform.

The thing with the marines is they don't fuck about. That could be a slogan for them in fact, the marines: we don't fuck about. As I arrived on the camp, on the phone to my best mate and manager, the aforementioned Nik, demanding this macabre social experiment be cancelled, I was a one-man Stanford experiment, I was the subject and the observer, and I wanted neither role. All I wanted, with burgeoning intensity with each camo-clad man I passed, was my mum.

Nik said I should stay, which incidentally has been his position whenever he's received these phone calls from sex addiction centres and drug rehabs. 'Come on, pal, give it a go,' he intones in his Old Trafford bray. 'Give the marines a chance,' he said. 'You'll learn from it.'

I've always had the problem of being unable to envisage the nature of a situation prior to its commencement. This means I'm in a state of perpetual shock while doing things that I've agreed to.

The marines is a pretty extreme example. When I came up with the idea to do it, or agreed to do it, I just had an image of myself as Rambo with a dressing-gown belt round my head, doing something irresponsible and impressive with a knife. That's it, a mental photograph of a moment. Reality doesn't behave like that. Although sequential time as experienced by humans is likely an illusion contrived by our animalistic experience of an expiring anatomy, it don't feel like that when you're on an obstacle course getting coated off by a drill sergeant.

There was no warm-up time. You know when you go to a fancy hotel? (If you don't, don't worry, these are the very kind of privileges that will be collectivised or banned, come the great day.) Well, when you arrive, there are some protocols: someone'll give you a drink, maybe you'll get shown round and given a little cold wet flannel in a packet to refresh you from your drive. These niceties ease you into your new environment. There's none of that in the marines. Within ten seconds of Nik hanging up on me, I was in a barracks surrounded by hard-looking fuckers doing marine shit.

They shouted hello and gave me a rucksack that was as big as I was and pointed to a car-boot sale's worth of khaki crap that I was expected to pack.

I'd been greeted – if that's the word, it was more like a well-drilled ambush – by five double-tough-looking skinheads in combat fatigues who I was informed were to be my instructors, and the only reference for comprehension that I could reach for in my head was the five martial-art animals that teach the Kung Fu Panda. 'It's okay,' I thought, 'I'm just in the film *Kung Fu Panda.*'

The first thing I was commanded to do, addressed by my surname, which I've never liked having bellowed at me, was put the giant pile of stuff, including three sleeping bags and a shovel, into the big, but annoyingly not big enough for the job, rucksack.

I squatted on the floor with the most Nazi-looking of the furious five looming over me, shouting encouraging slogans like 'Move it, you maggot.' To give you some idea of the physical dimensions of this hollering cyborg, I give you Dolph Lundgren from the film *Rocky IV*, or simply a wet dream of Adolf Hitler. He was so blond and tough, like an evil Milky Bar kid gone buff.

Now, I don't like packing at the best of times, I have existential problems with the concept. It involves for me a perspicacious sorcery with which I am ill at ease.

In my room prior to a trip, case open on my bed, possessions strewn about the room, I am confronted with an unknowable conundrum:

'Right. I'm me, but I'm not me now,
I'm me in the future,
on holiday in Crete.
Right, what've I got on?
Now put it in the bag.'

I can't see into the future; I just told you I can't envisage stuff. I can barely see into the present.

It was clear from Dolph's phlegm-flecked imperatives that I was not only expected to pack, but also to pack in a particular style, pertaining not to the contents but manner of my movements. I was obviously being too effete and ineffective, because he eventually began jamming stuff in himself. Gripping in his veiny claw one of the three sleeping bags, he thrust it into the quickly decreasing chasm of the rucksack like rewound footage of a vet angrily delivering a calf.

My query as to the necessity for three sleeping bags didn't even warrant a response, but really, why would you ever need three? Any camping trip that results in the loss of two sleeping bags ought to be swiftly cut short to prevent further calamity, an argument that my Aryan orderly brushed off with the same cold-eyed indifference that he afforded the scratch he got on his knuckle from one of my many gem-spangled rings.

Our eyes met as the blood rose, but I curbed my nan-like impulse to go, 'Ooh, are you okay, dear? Do want a plaster? That'll sting,' as I thought it would be bad for morale.

I was loudly informed that the reason we were packing this bag seemingly designed to cater for a disastrous and repetitive holiday was that at three in the morning, or 'Oh three hundred hours' as Dolph called it, we'd be getting up to do a 10k hike carrying a 75lb bag with seventy other trainee marines. As well as being startled by the extraordinary distance and punishing baggage, I was concerned that one military manoeuvre contained both imperial and metric measuring systems. 'Make yer mind up,' I thought.

The final futile instrument to be willed into the bulging knapsack was a collapsible shovel. 'Do all the marines carry shovels?' I asked. Dolph responded in the affirmative. 'Then in the event that one is required could I not borrow one of theirs?'

This enquiry that some may have seen as an indication that they were dealing with a strategic mastermind the likes of which we've not seen since Alexander the Great barely warranted a grunt. Instead of being awarded a Purple Heart I was sent off to a kind of broom cupboard to put on my fatigues.

I am at pains to point out that I was not granted the proper US marine uniform, which I was looking forward to wearing, but instead a kind of 'You forgot your PE kit so get something from the lost property' parody of a marine uniform. I was well vexed.

I also had to tie my hair up in a bun, so gone too was my hope of undertaking this rapidly growing nightmare as a kind of latter-day Cuban revolutionary. More Frank Spencer than Che Guevara.

I realised with a shudder how much of my sense of self I'd unwittingly invested in tight garments and rock 'n' roll jewellery when I emerged from the broom cupboard in my lost-property uniform. I was trying to distance myself from the clothes while wearing them, like a cat resists a plunge towards a full bathtub. The revulsion is magnetic.

Blessedly Pendleton is not bestrewn with mirrors or I may not have been able to proceed; as it was, the giant, pointless knapsack was thrust on to my back and I was marched – that's right, marched – to an obstacle course. The biggest obstacle being that I'd avoided PE as a kid.

My indulgent mum, a single mum of an only son, would let me skip games, pandering to my teary complaints as a former fat child herself. This, I suppose, is where a father figure would come in handy, a loving, authoritative, strong male to affectionately shove you into adversity. As it was, notes were written and physical activity strenuously avoided until I discovered that some exercise had an orgasm at the end of it. This syndrome of 'fatherless' boys is a much-cited problem that military organisations effectively resolve: personal identity put aside; a male ideal upon which to focus is provided and pursued.

Another word for obstacle course is assault course, and I can see how both terms have flourished because when I finally embarked on the horrific sequence of logs and fences and nets and ropes, assaulted is how I felt. They may as well've called it a humiliation course. The other marines – that's right, 'other' marines – hopped, zipped and sauntered across each awful vicissitude like butch Nijinskys. Then came my turn.

I hate doing things I'm shit at, especially in front of people who are good at them. The only way that obstacle course could've been made more traumatic is if they'd brought along a girl I fancied to watch. With each tentative tiptoe and stumble I had to inwardly assure myself that I was a good comedian and that my life was not pointless.

'I am addicted to comfort,' I thought as I tumbled into the wood chips.

I have become divorced from nature; I don't know what the names of the trees and birds are. I don't know what berries to eat or which stars will guide me home. I don't know how to sleep outside in a wood or skin a rabbit.

We have become like living cutlets, sanitised into cellular ineptitude. They say that supermarkets have three days of food. That if there was a power cut, in three days the food would spoil. That if cash machines stopped working, if cars couldn't be filled with fuel, if homes were denied warmth, within three days we'd be roaming the streets like pampered savages, like urban zebras with nowhere to graze. The comfort has become a prison; we've allowed them to turn us into waddling pipkins.

What is civilisation but dependency? Now, I'm not suggesting we need to become supermen – that solution has been averred before and did not end well. Prisoners of comfort, we dread the Apocalypse. What will we do without our pre-packed meals and cosy jails and soporific glowing screens rocking us comatose?

The Apocalypse may not arrive in a bright white instant; it may creep into the present like a fog. All about us we may see the shipwrecked harbingers foraging in the midsts of our excess. What have we become that we can tolerate adjacent destitution? That we can amble by ragged despair at every corner? We have allowed them to sever us from God and until we take our brothers by the hand we will find no peace.

My mate Mark Stone worked for Ford. When we left school my eyes were trained on the glimmer of far-off hills, one word, block high across the sky. Mark became an apprentice at Ford's in Aveley nearby. I never told him that I thought his pride gauche. That when he spoke of 'our place', meaning the factory where cars were assembled, to me that sounded odd. He felt connected to his work, and proud, as a man who loved speed and cars, that he knew how to make them. We'd bomb about in Essex lanes in his customised van – Ford, of course – and smoke draw. Mark was content, well paid, connected. I was signing on and fraught. Desperate, feeling only what I didn't have, that I was subject to some terrible injustice. That Olympus had erred and given me the wrong life. It was okay for Mark to work as a skilled labour and listen to hip-hop and do nights on doors in clubs in Dagenham and have rows and pull birds. I am fated for better things. Better things.

I got a grant to go to drama school, I got a habit, I got a cool jacket and cool friends. Mark would come up and visit me in London, still talking of 'our place'. He'd drop me off a bit of gear and indulge my fantasies of fame. 'I'll be your bodyguard, Russ,' he'd say, but we both knew he loved it at Ford's, with his mates, making things.

When Mark died on a motorbike at twenty-nine I didn't cry. I didn't go to the funeral, I was too busy making it to grieve for a mate that lived for making things. I was a junkie by then. Now I know what Mark meant by 'our place' and his easy pride in what he made. He knew himself, and in his heart that factory was his, it didn't matter where the profits went. I wanted power. Mark already had it.

They closed Ford's down, of course; they put their factory somewhere else where people work for less. The system they deploy doesn't measure pride or connection, it measures only profit. They talk to us all friendly, use our language, whispering in seductively avuncular vernacular, in their slogans, in their ads. They use our labour while it suits them, till it doesn't, then they're gone. Like Dracula on a jugular, they kill the thing they feed upon.

Where is this connection that Mark felt at his place, that I looked for in fame? That these marines appear to have as they skip by like this assault course is a poppy field, whilst I spit out the wood chips?

I feel embarrassed by their insistent encouragement. They treat me like I'm one of them, and I've always found that hard. Like I might leak lachrymose gratitude, like the Elephant Man or a blind boy in a story from my nan.

Up I get, though, and the course that beneath their stomped ballet rolled with them like an airport walkway, with me rises and undulates and slaps me about the face, a belated chastisement for missing games. They're nice about it, though, and as I accept their consolations I silently thank God for making me famous. 'Thank you for the gleaming bandages, the glamorous mummification, that I can die quietly here, behind the walls of my marvellous tomb.'

I sought ways on the camp to reassert my identity, which I was hoping extended beyond backcombed hair and lacquered-on pants. I spied a nesting robin travailing at an air-vent but stopped short of eulogising on this neat emblem of tenderness and nature in case the rest of the battalion thought it a bit poncey.

We went to the Mess, which was actually quite tidy and organised, to eat what passes for vegetarian food in the marines – I imagine that marines who don't eat meat are a small demographic. I then chatted to a few lads. Mostly they were working-class boys who were always destined to end up in a violent gang of some description and had sensibly joined a very well-funded one.

We went back to the dorms to do more marine things – time has blessedly relieved me of the details. I do recall, though, just before bedtime, being sat in my pants with the other lads around a podium while a senior marine read accounts of what in my mind seemed to be a daily round-up of marine acts of heroism around the world.

As I surveyed the faces of the sleepy adolescents, now dressed in combat pyjamas, which are much less intimidating than the day time get-up, I recognised that what was in effect happening was that we were being read a bedtime story.

This was to soothe us before we clambered into our thin sponge bunks. Instead of a tale of courageous rabbits or mischievous wizards, it was a harrowing logbook of violence and assaults; to those lads, though, it was a lullaby.

As I watched these lost-boys cocooned in their military cradle and concocted excuses not to fulfil my obligation to stay for three days but to weasel my way out, by any means necessary, I remembered what I'd heard about madrasas. Those are the schools in some Muslim regions – Pakistan, for example – that are often funded by Saudis; some I'm sure are legit and just teaching theology or whatever, but there are apparently, extreme versions. In these more off-book and antagonistic establishments, young lads are taken from their village (it could be a city, what do I know) and indoctrinated into fundamentalism to become hard-core soldiers. Or terrorists, depending on which side of Dick Cheney you're on. The lads are immersively indoctrinated into a militant ideology which must seem all the more appealing if received in total isolation. Apparently they never meet women, are amped up on hatred and only receive affection from the fellas that run the place, who will one day make their approval contingent on acts of homicidal or even suicidal valour.

This is how the perpetrators of the 2008 attacks in Mumbai were likely raised, their only access to love from handlers who groomed them into terror.

I watched a documentary about them, and the conversations between the lads doing the bombing and shooting in India and their superiors in Pakistan were perversely touching: 'You're doing well, brother. Now torch the room, in God's name.'

Me and an ex-girlfriend watched this documentary, *Terror in Mumbai*, whilst in the Taj Hotel, the location of considerable carnage that day. Hostages were killed there; one wing was set ablaze. She insisted we snuggle down in the darkness of a room where the atrocities took place and watch the harrowing affair unfold on film.

It was eerie to see the corridor outside our room in grainy CCTV, with armed young men bustling through and kicking down doors.

Most disturbing of all is the innocence and humanity of the killers as they nervously conduct the execution of hostages. One lad tentatively negotiates with his handler to see if there's any way he can avoid killing them, by now infected with the inevitable empathy that we feel even when powerfully conditioned against it.

The mundanity too is striking: he sounds like a schoolboy trying to get out of sports day, rebutted by an austere mum.

'Do I have to kill them, brother?'

'Yes,' replies his impatient superior, 'just get on with it in God's name.'

I imagined the killer as a seven-year-old boy with no route to affection but via these bellicose uncles. How severely behaviour can be shaped by environment; as surely as we learn language, we have our compass set in the amoral abyss by our early inculcators.

You hear a muffled gunshot and the lad shakily returns to the phone for his approval. 'Well done, brother.'

When they arrive at the opulent and then easily penetrable Taj Hotel, you hear when they report back to base their utter amazement at the consumer treasures within:

'Brother, you won't believe the size of the TVs in this place.'

'Don't get distracted in God's name, brother,' replies the irked handler as if dealing with a wayward Cub Scout enchanted by a lily.

The marines, after their bedtime story, have a kind of final head count, I guess to check no one's absconded. We stood by our beds, the seventy of us, and each had to sequentially shout the corresponding ascending number to ensure we still totalled seventy. I was the penultimate marine – well, not quite marine; something less than that, a sub-marine. I watched with dreadful certainty as like upward tumbling dominoes each lad hollered their number: 'Sixty-five, sixty-six . . .' It's getting closer. 'Sixty-seven, sixty-eight . . .' Why yes, of course, now it's my turn, and in my pants in a room full of marines I chant 'Sixty-nine' like Kenneth Williams. It's all I can do to stop myself winking.

We then settle into our brittle sponge beds for the night – individually as I remember; I think gayness was still frowned upon in the military at that time – for what seemed to be barely a teaspoon of sleep before being awoken at 3 a.m. to participate in a rehearsal for Armageddon.

Out in the floodlit concrete expanse, battalions moved in inhuman harmony. Clichéd sounds all about me – unified boots on hard floor; rifles twirled and hugged in a murderous tango. They sang those call-and-response songs that they do in *Full Metal Jacket* or *Platoon* that are mostly incongruously misogynistic limericks, speculating on the likely characteristics of different nationalities of vagina. Eskimos: cold; Indian: spicy; Vietnamese: initially appealing but ultimately an unruly quagmire that leads to humiliation. I made the last one up. In fact I may've made the whole thing up, but it was that kind of mood, a bit nationalistic and blokey, as I imagine one might expect from a nocturnal drill in the US Marine Corps.

I suspect you'd be given short shrift if you complained on the basis that you were finding the whole experience a bit sexist or too tough. I think within minutes you'd find yourself the subject of a hurtful ditty, and that's just for starters.

It felt like the end of the world. I get prophetic flashes. There, I've said it. There are times when I see reality unfurl, not like the future is revealed, more like the past, or the present, like I can see the projector from which the spectacle is emitted. In the moment I feel dread. I watched them, maybe it's my own cultural indoctrination: I've watched a lot of films and gone on a lot of conspiratorial websites, so my mind too has been narrativised, I'm not free from tales and agendas. I saw the earth crack open and yawn belligerent fire and the sea take back her bounty. The animals in nightmarish calm know the end is nigh and move to high lands. The unduly unfurled flags are lashed by rain and untethered from their masts by lightning.

All nature converges; the purple sky bears down on the cleaved soil as Earth roars. The furious ocean envelops her lover, as long somnolent beasts rise up from the deep. Things don't fall apart; they move suddenly inward in vengeful implosion.

Alone in this dark reverie I stagger through the sepulchral ballet, as men move as dead men do, in dumb harmony.

The rhythm of my own two feet silences my dreaming. Now I am them and the dawn rises. We march through verdant and dusty Californian hills. I look at the others and try to stay in the middle. Some of them are so strong and young: athletes. These men are training; for me this rehearsal does not lead to a performance, it leads to a swift and grateful departure and a wry reminiscence. For them it leads to death.

They're so young. Once in a while they pass and sometimes vary in colour. Mostly, though, they are indistinguishable and young as they march past. Sometimes one will be wearing glasses and, like in a lazy movie, this is a placeholder for character, for individuality, vulnerability.

Senior marines marshal the pups; they have thicker necks and more certain voices, even the fog on their breath is more forthright, molecularly tighter. Drilled exhalations, their breath no longer theirs to give.

My mates are filming me and offering encouraging looks and sweet smiles, but I swear, twerp that I am, I have already Stockholmed myself into deep fraternity with the troops.

'You pansies,' I hear myself think of my former friends from yesterday on Civvy Street, 'you don't know what it means to be a marine.'

There are deep codes awoken here as we march in unison, our metronomically beating feet hypnotising away individualistic need. Lurking at the bottom of the pond of my mind, among the weeds, is a slumbering thing not nurtured by MTV or Pfizer or Coke or our other neon-pagan deities. It jolts in the dirge at the ancient siren.

At the end of the 10k hike I feel all proud and misty-eyed, choked on camaraderie. The commander of Camp Pendleton gives me the lid of a wooden ammo box with a brass plaque on the top that says I'm brave. I inwardly flood. It is the kind of engraving you'd have at the bottom of a pub darts trophy, any sport's trophy; I've never had a trophy so I am especially susceptible. Like all these fatherless boys, in Pendleton or Pakistan or Birmingham or Compton or Cardiff, any token of belonging is embraced.

I truly felt, ultimate objective aside, that the marines had something beautiful about them. Fraternity, initiation, mentoring, honour, valour, duty, beautiful male attributes in a society in which masculinity is maligned. I can get a bit like that, a bit D. H. Lawrence, a bit jazzed on unexamined humanity. When I chatted on camera to a pair of perfectly assembled teen marines who sat handsomely in their fatigues, rifles pristine and bolt upright at their sides, I was overwhelmed by the salvation that the military offers to boys that may otherwise have fallen through the cracks.

When they spoke of the ordinary deprivation of their origin and how it had been replaced by noble codes and duties, I teared up a little. By now I had put on my normal clothes and let my hair down – having made my point over ten kilometres I needed to assert my cherished individuality again. I was envious and admiring of these reformed and gracious lads who had had their lives turned around. I understood the pride – yes, pride, in both senses: honour in identity and unity of group – that the on-looking sergeant had engendered.

'The marines is unequivocally a good thing,' I concluded. Then I realised that if at any moment that sergeant sharply barked, 'KILL MR BRAND,' the boys would unthinkingly, unblinkingly, in one well-oiled, instantaneous clockwork blur, stand, aim, shoot me dead, then sit and resume answering whatever question I'd been asking when they shot me.

The training removes the gap that exists between command and action; the protocol is inserted at an instinctual level, way down in the swamp of the mind.

The manipulation of ancient codes, the management of instincts, this is the mode of our day. The same way the computer I type this on has pop-up reminders to back up my phone or observe a birthday, we have in our own programming inherent alarms and systems. Procreate, form bonds, suspect strangers, be wary in new lands.

The same way our once useful drive to consume scarcely available fat and sugar has become a debilitating hindrance in our menagerie of abundance, so too do our other instincts misfire, here in captivity.

These young men that are trained to kill are a fine example. What is training other than the emphasis on a particular set of behaviours? One need spend but a moment watching Andy Murray to recognise that his energy resources have been exclusively directed at proficiency in tennis to the observable detriment of other capabilities. In a press conference he stares with juvenile unease at his heavily sponsored shoes. On the court he is alive and firing.

I expect Andy Murray sacrificed a lot to achieve his excellence. The essence of sacrifice is yielding to a higher purpose. In his case, sporting supremacy.

In martial environments like the marines or extremist training camps, pertinent information and behaviours are exalted; information and behaviours that are detrimental to the common cause are eliminated as best as possible. Humanity echoes still, though, around the mind of an assassin as he looms above his hostage. Some irremovable cue – a tear, a cry, a smile like your mother's – and the training peels back like old paint.

I suppose the discomfort around homosexuality in the military is an acknowledgement that a competing primal force like sexuality can reasonably vie with the tribalism and competitiveness harnessed by these militia ideologues. Sexuality and love.

CHAPTER 21

Checking the Phone

I don't write this from a Teflon edifice of haughty objectivity: the World Cup is on at the moment, England have just gone out in the group stages, and I have been yanked by atavistic strings into all manner of patriotic contortions. I watched England's decisive match against Uruguay and weighed my personal requirements against the needs of the team.

'What would I give up for Ross Barkley to score, to put England level, to keep England in the tournament? What would I give of myself for this greater good?'

The fact is that in that pub under the ninety-minute spell, shoulder to shoulder with strangers with shared intentions, these psychological offerings were de rigueur. Everyone was thinking it. Everyone there felt the indescribable yearning.

Those feelings and urges lie latent, like flowers for Diana. Before she dies, on a garage forecourt sit mixed carnations, indistinct in a green bucket. Then the news: Diana has died, the emotion is provoked, the sediment stirs and now these petrol-infused and hopeless blooms have a destination. They are glumly collected on route to Kensington Palace and left in the cellophane tide that crashes like a drenched, insistent knell at the gates.

The British people's demands become childish. 'Why isn't the flag at half mast?'

'Where is our Queen?'

In the madness of abstract bereavement we demand palpable signs, demented and priapic, roused to fury by the mourno-graphic onslaught.

The situationists are right, we are drifting through space like Sandra Bullock in *Gravity* (a film in which gravity hardly ever appeared – what a swizz), no moral context, no cohesive story, no God, no one another.

The sudden withdrawal of the beautiful face of a seemingly kindly stranger is too real for us to bear.

What were the English before England, before the Romans, before the Normans, before the Celts? What name did we give ourselves? What calendar did we mark? What princess did we grieve for then?

In Albion when the sun rose, in Albion when the grass blows, in Albion when you hear sparrows in the hawthorns, who is your God then? Before there were three lions on a shirt and one swoosh on a shoe, and an apple on your phone, who was your God then? Before Google and Gaga and Yahoo and Fanta, at what altar did we kneel then?

When we had Galahad and Merlin and Guinevere and Arthur, was there still this lack, like a heart with alopecia?

Is there an emptiness in you as you walk your land, uneasy feet on uneasy streets, uneasy in the bedroom, uneasy even in the mirror, an uneasy creep to uneasy sleep, pulling the bedsheets up close; checking your phone, checking your phone, checking you're not here all alone, to die alone?

How long can you go on like this? Have you made a pact? Will you hang on and hope you endure like Methuselah?

I read some chump's upended brain dump: 'Does Russell Brand know the Revolution he's demanding would render his million-aire, movie star position redundant?' You query this even as the tomb calls?

'How can he talk of Revolution, riding round his ivory tower on his high horse?'

Do you not see the gathering carrion, the black-and-white magpie sky? I know the band on the *Titanic* played on. Do you want to expire watching MTV, biting down on Hubba Bubba like a gum bridle, as you canter to the knacker's yard?

CHAPTER 22

"Corporacide"

I went on a march to end austerity. I tell you, the marines march with more purpose. When Isis move on Damascus, they stay on the saddle, not fallen like Saul. When we march, we march for change, the march shows unity and it shows movement. I felt neither: I saw intransigent lines and people contentedly perched on either side.

Peaceful protest needn't be flaccid. I felt that what was missing was faith, real faith, faith with intention. Activism too, it seems, will be increasingly played out on the cyber battlefields drawn by Anonymous and other Hacktivists. Nerd warlords like Edward Snowden, Aaron Swartz and Jeremy Hammond have staked their lives and freedom in the conflict that with my limited imagination I can only envisage as Tron. Whilst the immaterial land of the Internet is corporately colonised, an invisible army fights to prevent digital flags being planted. By supporting vanguard organisations like these, as well as more traditional protest movements, consensual momentum will eclipse the brittle scaffold of convention.

Whilst I like stability, routine and comfort, I know I can handle disruption and that is, I suppose, a good thing to know if you want the world to change.

Of course there is a perennial war to fight against hypocrisy and sin and old programming. I can keep the patriotism and conformity under relatively good control when in England as it's trumped by anti-establishmentarianism. In America, though, I'm like some St George's flag-draped John Bull, Enoch Powell character, defending the honour of the crown, shouting down Yankee insurgents.

When the royal wedding was on I watched it, I nearly got hooked on *Downton Abbey*, I took part in the Olympic Closing Ceremony – all because of some infantile hook I've been unable to unsnag from my cheek. These techniques work. When I met the Queen I almost curtsied; I have to force myself to resist the Disney charm of the royal family. They are part of a cultural narrative that's as lazily entrenched as the spaceman wallpaper on my childhood bedroom wall. Their presence lights up the deeper pathways of my mind too, my yearning for structure and hierarchy. Then more innocuously and rationally, every day I read stories about Harry's bonhomie and Will's imperial grace. The ordinariness of the new one, George, tethers this pantheon to the quotidian as child seats are fitted and first steps taken. But if wisdom is acting on knowledge, they have to go. This luminous centrepiece of our neon matrix. That class is okay, natural, normal, good. They are a symbol of ideas that do nothing but hurt. Privilege, excess, violence, oppression, nation. The abolition of the monarchy would be a powerful symbolic victory for a new world. A significant and necessary victory, though, would be a demonstrable cowing of our real opponents, the real masters of our universe: global corporations.

We are constantly goaded and pricked into localised resentment of impotent targets on the basis of their nationality or sexuality or physical 'difference'. The common thread shared by those consistently targeted is that they have no significant wealth or power.

Immigrants, for example, are not a wealthy demographic of

fat cats, living it up on the spoils of the 2008 financial crash. Typically they are the most vulnerable, underserved and exploited strata of society. I chatted to a cab driver yesterday and he said he felt that Ukip represented him because of their stance on immigration. 'It's not all immigrants,' he stressed, 'just the ones that come to this country, exploit our resources and give nothing back.'

I of course told him that what he was describing, whilst an appealing story, is a barely relevant fragment of the whole truth. That the charge of exploiting our country, not contributing and using our resources is much more legitimately levelled at multinational corporations. Vodafone, Starbucks, Boots, Topshop, all massive organisations that exploit our country and its infrastructure without giving back.

Their impact is far more significant than that of immigrants. Philip Green, who owns Topshop, is one of the wealthiest men in this country, yet he pays less personal tax to support the nation from which he extracted his wealth than the cleaners who work on the floors of his store.

I would love to say to every working person being pushed to the right by the inefficiency, indifference and corruption of our politicians, 'You are looking in the wrong direction.' Every time anti-Islamic fervour is stirred, our true exploiters rub their hands, knowing their marauding can continue.

As I keep saying, I am from Grays, I am from a place where Ukip have been voted in. Barking in Newham, east London, where I lived with my nan as a kid, has always had occasional right-wing flare-ups. This frustration you feel towards immigrants and Muslims, this sense that you are being duped and ripped off, just for a few years can we all come together and focus this antipathy on its rightful recipients? The banks, the government, the big corporations.

If you want to reapportion money and power you have to

target the people and institutions that have it, not other poor people who are slightly different. Just for a few years let's focus together on the people that have the power. Bring the passion of the terraces to the places of their work. Fill the streets with ordinary people of every colour, alignment and faith, and together demand our country back. Demand a fair deal. Demand that which is already ours but will never be freely given and can never be achieved until we overlook the superficial differences and distinctions that they lower like a veil between us and unite to overcome them. Then if in a few years, if that hasn't changed the world, let's go back to killing one another.

For now though, let's kill a corporation.

This idea I'm at pains to point out, like all the good ideas in this book, is not mine. I've always suspected that there were loads of viable social systems out there that were kept hush-hush because it would subvert the current order, and I was right.

Already we have realised that we could radically alter trade agreements to support the needs of the people and the planet, like localised, organic farming instead of assisting big businesses profit from mad endeavours like importing and exporting the same quantities of food and sending apples across the globe to be polished like spoilt brats before being sent home.

We have learned that we have to impede energy companies' ability to profit from irresponsible practices in oil refinery and fracking, and convert to responsible renewable energy.

We have learned that cancelling personal debt would stimulate the economy more than any 'too big to fail' bank quantitive easing.

That the money given to these corrupt institutions could easily be given to pay people to build a better society for us all.

That wealthy institutions and individuals denied the right to entomb themselves with private security would become more accessible and responsible.

That titles are used to create acceptance of exploitative hierarchies and we should remove these outmoded symbols of inequality and oppression.

That centralised and detached power, whether from the private sector or the state, disempowers people and that we need to be responsible for our own communities and government, which we can now achieve through technology.

From highly respected experts like Thomas Piketty and Naomi Klein we have learned that, importantly, this change will not come without cohesive, unified resistance. We all need to come together and confront our shared enemy. The opponents of each of us, that come to our countries, use structures built by our efforts and give nothing back in return.

And I'm not talking about immigrants.

The idea to kill a corporation comes from the magazine *Adbusters*. In the issue I'm reading at the moment, the July issue, they point out that the 100 largest corporations in the world produce $7 trillion in sales and have $10 trillion in assets. With this money they control governments through lobbying and donations, fund academic research so that the 'scientific' view of the world adheres to their perspective, e.g. 'there is no climate change', and most importantly dominate consciousness by graffitiing our shared spaces and media with their peculiar philosophies.

The magazine observes that a corporation is like an immortal being, a god; corporation means 'body', but a dispassionate, unloving god, untethered from the earth, with only one obligation: make money. That is its function.

When they were first set up, corporations had built-in expiry as they were only designed to fulfil a specific task, like pave a road or build a tobacconist. They then lobbied for the right to exist beyond the completion of specific tasks; this is when they began to incorporate other roles and grow.

A corporation's role as a 'profit maximiser' for its owners is similar to the dispassionate description of *Homo sapiens* – that's you and me and our mums – as 'utility maximisers'. Creatures that care only about what's useful. That's a bloody inaccurate description of my mum: she wastes about 90 per cent of her time faffing around after her dog, a total prick by the name of Bobby that I, to my shame, bought her.

He is a vicious little canine jihadist, once described as a 'fluffy piranha'. Any utility that he's providing is a mystery to me. I think he's a punk.

Corporations haven't been around that long, only a couple of hundred years, and I think one of the problems we have in our hypnotised state of despondency is that we forget that we are not listless little subjects but glorious creatures that can imagine new lives for ourselves. Succinctly, all we have to do to rid ourselves of a problem like corporate tyranny is to imagine doing it, then do it. As dear, beautiful, morally unimpeachable Che Guevara said, 'Those who do not dream will never see their dreams come true.'

Sadly I think that it is also a lyric of that song 'Talky Talky Happy Talk Talk' but I'm pretty sure Che was first, and certain that if the creators of the song quibbled he would shoot them with a Kalashnikov without knocking the ash off his cigar.

Corporate charters weren't put together by legislators but by judges. I suppose that means they were not established in conjunction with the constitution and that's how come they're such devil-may-care gadabouts.

This change happened in the 1890s, prior to which, as *Adbusters* explained, corporations had a clear role and a definite period within which to fulfil it. I suppose that meant they could never swell into giant society-guzzling ogres. Even if they did, it wouldn't matter; they'd just complete their project, build a sewer or a dam, then disband.

In the 1890s, all that changed because judges, presumably in wigs and capes, decreed that the 'limited' lifespan of a corporation could be discarded. I once chatted to a judge that as a using addict had injected himself with heroin, under his robes, whilst sentencing people to harsh prison time for – drum roll, please – using drugs. So we can't take them too seriously. In fact all those places where they bang little wooden hammers and have flags and crests and shout 'Order, order' are in my view trying a bit too hard to seem serious. Have a bit of faith in yourselves. If what you're doing is patently not bollocks you won't feel the need to whip out Bibles and dress up like old-lady pirates.

With the abolition of these limitations a company that was created to spend four years building a bridge was no longer euthanised but allowed to live for ever – and to pursue any kind of money-making venture that it fancied, like Donald Trump with a trolley full of spare kidneys and livers. Note I didn't put spare hearts, as I was thinking about doing a joke like 'he doesn't even have a heart to begin with', then I thought, 'Nah, fuck it, Russ, you're a professional comedian and don't need to flounder around with that kind of "earnest" joke which has stymied the left since the sixties.' Once in a while you'll get a George Carlin or Bill Hicks or whatever, but for some reason changing the world is assumed to be a serious business and exempted from humour. John Cleese says that's because people mistake solemnity for seriousness, that by being all stern and joyless their ideas are somehow levitated.

Ol' Radhanath Swami once told me a story from the Bhagavad Gita about Krishna as a boy that exemplifies the necessity for lightness and joy when confronting dark power.

As is often the case in mythical tales, a village was besieged by the mischief and evil perpetrated by a tyrannical and wicked serpent.

231

This serpent was a real arsehole and was living in the lake where the villagers got all their water. He had multiple heads – that means he was a hydra, a many-headed monster – and he had a few wives too. Oddly they are depicted as human, and if you don't mind my saying so, quite fit. When I saw them, in the form of a statue depicting the event, I was peeved that this venomous troublemaker got to live in his lake with such top-notch crumpet. To say nothing of the fact that there were two of them. In the proper version of the story, when told by a monk (to me in my garden), this aspect of the tale is skimmed over: 'He lived in a lake with his two wives and—'

'Wait up, mate. Two wives? Don't they argue? Does he do it with 'em both at the same time? Do they do stuff to each other?'

The polygamous private relationships of the antagonist were of more interest to me than the fact that he was a many-headed, evil lake-snake in a story about how to live in alignment with God.

Eventually, after I'd perved for a good while on what ought to have been a secondary detail, I allowed the embarrassed swami to continue. The villagers were all ill, some were dying, and morale was at an all-time low because of this infected water, and for all I know because the fiend behind this cruelty was living 'la vida loca' down there with his doublemint, double-your-pleasure twin brides, so they turned to Krishna, who although just a kid at the time was, as 'the Supreme Godhead', already the go-to guy in such matters. Krishna is an all-loving deity, supremely powerful, who plays all reality into being with his flute. That could be a way of saying he is the divine source of original vibration, which is the same as saying 'In the beginning there was the Word', or from 'nothingness' came a big bang, or a powerful creative sound.

I've always liked Krishna as a god because he's jolly, dresses cool, hangs round in fields and forests with fit women and animals, plus he's blue.

The villagers ask for Krishna's assistance in dealing with the scaly bigamist at the bottom of their reservoir and he of course agrees. He swoops over the lake, playing his pipe and goading the serpent like Muhammad Ali. The serpent, rowdy and easily wound up, comes smashing through the surface of the water like a beanstalk, all fangs and fury. Krishna stays cool.

He is the avatar of absolute power, so that must take a lot of the pressure off him in situations where mortal combat is involved. Anyone who's ever developed a movie script will know that your protagonist's vulnerability is vital for 'jeopardy' or there are no 'stakes'. Like Superman has to have kryptonite or we know that he's invincible and don't worry when General Zod says he's going to give him a good kicking.

Jesus as protagonist in the Gospels is good because like Superman he's been sent from another dimension, like Superman he's decided to dedicate himself to saving humanity, and like Superman he's got special powers: heal the sick, walk on water, food multiplication. His vulnerability is that he is part man, and as such can be speared, mocked and nailed up and, at least carnally, sacrificed.

Krishna, we always suspect, will be okay because his defining attribute is omnipotence. Perhaps that's why in this tale he is depicted as a child, only partially formed.

The fuming amphibian ensnares Krishna and coils about him, squeezing the god as if prey. The onlooking villagers gasp with fear, and presumably guilt as it was them that put him in this quandary, whilst the serpent's wives cheer him on like molls or Essex girlfriends in a car park row, 'Go on, Dean, kick his head in.'

Krishna of course is untroubled by this attack. Where most would be asphyxiated – one of the worst ways to die, I'll bet; I was once choked by a big Scotch bouncer and it was fucking awful, all my bravado leaked out of me and I squawked oesophageal apologies like a repentant tracheotomy patient – Krishna instead, using his secret and plot-ruining weapon, omnipotence, slims himself down to the size of a panatela cigar, slinks out and leaps on to one of the serpent's heads.

He then resumes his normal size and begins to dance a jaunty, spry and by all accounts powerful jig across the villain's brow. As he plays his pipe and dances, the serpent becomes at first bewildered, then weakened and eventually despairing. Krishna's gentle but potent dance is killing the beast.

Crucially, at no point does Krishna seem agitated; he does the whole thing in a spirit of great fun, as if there were no consequences, nothing to worry about at all. The serpent flails and spasms and droops, hopelessly spewing his venom. Evidently Krishna is enjoying himself so much that he scarcely even notices, he's completely in the moment. Eventually the serpent's wives – let's call them Carol and Sue – participate in the story in a meaningful way by begging Krishna to show mercy.

Krishna, who, let's face it, is a damn fine fellow and the source of all wonder and heavenly glory, agrees. The subjugated and battered snake has been irreversibly changed by the encounter. Far from seeing his pummelling as a humiliation, he has been converted by Krishna's grace and says he'll be no more bother and, if memory serves, continues to live in the lake but now in a more community-spirited capacity, like a lifeguard. I don't know if he kept his wives.

The point of the story is Krishna's joy – that he doesn't become the thing he's trying to defeat. He, on his own terms, thwarts the monster and creates love from hatred.

I'm sure there are other analyses that could be drawn; for example, we could regard the snake and its many heads as a kind of corporation – one body, many faces, polluting the common good for its own selfish needs. I don't know where the polygamy fits in. I know, though, that the manner in which these institutions are overthrown should be in themselves a defiance of their dogma and that the systems that follow cannot be an echo of their droning hypnosis.

When corporations were first established people objected as these new entities had the same rights as a citizen, but were immune to human controls – you can't imprison or execute a wayward corporation. They're like evil lake-snakes.

Adbusters propose a return to the earlier corporate incarnation: entities with a limited function which expire at the completion of that function. This would mean a completely different cultural and economic landscape; corporations and brands would be relegated to a functional position in society, where they serve us instead of dominating us.

Adbusters, as a means to reach this improved version of the corporation, suggest as a symbol, and to show we're serious, the killing of a corporation. Make them subject to the forces that control humanity. However great and powerful we become, however mean we are, in the end along comes death, all nonchalant in his hoodie with his long handled dagger and levels the playing field right out.

Much of the irresponsible and destructive behaviour engaged in by corporations is likely because they are never punished. No corporation has ever been killed. It doesn't matter how much they pollute, lie, steal, or even when they murder their customers, the consequences are minor. I agree with *Adbusters*, it's time to kill a corporation.

They suggest a bunch including General Motors. General Motors, as the name suggests, are generally speaking interested in producing automobiles. Perhaps they are being a bit too general and should be a bit more specific. Perhaps it is this somewhat vague and blasé approach that led to one of the more notorious crimes in their history. Put briefly, they accidentally made an ignition that shut down and killed people, installed it in one of their cars and then sold loads of them.

Some people died as a result and their families, disappointed by the loss of their loved ones, complained. GM of course apologised, they're not monsters, but then had a conundrum on their hands. Should they recall all the vehicles that had the faulty, murderous ignition – which would be pricey, if you value economic cost more highly than the cost of the loss of life to a family?

GM do. They have to. They're designed to. They are legally obligated to make as much money as possible, that means in a situation where human life is weighed up against a fiduciary deficit there will be blood. In a way the allegorical device of a man-made machine that goes wrong and kills people is too on the nose to be helpful. Twelve more people died, GM effectively did nothing.

Now, let me remind you, this is your planet, you can change it if you want to. You can change it by doing loads of drugs, or having it off with loads of women, or going on a murderous rampage with a licensed weapon. Doesn't it make more sense, though, to change it by binding together with your fellow man and working to create a society that's fair and just? Of course it does. Let's kill General Motors. Let's take it back from its shareholders, scribble out the name and the logo and use its resources for something more valuable.

In Michael Moore's excellent first film *Roger and Me*, Moore explains how GM used to employ loads of people from where he's from, in Flint, Michigan. His dad and a load of his uncles worked there and it was all cool; people were doing fine. Then when GM discovered it would be more profitable to move their production to Mexico and fuck off the town and all the loyal workers that'd toiled away their lives at the plant, they barely paused to say 'Ay caramba', if you can tolerate a little racism.

They had to, they are an entity designed to make profit at all costs. They're a bit like the Terminator in the film *The Terminator*. Terminator, as his name suggests, is a robot designed to terminate people. It's no good getting all cross if you leave him to look after your rabbit when you go on holiday and come home to discover he's terminated it: that's his job. You should've asked a neighbour.

So we should say to GM, right, this company of yours, you've had a good innings, but frankly we're upset about the pollution, the disloyalty, and not to put too fine a point on it, the killings, so we're shutting you down. You don't have a GM any more, there is no GM any more. Stop crying, you should've thought of that when you didn't recall those faulty units because you calculated it'd be cheaper to compensate the victims than tarnish the brand.

We have a couple of options for what to do with the assets that GM have, their factories, plants or any resources they own. We could sell them off and use the money to compensate victims and former workers, or we could collectivise it and run it as a worker-owned cooperative.

The people that run the factories, design the cars, work in the canteens, do the admin, all that (I'm not an expert, who knows what they get up to), will own and run their company. Each region will be autonomous and fully self-supporting except in matters that affect other areas of the organisation or the planet or humanity as a whole.

They can democratically elect a board from the workforce who will serve for a limited time period and are kicked off if they fuck about. They can call their new company whatever they vote for – I'd suggest 'We Don't Kill Our Customers Motors' – and get on and responsibly make automobiles for American people. I wouldn't worry too much about exporting them, as other countries have their own fucking cars, that they can reclaim – like in Germany, for example, the people could take back Volkswagen in much the same way and call it 'We Don't Make Cars For Hitler Motors' or whatever.

These companies might consider observing a new charter, which they can collectively devise, to make cars responsibly. Might I suggest, for example, not deliberately making cars that break down in a few years so they can sell more of them. Built-in obsolescence, the deliberate and ubiquitous practice of manufacturing shoddy and expiring products, can be outlawed. It doesn't serve us, it only serves them.

Other corporations that *Adbusters* suggest bumping off include Philip Morris, the fag company. One million people have died of smoking-related diseases, and as I keep saying, because it is such a clear demonstration of the priorities of big business, they knew for ages they were killing their customers but were as addicted to the money as we were to the nicotine.

They had no obligation to obey human codes. If I, me, ol' Russ, knew that the milkshakes I was selling caused blindness because scientists kept telling me and because the people drinking my shakes were having trouble finding their way back to the store, yet carried on selling 'em, I'd expect consequences.

Especially if I aggressively went around getting anyone I could to drink my 'cataract smoothies' through sexy adverts. Then, if when the jig was finally up, because the lie had become too obvious to ignore, I went to countries where the laws protecting people from my myxomatosis brew were more lax, like the Philippines, and started flogging it there, I'd expect, at some point, people to come together and say, 'Alright, ol' Russ, enough of this now, we're going to have to shut down your milkshake business.'

If I indignantly responded that my milkshake business was a

proud 'national institution' and a 'tradition' or 'a way of life', out would come the butterfly nets and I'd be in for a spell of basket weaving.

Today in Britain, America and other mostly white people countries, fag firms have to write a message on the box to the effect of 'Sorry we lied to you about our snout for generations. Here's a list of ways this stuff is going to make your life worse if you smoke these.'

So instead they are promoting cigarettes all over Africa and Asia, new markets where people are less informed on the subject and there are no warnings about cancer and the other known negative side effects of smoking.

We should probably kill Philip Morris. Difficult to know what to do with the factories, given it's a product that kills people and the market is flooded with alternative brands. We could make it super-reasonably priced with our new, efficient worker-owned model. We could also sell fags with weed in them – people seem to like that.

Or we could use the money raised from selling assets to compensate their victims (costly) and retrain their workers to do other, skilled jobs. This is an option; there are many options.

Why stop there? There's loads of corporations all over the world, exploiting with impunity. We could knock 'em off like seal cubs – Exxon? Goldman Sachs? Boots? Yeah, Boots. If they don't pay tax, we'll reclaim their assets and give them to the people that work there to run.

This idea that society will fall apart if there isn't a snidey gang at the top of the financial pyramid needs to be challenged. We're ready to challenge it.

CHAPTER 23

Co-Operate

The answer to the quandary of how to reorganise society isn't new leaders within the same system, the answer isn't leaders at all. The answer is, of course, simple: we can run our own lives and our own communities. We're not idiots, we need to establish a few immutable, non-negotiable principles, mostly to respect the planet and individual freedom, then look at who is benefiting from things being the way they are now and, using no violence when we approach them and no titles when we address them, politely insist they give us our planet back.

As you know, I'd prefer we just spontaneously began co-operating on the basis that we are all manifestations of one sublime vibration, but that ain't gonna butter no spuds on *Newsnight* or Fox News, so I will now reluctantly, and possibly badly, describe to you, in a little more detail, how we could own and control our means for production.

My mate Adam Curtis, the documentary maker who I've gone on about a bit because of his amazing films and weird, clever, sweet personality, told me this: 'The problem with Marxism is that it placed economics at the heart of socialism.'

Now, even if you don't understand that, simply nod and agree as if you were already thinking it.

What it means is, I reckon, that every subsequent political

ideology, especially successful ones, like capitalism, have similarly placed economics at the centre of their philosophy. The economy is just a metaphorical device, it's not real, that's why it's got the word 'con' in the middle of it.

There are generally speaking, like General Motors do about their generally not, but sometimes a bit, murderous cars, two ways that the 'means for production' can be owned.

Currently the most popular method is privately owned businesses with invisible, irreproachable bosses, often residing in tax havens, or nationalised industries, where incompetent and detached politicians run things.

Both these methods lead to an odd sense of alienation and disempowerment. No real pride in the work or the product, no real power to complain or change things. That works incredibly well for the people in charge but is a drag for the poor sods doing the graft.

Upon which unchallenged basis too are profits hurtled with thoughtless expedience into the pendular pockets, swinging like a velor scrotum, of the thumb-twiddling plutocrat who by happy accident owns the firm? The profits should be shared among the people who do the work.

An elected, rotating board can do the admin. I should note that I mean the board members rotate, not that the person in the role whirls dervishly in his chair.

Another tradition of the abstinence-based recovery groups that I much respect is 'leaders are trusted servants, they do not govern'. Even in the policy-bare days of the Paxman interview, I alluded to an attitudinal shift towards civil service and governmental roles. It should be clear that these positions are about serving the people. We are not some binary crowd to be shepherded and shushed; we are not children who need to be reprimanded and praised; we are the people, the power is with us.

In this version of reality, we would have autonomy and

freedom at work. If we had jobs at Carphone Warehouse in Lakeside, we'd chat among the twenty or so staff and elect two or three people to be over the admin. At the end of the year we'd vote to see what to do with the profits and whether we wanted to make infrastructural changes.

We might also like to consider that given we are no longer syphoning off all our profits to a vampiric board, we can give more money to ourselves and work less hours. The only people who tell you this is impossible are the people who benefit from things staying the way they are. Start to take notice of who the people are who are telling you that things are fine now, watch them, remember them, because change is coming. When people say, 'The system works,' they mean 'The system works for me.' The slags.

This business model is up and running all over the world. Typically they are described as 'co-ops'. My mate John Rogers, who's a bit of a hippie, lefty, druid, scruffbag-type fella, did some research. Let's go through it together:

'Autonomous, democratic control of the economy driven by equality, fairness, environmental and ecological responsibility is not idealistic, pie-in-the sky, utopian daydreaming, it is a system currently in use by some of the most successful companies.'

It is important to keep reiterating and asserting that alternatives exist and flourish. The reason we grew up thinking socialism was a tarnished and hopeless ideology and only heard pejorative reports of the most extreme examples of it is because if we aspired to it Margaret Thatcher's head may've ended up on a spike. This is the last thing she'd've wanted – typical.

'A cooperative is an autonomous association of persons united voluntarily to meet their common economic, social and cultural needs and aspirations through a jointly owned and democratically controlled enterprise.'

That doesn't sound too scary. I once participated in a capitalist experiment with the renowned street artist Shepard Fairey. We hired a unit in the Beverly Center in Los Angeles and ran a shop called 'Buy Love Here'. The concept was to test the nature of consumerism by stocking items donated by famous folk like 50 Cent, Cameron Diaz, Mike Tyson, Jason Segel, Katy Perry and a load of others but not mark them out as such. There were loads of other donated items too, loads of shoes and T-shirts and jumble.

People were invited to take anything they wanted from the store but they had to leave something in return. There was no imposition of equivalence, no price; people could take what they wanted and leave what they felt like.

That was how it was supposed to work. The problem was, I was involved. Even though, along with Shepard and my mates, I had come up with the idea, a gentle examination of consumerism in the very heart of the problem, I was incapable of behaving in the detached and objective manner that a social experiment such as this required. I was worse in fact than that lunatic Professor Zimbardo who conducted the Stanford prison experiment from the hardly neutral post of prison warder. I jokingly criticised him earlier in the book without acknowledging that I've committed a similar transgression.

Within seconds of the shop's ostentatious opening – we had brown paper ripped down from the shopfront windows by models – I was carrying on like a fastidious little capitalist, sticking my nose into every purchase, barking at the 'staff' and secretly trying to put aside Cameron Diaz's bikini. I was like Arkwright from *Open All Hours* – or JR from *Dallas*, if you're American; it says much of our two nations that those two figures are comparable.

I was completely incapable of behaving in the Zen and non-judgemental manner that the experiment demanded if it were to be valid. It brought out the very worst in me. I hated the fact that someone could bring in an old tennis ball they'd found in a dog park and swap it for my ex-wife's frock. I completely forgot the point of the experiment: to see if people would behave fairly if given the option. I was incapable of letting it be.

I recall reducing one poor woman to tears as she tried to swap a hairbrush for Iron Mike Tyson's toaster. It was a shambles. Loads of TV people turned up to see me in a tight yellow Shepard-designed T-shirt, frolicking with the models and bickering with the staff about flexitime.

I frog-marched some poor woman to a nearby jeweller's to see if the diamond ring she was trying to swap for one of Shaquille O'Neal's big shoes was legit (how many of those things did he give out? They're everywhere). This completely violated the idea of trust, which was meant to be at the heart of the concept.

The only thing the experiment proved is that I should never be allowed to run a shop. More broadly, it indicated that we need to safeguard against domineering individuals tyrannising systems designed for the community.

Here are some further co-op guidelines that if deployed may have prevented the Buy Love Here disaster:

'Cooperatives are based on the values of self-help, self-responsibility, democracy, equality, equity and solidarity. In the tradition of their founders, cooperative members believe in the ethical values of honesty, openness, social responsibility and caring for others.'

Sounds a bit airy-fairy but these ideas would've prevented me squirrelling away the donated offcuts of well-meaning celebrities for some imagined reason.

This is all we need to know to run a co-op:

1. Voluntary and Open Membership
Cooperatives are voluntary organisations, open to all persons able to use their services and willing to accept the responsibilities of membership, without gender, social, racial, political or religious discrimination.

Voluntary? Do we get paid for working in these places or what?

2. Democratic Member Control
Cooperatives are democratic organisations controlled by their members, who actively participate in setting their policies and making decisions. People serving as elected representatives are accountable to the membership. In primary cooperatives members have equal voting rights (one member, one vote) and cooperatives at other levels are also organised in a democratic manner.

Okay, so I suppose we could vote on whether or not to make money. See, I've gone into a capitalist frenzy and we're only on point 2.

3. Member Economic Participation
Members contribute equitably to, and democratically control, the capital of their cooperative. At least part of that capital is usually the common property of the cooperative.

I see. We have to foster a different attitude to property. It's hard when you've spent your whole life being defined by stuff, logos and brands to step back from the ideology of consumption and remember that what we were trying to access through these acquisitions was a sense of fulfilment better delivered through belonging and community.

4. Autonomy and Independence

Cooperatives are autonomous, self-help organisations controlled by their members. If they enter into agreements with other organisations, including governments, or raise capital from external sources, they do so on terms that ensure democratic control by their members and maintain their cooperative autonomy.

So there is opportunity for growth and collaboration but within democratic and responsible guidelines. I'm beginning to see that these principles are explicitly designed to inhibit predatory people like me.

5. Education, Training and Information

Cooperatives provide education and training for their members, elected representatives, managers and employees so they can contribute effectively to the development of their cooperatives. They inform the general public – particularly young people and opinion leaders – about the nature and benefits of cooperation.

This model is designed to perpetuate further cooperatives. I expect the entrepreneurial spirit could still thrive, but not at the expense of more important collective values.

6. Cooperation among Cooperatives

Cooperatives serve their members most effectively and strengthen the cooperative movement by working together through local, national, regional and international structures.

Daniel Pinchbeck was talking about how these kind of organisations could now be communicated and collaborate on a global level using the incredible technological advances of the last few decades. Now, though, for the benefit of us all, not just an elite, and with the removal of dumb ideas that increase pollution and waste, like those bloody jet-setting apples.

This cooperative model, in conjunction with localised farming freed from oppressive global trade tariffs, as explained by Helena Norberg-Hodge, would improve life remarkably for us by creating job opportunities and autonomy and wealth and leisure – and for the planet, mostly because we'd stop that mad international waxed apple ricochet.

7. Concern for Community
Cooperatives work for the sustainable development of their communities through policies approved by their members.

The values of community development, democracy and opportunity are emptily bandied about from politicians' mouths every time I see them on my telly.

They're forever up on podiums, thumb on top of index finger, like Clinton was taught to do, telling us they want us to have opportunities and build communities and participate in democracy. Telling me I'm irresponsible for not voting. Gloating that they're participating by door-stopping and flesh-pressing and press-fleshing and baby-kissing. As soon as the red light goes off, their expressions change and they go back to their true agenda: meeting the needs of big business. It isn't even their fault; it's a systemic corruption that they unavoidably serve.

By the time you get to be an MP you've spent so long on your knees, sluicing down acrid mouthfuls of Beelzebub's cum, that all you can do is cough up froth.

We can't blame them or even condemn them; we just have to ignore them. Elsewhere in the world, modest versions of these ideas are already implemented. Whether it's Portugal, where drug users are no longer pointlessly criminalised; or Switzerland, where democracy is already more inclusive and referenda on civil issues are a regular occurrence; or Iceland, where corrupt bankers were booted out and told to sling their hook re bailouts; or Germany, where large companies, including Bayern Munich FC, have workers – and in that case, fans – on the board of directors.

It's worth noting that Iceland – y'know, Björk, aurora borealis – Iceland in 2008 had a Revolution. They peacefully overthrew their government precisely because of the financial piracy and debt enslavement which the rest of the world continues to be tortured by. They did this by mass civil disobedience and the replacement of their corrupt parliamentary system with an assembly of representatives taken from the population. Not people who'd been conditioned and groomed to compliantly abide by the system that exploits them.

They refused to pay back the international debt they were told they owed, and because they were unified there was nothing anyone could do to stop them. If it worked for them, it can work for us.

These modest measures are working. These suggestions don't just amount to 'play nice', like some equal-opportunity PC crap to hold out a hand to the disadvantaged; they work better. The German economy is the strongest in Europe, perhaps because its workforce feels invested in its efforts, instead of trolling around like eunuch mannequins, castrated and hopeless, waiting for a two-week holiday.

What we must now demand is a radically altered society. We've gone way off track, put some absurd people and institutions in charge of our planet, and it's time for radical change. That change cannot come from within the system. The successes I've listed above are improvements, and improvements are better than a kick in the balls from Bobby Charlton, but I think we can aim higher than incremental change or modest reform. I think we'd all be a bit disappointed if all this talk of utopia, ditching capitalism and Revolution boiled down to 'We want to be a bit more like Germany' – fuck that.

Remember we have no choice; there are ecological imperatives that have done our thinking for us. The planet is in trouble; there has never in all the history of our dopey, lovely species been a time of such inequality. The time for change is now. Will that change be delivered by David Cameron or Ed Miliband or Hillary Clinton or Barack Obama? Of course not, look at them, just look at them, you're not an idiot, you can see what they are; look at their eyes, they are all avatars of the same neo-liberal concept, part of the problem, not the solution.

We have to immediately dispatch with the notion that we'll get any dice whatsoever from people who already have jobs in oak-panelled rooms with leather seating.

Cast your mind back to the end-of-term glee that accompanied Barack Obama's 'Yes We Can', 'Time for Change', 'Ain't We Neat' election. There was such hope, such optimism, but what happened? Nothing. Nothing was ever going to happen, nothing could happen in that context. That's the whole point. The joy of Obama's presidency after eight years of Bush amounts to an insipid blow-job at the end of a rotten evening. Very nice for a moment, but who's going to actually mop up the mess?

We are, obviously. All else has failed; it's time for a Revolution.

CHAPTER 24

Plug Me In

A Revolution is where a political system is overthrown from outside the formal political structures that already exist.

The 1997 UK election that swept Tony Blair's New Labour into power, jolly though it may've been, wasn't a Revolution; it was at best a refurbishment. It was comparable to the election of Obama or Clinton: a bloke with a nice smile and an angle is swept into power after a more obviously despicable regime and then behaves more or less exactly like his predecessors. We shouldn't be disappointed. No version of 'bloke with nice smile', or different-colour skin, or accent, or vagina, will work. True change has to subvert the system that produces these people.

Joseph Campbell has a lovely analogy to help us understand mortality. He explains that a school janitor, in charge of minor repairs, on discovering a light bulb has broken, doesn't collapse into a quivering puddle of grief, warbling, 'That was my favourite light bulb, and now it's gone.' The janitor, if he's any good, knows that a bulb is just an expression of the electricity that illuminates it and simply unscrews the dead, useless bulb, tosses it away and pops in a new one.

Here I will use Campbell's maintenance fable to deliver two points: 1) we human beings are the temporary expression of a greater force that science as yet cannot explain but is approaching in its fledgling understanding of the harmony and transcendent principles of the quantum world, and 2) all political figures are the expression of a refined systemic energy and cannot therefore ever convey a significantly different ideology; it's not their fault, they're just not plugged into it.

I chatted to a boy from an expensive British private school yesterday. The boy was smart, alert and funny. The most obvious result of his education, though, was an adamantine, unblinking certainty that things are the way they should be. That there are no alternatives to the current political system. Anything else would be mayhem, violence and corruption. I suppose that must be one of the key priorities of any elitist educational establishment: indoctrinate the pupils with a turgid and absolute sense that change is impossible, that privilege is correct because it exists in a realm beyond morality. It seemed like even to countenance an alternative would be a kind of blasphemy. These ideas had been wedged into his head and no room was left to ponder alternatives.

Whenever I'm surprised by some unrecognisable behaviour or trait, I try to think of comparable phenomena within myself. Paedophilia is the most obvious example. Every time another icon of my childhood is slung into jail for diddling his audience, my peers, I am astonished. Whenever we hear a gut-wrenching tale of child abuse, we are sickened by the aberration. Our impulse is revulsion, disgust, to recoil from these monsters and their practices for fear of some indiscernible contamination. Like perversion is radioactive.

Clearly the ancient urge that motivates my own compulsions that are conveniently socially appropriate, are comparable to the drives of a paedophile, if aimed at a socially acceptable target: adult women.

When paedophiles talk about their obsession they always say they have no choice and that the urge is overwhelming. I don't think there's anyone in the world that can't identify with that urge or obsession; the distinction is the object.

Sometimes I tell myself not to smoke a fag or eat a chocolate biscuit but the urge overrides my will. Fortunately the subject of my desire is not taboo and doesn't have a negative effect on others – unless you're comparing passive smoking to child abuse. When I was single and lived a life of nocturnal excesses I got out of the habit of curbing compulsion; if I wanted to indulge a behaviour, I usually could. How pitiful if for some reason beyond choice and will, the subject of your urges were forbidden.

Judging from the number of people who've experienced abuse as children, this desire is incredibly common. What of those that feel forbidden lusts but don't act upon them? Those who suffer paedophilic urges but suppress them? What do they get, a medal? A parade? Even wanting, imagining sexual contact with children is disturbing, only marginally less than the act. Really, then, it's just an unpleasant thing that exists, that doesn't seem to be hugely curtailed by penalties or current therapeutic solutions. If our objective is to limit the number of children subjected to abuse, we must be open to new ways to treat the perpetrators, as well as the victims. Not just out of some wet liberal notion of tolerance but because it will yield better results.

Come with me now on a brief, new age, hippie ramble which may be of no help and if you're reviewing this book for the *Daily Mail* or are a concerned parent picking it up in a teen-ager's room will have you apoplectic. Don't look under the bed, for God's sake. The horrors that lurk there will dwarf this eastern liberalism. Although do kids these days even have things under the bed? Isn't all their porn, booze and weaponry stored in a digital cloud floating around the house, about to burst and drown us in a contraband downpour?

Back to my jumped-up, hemp-dusted theory: if we consider humanity to be not a disparate and separate conglomerate of individuals but the temporary physical manifestation and expression of a subtler electromagnetic, microcosmic realm (thy will be done, on earth as it is in heaven), like in Campbell's light-bulb allegory, then all resultant phenomena emanated from a single source so we are all jointly responsible. If we are all one human family, and there's not a theory out there from any denomination that opposes a single human source, then we cannot reach solutions based on 'separateness' or 'otherness' – it's mechanically incorrect.

As the TM Foundation's Washington experiment demonstrated, the transcendent consciousness of a group of meditators had a positive impact on the city's crime statistics. There is no real gap between my consciousness and your consciousness. The separation is a retrospective, sense-based application.

We've all seen the heartening and peculiarly uplifting news story of a recently bereaved parent who somehow instantly forgives the killer of their child. Someone who has somehow overcome the initial rage, hatred and urge for vengeance that accompanies such tragedy. Seemingly though, beyond that pain is a kind of sanguinity in forgiveness. How do they do that? From where is that strength sourced?

Resentment is painful to carry, justified resentment no less so. All resentment has to be relinquished to find peace. As it says in the St Francis prayer, 'It is by forgiving that we are forgiven.' If we want to be free from pain, we have to forgive everyone we believe to have wronged us, to find love beyond the pain, as these heroic parents do. In this forgiveness is the acknowledgement of our unity. That we are one human family. One consciousness. One body. Increasingly I learn that spiritual principles only have value in adversity, when applied in opposition to a powerful contrary tendency.

It is precisely when I want to kill or fuck I have to look within and see if there's another way. For years I lived by subduing my sensitivity. Eckhart Tolle says, 'Addiction begins with pain and ends with pain,' meaning that pain is behind compulsive behaviour. Eleven years clean, I still feel the urge to medicate pain. Whenever events don't go my way my first instinct is to annul the feeling, to look for an external resource to solve the problem. The second part of Eckhart's edict kicks in here, addiction 'ends with pain'. Medication of any kind offers only a temporary solution; it always leads back to pain and becomes therefore predictably cyclical.

The myths of Sisyphus, Prometheus and the sun-god Ra all recount this cycle of perpetual struggle.

Sisyphus was a Greek king who irritated the gods, mostly through hubris: he was up himself and constantly trying to pull a fast one. His primary offence as far as I can see was an attempt to cheat death itself when he was taken to the Greek underworld and chained by Hades, the bloke who looked after it. Actually Hades was a god, not some subterranean lavvy attendant; bloke might be reductive. Interesting that in Greek myth both hell and its chief administrator, which for us would be the devil, are seen from a much less pejorative perspective.

In Hellenistic myths 'the underworld', where the dead are sent, is a complicit part of the human experience, not a fiery penitentiary, and Hades is a more neutral character, not a cackling horned beast, jabbing you with a trident. I prefer pagan ideologies like Hellenism: they're more obviously symbolic and inclusive of human frailty. Monotheism is a bit too judgemental and reductive. It even sounds dumb: 'monotheism' – it's only got one idea, what a durr-brain.

King Sisyphus, who has spent his whole life tricking people, engaging in scurrilous wars, having it off with his enemies' kids and generally being a real dick, really takes the biscuit when sent to the absolute terminus of the underworld. When enchained by Hades he dupes the deity into releasing him using the oldest trick in the book, the ol 'Mate, show us how them chains work' number. Hades, who in my mind should be sacked on the spot by god of gods, Zeus, for this fascinating incompetence, falls for it and in no time at all is chained up himself, like Elmer Fudd or something.

Having made a mockery of Hades and the underworld, which amounts to 'laughing in the face of death', Sisyphus comes back to the land of the living and starts kicking off again like a royal hooligan – so like Prince Harry, I suppose, or Uday Hussein.

All the while Hades is chained up, clenching his fist and cursing that 'damn rabbit', no humans can die, so the earth is becoming overpopulated, the sick are suffering and we are learning that death is a necessary part of the life cycle.

Zeus, not before time, decides to step in. To demonstrate to Sisyphus the necessity and even favourability of death, Sisyphus is given the task of carrying a boulder from the bottom of a hill to the top again, then Zeus in a trick of his own, which might simply be 'gravity', returns the boulder to the bottom, where Sisyphus must resume his fruitless and unending labour.

Søren Kierkegaard, the Danish brainbox, reckoned it was a good metaphor for addiction to materialism and sex: 'It is comic that a mentally disordered man picks up any piece of granite and carries it around because he thinks it is money, and in the same way it is comic that Don Juan has 1,003 mistresses, for the number simply indicates that they have no value. Therefore, one should stay within one's means in the use of the word "love".'

This analysis is resonant: this book, to a point, is about my own disillusionment with the material offerings of fame and fortune, which include money and sexual opportunity. My mate Matt once said he heard me, from his place on the couch, skylarking and jesting with some female companions in my room and assumed I was adrift in hedonistic glory.

He then reported that I left the room, deadpan and hollow-eyed, sombrely walked past him, fetched some lubricant, either mental or anatomical, from the kitchen and glumly trotted back to the bacchanalia. When the door closed he said the trumpeting of decadent splendour continued as before. Whilst I don't recall that particular incident, I do recollect that what began as the pursuit of pleasure, or at least an escape from pain, became a joyless trudge through flesh, at the summit of each coital march, no certainty other than the process must begin again.

How Sisyphus and his myth of pointless endeavour chimes with me now is as a tale of recognition of the cyclical nature of all things, even and perhaps especially enlightenment. This commitment must be renewed daily; it is never permanently arrived at.

The poet Rumi has a line 'Tomorrow you will awake frightened and alone.' When I heard that recited, I thought, 'Fuck. I will an' all, I always do.' Each morning a new commitment is required to hand over my will, to relinquish my own ideas as to how my life should be, knowing that method always leads to trouble.

Bill Hicks said, 'The world is like a ride in an amusement park. It has thrills and spills and is very brightly coloured, but it's just a ride. Some people have remembered and they come back to us and say, "Hey, don't be afraid, this is just a ride" and we . . . kill those people.' Rumi, Kierkegaard and perhaps Bill himself have left clues and codes for us to help us to disentangle from the painful and material, sensorial fixation. All prophecies stripped of acculturation and geographic ornamentation seem only to be saying, 'Journey within, look behind your feelings, beyond your pain, fashion your world from what you find there.'

What we inhabit now is a world built upon the feelings and fears that the prophets are telling us to overcome.

Sometimes when I'm alone and West Ham have been particularly shit, I shamefully fantasise about supporting . . . maybe Arsenal. I can't do it for long though because it feels wrong, disloyal, perverse, indecent, like incest or something incalculably taboo. Like prepubescent fingers in a matriarch's knicker drawer while the babysitter watches *Bullseye* downstairs.

Reality responds to consciousness. Reality may only be consciousness for all we know, for all we can ever know, so we must be free to imagine new worlds. Of course we will be attacked. 'Oh yeah,' they'll say, 'what will they look like? How will they work?' The current system, of course, was given time and space to evolve and was not subjected to scrutiny from some haughty panel in an aloof gallery because they were the people who devised it.

There have of course been loads of successful revolutions in history, where people have come together and overthrown a system that no longer represents them. The problem, you will have noticed, is that they are usually replaced by another system that doesn't represent them. Like in Egypt in 2011.

What this implies is that any worthwhile Revolution has to have an inbuilt protection against any demagogic exploitation and that the will of the people needs to be perpetual and perennial, constant and continual; not some blind orgasmic flash that yields to post-coital lethargy.

As Bob Dylan wisely said, 'Don't follow leaders.' Leaders will let you down, the role itself corrupt. He did go on to say in his very next line, 'Watch your parking meters,' which many might think undermines the line that preceded it. I disagree, we could regard it in a few ways: for one, Bob, by saying something nuts and trivial, is demonstrating that we oughtn't start looking to him as a leader or kind of folk prophet. 'I like this Dylan guy, he's able to spell out a rhyming ideology in an appealing nasal twang, tell me more. Watch yer parking meters? No, the man's a twit.'

Or he could be saying that it is these mundane, municipal inconveniences, like parking meters, that truly outrage a modern, urbanised population.

Are you not more incensed by ATM charges than by oil spills and deforestation? When it comes to the crunch, aren't you more wound up by Apple mendaciously changing their chargers every fucking time they bring out a new device than apartheid? I mean, how much money do they want?

Do they have to wring us out like a vagrant vampire with a tampon in his fangs? When will it be enough? Aren't you, deep down, more pissed off about unnecessary and financially motivated parking fines than child sweatshop labour? I am. I know I'm meant to care about children in Palestine, and if you sit me down and explain it to me I get annoyed, I might even squeeze out a furious tear, but when I can't use my phone abroad because of some intricate admin around roaming, I'm ready to pick up a gun.

What's terrifying is that our petty frustrations and these awful global transgressions are intimately connected by the same dominant, profiteering system.

These miserable inconveniences somehow prevail.

That's why the *Daily Mail* and Fox News are so effective, because they reach right through our liberal bullshit and into our dark, animalistic, selfish, well-nourished core. And as Solzhenitsyn and the Native American wolf allegory demonstrate, we all have that capacity for darkness within us. The devil has all the best tunes and Fox News has access to the most responsive buttons.

This is why spirituality is not some florid garnish, some incense fragrance wafted across our senses, but part of the double-helix DNA of Revolution.

There is a need for Revolution on every level – as individuals, as societies, as a planet, as a consciousness. Unless we address the need for absolute change, unless we agree on a shared story of how we want the world to be, we'll inertly drift back to the materialistic, individualistic magnetism behind our current systems.

CHAPTER 25

Give My Regards To The Basket

My conception of Revolution, probably like most people's, comes from old-fashioned ones where the state is overthrown by a vibrant, sexy, chanting horde and then reassembled, like the eighteenth-century French Revolution.

This was pretty hard core as revolutions go, because an all-powerful leader, Louis XVI (I'm pretty sure that means 'sixteenth'), got his head cut off. Once you've called fifteen kings Louis and it's still the only name you can think of, it's quite clear you're an institution that's bereft of ideas and a bit of noggin chopping is required.

I note that if that baby royal they've just done in Blighty were to ascend to the throne he'd be George the seventh. Seventh?! We've already had six and we're gonna have another one. How long do we intend to let this silliness persist? Surely it's time for us to invest in a Fisher Price guillotine.

At the time of the French Revolution the powerful were corrupt and wealthy whilst the poor were becoming more and more disenfranchised, with no legitimate means for creating real change. Well, apparently that's what's happening now, according to Ol' Piketty. Our system, capitalism, is designed to behave like this: it generates wealth for the wealthy and further impoverishes those with nothing. Asking it to behave differently is like asking a microwave to wash your car.

In pre-revolutionary France, if the *Dogtanian* cartoons are to be believed (and if we're going to start questioning their veracity, my entire philosophy will unravel), the clergy, monarchy and aristocracy had become too rich and unaccountable and the French got so wound up that the axes came out.

There had been unpopular wars, bad harvests and a financial crisis, yet the upper tiers of French society were scoffing croissants like there was no tomorrow. It turned out they were right: for most of them, there wasn't – they all had their head lopped off in the Revolution.

After which there was a lot of faffing and enlightenment-inspired political thinking until the post-revolutionary ideas that dominated were nationalism and democracy.

These ideas have evolved to become veils behind which a comparable elite are able to enforce an exploitative system that benefits them to the detriment of everyone else and the planet.

Instead of clergy and aristocracy we have corporations and the financial sector. Instead of bad harvests we have the decline of the manufacturing industry, and instead of a financial crisis we have, well, a financial crisis.

When the French folk chopped off the king's head it sent shockwaves around the world, it was an unprecedented event, a hybrid of the 9/11 attacks and the death of Diana.

If the *Sun* had been in existence then there definitely would've been a commemorative pull-out and Elton John would've sung a sad reworking of 'Candle in the Wind' at the Bastille:

> Goodbye Louis's head
> Even though I am so glad you're dead,
> I hope Marie Antoinette is next,
> For offering cake for bread . . .

You get the idea. Anyway, aside from a lovely, carnivalesque period where Paris became a sort of urban Glastonbury, with folk hanging out and sharing, and some bloody helpful ideas about human rights, recognisable power structures were soon reasserted under transitory leaders like Maximilien Robespierre, who sounds like an untrustworthy, Gallic Transformer, then a few committees, before Napoleon took control of the situation and became emperor – which doesn't sound sufficiently different from 'king' to have warranted all the bother. Except he was really good at wars and did his own butchery. Plus he was well into his missus, and wrote her filthy letters insisting she kept her privates unkempt and unwashed. So there you go.

That may not be the most academically satisfactory rendering of the events around the French Revolution, derived as it was from the adventures of Dogtanian (and the three Muskehounds), one episode of *Blackadder the Third* and several 'hunches', but whatever it was that went down in revolutionary France it has led to what's happening in France now, and France now is once more as in need of a Revolution as anywhere else.

In the 1970s, the Chinese leader Zhou Enlai was asked if he thought the French Revolution was a success. 'It's too early to tell,' he said. Very clever. Well, I don't bloody think it is and neither do the French; they can't go half an hour without a riot, or getting swept up in nationalism or crazy upside down Sieg-Heiling crazes.

Professor John Dunn thinks our yearning for Revolution is a secular version of a messiah fetish; the same as Mary Midgley's assertion that Dickie Dawkins's Selfish Gene theory is a retelling of the Protestant Genesis myth – that the sins of the father will be visited on the progeny and that man is condemned to follow a predestined path outside the uteral comfort of Eden. Or Joseph Campbell's observation that all creation myths have a 'cast out of paradise' component that is resonant for human beings who are 'cast out' of the lovely, cosy womb where all our needs are automatically met and into this mad, chilly world.

All anyone's got is theories, usually distorted by what they've been through or what they want.

This book, for example, was written by someone from a suburban, broken home, raised in Thatcher's Britain, where inclusive ideas and family values were dismantled. A culture in which fame and celebrity became deified and drug use among the young extremely prevalent. Where modern manifestations of tribal identity like trade unions or guilds became redundant, manufacturing industries disappeared, neo-liberalism emerged and the welfare state was all but abolished. You could probably predict the contents of this book by looking at my weekly shopping receipt from Tesco's. Alright, Waitrose.

I'm dying to paint myself as a lowborn, WatTyler, Essex messiah; fortunately, I'm not quite that mad. I know that that heroic myth is part of my programming. That I'm a quite funny, normal bloke, that there's a bit of bad in the best of us and a bit of good in the worst of us, that any centralised power structure with an egocentric figure at its helm will become corrupt. The only solution is to develop a template built on ecological responsibility and equality.

It could be that our longing for Revolution is like our longing for perfect love: the impulse we all have for union that was for so long met by religion. However we assign these yearnings, it is difficult to ignore the obvious need for change. Some of us will ascribe it to romantic love, some to consumerism, some to utopianism. It doesn't really matter. What is important is that for the first time in history we have the means to implement a truly representative system, the means to globally communicate it and the conditions that require it.

Whilst a mystical and faith-based component may be helpful in bringing about significant change in consciousness and the planet, we must remember the objective is simple: to make life on the planet, and for the planet, better.

To be against this Revolution you have to believe the system we have now is the best possible system, and I know there can't be too many people who believe that. There aren't enough places at Eton.

The Revolution that most decent folk are into, including George Orwell, who joined in with it and Noam Chomsky, is the Spanish Revolution of 1936. In this recent uprising there is much that will be of use to us, and although it eventually ended up being crushed by fascists, let's optimistically assume that there is no modern-day equivalent of the Nazis who lent Franco's triumphant army military hardware that ensured his victory.

I was once sneeringly instructed by a privilege-glazed bellend to 'read some Orwell' because I said democracy in its current form was pointless. Well, I have, and it turns out that Orwell agrees with me. In his autobiographical book *Homage to Catalonia*, Orwell describes his experiences in Spain in the midst of their Revolution:

> This was in late December 1936. I had come to Spain with some notion of writing newspaper articles, but I had joined the militia almost immediately, because at that time and in that atmosphere it seemed the only conceivable thing to do.

George's writing holiday went way off track; right from the off, he's been swept up in revolutionary fervour. I like that he says he joined up because it was 'the only conceivable thing to do'. He can't've imagined that when he was doing his packing. I bet he just took some Tippex and colouring pens; within an hour he was tooled-up and killing fascists. He should've written a complaint to his travel agent.

It was the first time that I had ever been in a town where the working class was in the saddle. Practically every building of any size had been seized by the workers and was draped with red flags and with the red and black flag of the Anarchists.

Ah, the sense of carnival and community is intoxicating. Also, it's clear that we've been fed a lot of old codswallop about the Anarchists. Far from being a bunch of glue-sniffing ne'er-do-wells, they're salt-of-the-earth community organisers.

Almost every church had been gutted and its images burnt. Churches here and there were being systematically demolished by gangs of workmen.

Well, I can't say I approve of all this sacrilegious church smashing, but I suppose the Spanish had endured considerable hardship at the hands of that institution, the Inquisition and whatnot, and were clearly keen to see the back of it. I don't know why they had to demolish them, though; they could've made them into multi-faith meditation centres – like you get in airports.

Every shop and cafe had an inscription saying that it had been collectivized; even the bootblacks had been collectivized and their boxes painted red and black.

This collectivisation is the most exciting and replicable aspect of the Spanish Revolution, if you ask me, and dear George (whose work I am currently desecrating like an anarchist chiselling away at La Sagrada Familia) the revolutionaries of Barcelona had removed the invisible structures behind industry and placed control in the hands of the people doing the work. There's no reason why, say, Pret A Manger couldn't be owned and run by the people that work there. The people that do the deliveries could own and run that operation. There may be some fundamental change to the menu due to the shipping of ingredients – you might not have all-year-round strawberries for your yoghurt and granola, but fuck it, man, I'll live with that for freedom. The idea that you can't have services or choice without international corporations crouched in the shadowy abstract is bollocks, and as those seventies incarnations of anarchy the Sex Pistols said, never mind that.

You can still have Pret A Manger without Ronald McDonald, their silent partner, craftily collecting the profit.

Waiters and shop-walkers looked you in the face and treated you as an equal.

Lest we forget that the return of dignity to ordinary working people is the driving force behind our demand for change. Who is offering this? Hillary Clinton? Ed Miliband? That poor doomed sod in France, Hollande? None of them are, because none of them can. True freedom cannot be offered from above, it must be taken from below.

Servile and even ceremonial forms of speech had temporarily disappeared. Nobody said 'Señor' or 'Don' or even 'Usted'; everyone called everyone else 'Comrade' or 'Thou'.

Fuck me, Matt Stoller, you old bastard – with his policy of abolishing titles he is spoiling us. In egalitarian cultures people naturally dispense with the social accoutrements of power, calling people 'Mister' or 'Doctor', being punched with a giggle-some flush on hearing your teacher's first name. These niceties have no place in the real world.

Tipping had been forbidden by law since the time of Primo de Rivera; almost my first experience was receiving a lecture from a hotel manager for trying to tip a lift-boy.

Who won't be glad to see the back of that? I never know how much to give. I'm famous, so I go high. Sometimes, though, people are offended; far better to acknowledge tipping as a patronising and derisory form of payment, unnecessary in a society where people are already treated fairly.

There were no private motor-cars, they had all been commandeered, and the trams and taxis and much of the other transport were painted red and black.

This is where it gets tough for our consumer generation. I know a lot of blokes who won't fancy giving up their motor. Plus the colour scheme seems needlessly upsetting. I'd suggest involving Banksy or Shepard Fairey when it comes to the design element. Plus, if you have self-governing, decentralised syndicates then you can just join one that still endorses car ownership, if you're not ready to let go yet. That's the beauty of governing yourself: no one can tell you what your society should look like.

Me, I don't have a car so I'm mellow. Suffice to say, I won't be joining a syndicate that collectivises Dior boots.

Down the Ramblas, the wide central artery of the town where crowds of people streamed constantly to and fro, the loudspeakers were bellowing revolutionary songs all day and far into the night.

Sounds alright for the young folk, as long as there's somewhere quiet for the likes of me, teetotallers that like to meditate. Shame they demolished all the churches. Bloody anarchists.

This depiction of Las Ramblas being communally owned and communally used, not a de facto billboard for big business or tourist titbits, is a tearjerker. When I was last there I bought a goldfish in a tiny bowl with a lid on it, then smuggled it home in my jacket. In addition to some heroin up my bottom, all in all, a city break gone awry.

> In outward appearance it was a town in which the wealthy classes had practically ceased to exist. Except for a small number of women and foreigners there were no 'well-dressed' people at all. Practically everyone wore rough working-class clothes, or blue overalls or some variant of militia uniform. All this was queer and moving.

After my time in the marines, which was incidentally about twenty hours, not, as I continually suggest, a three-year tour, I learned that much of my identity is wrapped up in my clobber and haircut. Orwell's description then of an anarcho-syndicalist utopia in which everyone is dressed like the Tetley Tea Bag Men is terrifying for me. How important are these trinkets and delightful accessories that I prize if their true price is freedom? Where did this affection for waxed jeans with unnecessary zips in them come from? 'There's someone in my head but it's not me', said Pink Floyd. Is that possible? Is it true? Do I want things and pursue things because of conditioning? A kind of psychological implant? Almost certainly. Can I be free of this programming? Of course I can. Anyway, I'm sure for those of us of such a persuasion, locally made, ethically sourced, sexy-as-hell attire can be provided if need be in a post-revolutionary world.

> There was much in this that I did not understand, in some ways I did not even like it, but I recognized it immediately as a state of affairs worth fighting for . . .

269

It seems that even Orwell was put off by the outfits. He was very much a cords-and-tweed-jacket-type fella, but he's prepared to put aside sartorial preference for a society that's closer to our essential nature. This somewhat scruffy Spanish idyll appears to be that, an expression of higher human values. Capitalism is not the manifestation of our nature. 'Capitalism is the extraordinary belief that the nastiest of men for the nastiest of motives will somehow work for the benefit of all,' said economist John Maynard Keynes; we are now witnessing its implosion. What we have to decide is what will follow it, something just, or something more draconian than we have ever dared to consider.

> So far as one could judge the people were contented and hopeful. There was no unemployment, and the price of living was still extremely low; you saw very few conspicuously destitute people, and no beggars except the gypsies.

Even in a society built on cooperation and mutual aid, the gypsies opted out. You've got to hand it to 'em, they're sticking to their creed.

> Above all, there was a belief in the revolution and the future, a feeling of having suddenly emerged into an era of equality and freedom.

This is what we're after. This is worth giving up the rooting tooting boots for: belief, togetherness, equality. This is why people get obsessed with festivals, or clubs, or drugs, or football, or other temporal approximations of togetherness; these distilled vials of the elixir are craved by our starved souls. I'm as materialistic as the next man, probably more, given that the next man is George Orwell, and I am prepared to relinquish my trinkets for a shot at living in that ramshackle paradise.

Human beings were trying to behave as human beings and not
as cogs in the capitalist machine.

Orwell wrote this in the mid-thirties. Consider how radically
capitalism has advanced since then. In his great dystopian fiction
1984, Orwell described a totalitarian regime where humans were
constantly observed, scrutinised and manipulated, where freedom
had been entirely eroded, omnipotent institutions dominated
and every home glowed with the mandatory TV screen streaming
state-sponsored data. Well, he was spot on, aside from a bit of
glitter and the fact that we voluntarily install our own screens.

Orwell saw this brief period in Spanish history as a potential
template for an alternative future. Ordinary workers took over
their businesses and factories, and ran them democratically.
Naturally, they were brutally massacred by a multitude of
enemies – the fascists, communists and liberal democracies all
coiled about them in a terrified asphyxiating clench.

I'd never heard of this Revolution; the reason for this is of
course because it's so fucking inspiring. The revolutions that
we're taught about are ones that wind neatly back to repression
of one flavour or another and convey the bleak despairing
narrative that makes the forms of impoverishment we live with
now, whether financial or spiritual, seem preferable. No one,
absolutely no one, will tell you that an alternative is possible
and the ways and means are strewn all about us.

A lot of other political struggles and social uprisings labelled
'revolutions' are in my mind unworthy of the term, in that they
were simply a hegemonic exchange. Whether it's the Russian
Revolution, which led to Stalinism, or the American Revolution,
that led to corporate oligarchy. The Revolution we advocate
ought to have two irrefutable components: 1) non-violence,
and 2) the radical improvement of the quality of life for ordinary
people.

I still get choked when I reflect on the American Revolution: the violence, the humiliation, the wasted tea.

The US was a British colony, and a damn fine one. For some reason around 1775 the Americans, or Brits abroad as they rightly were, as America hadn't been invented yet, decided that paying tax to the British for no discernible reason was no longer appropriate. It is interesting to me that what irked them ultimately was the geographical abstraction. 'We're not paying tax to that unresponsive entity that doesn't represent our interests, especially as they are distinguished from us by the Atlantic.'

The Atlantic allowed the emerging nation to see themselves as separate. The same problem of course exists today: unless you are the CEO of a major corporation, you too in 2014/15 are paying taxes to a government that doesn't represent you, they represent the interests of big business. The only difference is there isn't a convenient and obvious distinction as demonstrated by the ocean. There is, however, an ocean of inequality that separates us, an Atlantic of indifference.

The geographic dislocation also enabled the – okay, I'll call 'em it – Americans the advantage of being able to see that they could run things without their 'leaders'. They already were: their leaders were thousands of miles away, wigging it up in Westminster. The same is true now: we are already running our own lives; the infra-structural duties carried out by big companies that run our energy networks or whatever are not in their hands because they possess some secret wisdom, it's because they can make a profit from it.

Why are we giving all this money and power to Tesco's? Or Walmart or Corte Inglés? They are no different from the colonial masters of a bygone age, unresponsive and exploitative overlords. Where is the sacred text that says they are allowed to glean such profits from our land and farm our labour and our minds so that Tesco can take one pound in seven and the Walmart kids can have as much wealth as half of America? Show me where that's written down and I will tear it up. It's not serving us, it's not serving the planet, it's not even serving them, it's time to wake up and take back authority.

Their commercials, their logos, their slogans all mimic familiarity, imitate the human emotions and connections that they have hijacked and drained. 'Every Little Helps'? We're taking the fucking lot.

They spend millions designing typefaces, symbols and campaigns that eerily ape the local, informal economies that they bludgeoned into mush to achieve their towering monopolies.

These corporations do not believe in nation. They register for tax wherever it's expedient, then drape themselves in patriotic slut garb during the World Cup. They are laughing at us, our traditions, our beliefs, our vulnerable human love. We are like a swarm of battered spouses unable to believe that a better world is out there because we're cowering and flinching and reaching out for stinking trinkets. We can still have things. We can still have Xboxes, waxed jeans, football teams, magazines and beauty queens if we want them, but we might find that we don't want them as much when we're free.

After the British people that were in America beat the British people that worked for the king at fighting, many assumed that George Washington would appoint himself the new king, but he argued instead to have a constitutional republic. Which seems damn decent of him until you realise that all that really happened is one elite replaced another.

John Jay, who was the leader of the new constitutional convention, said, 'The people who own the country should run the country.' Another squandered opportunity then. Let's make a promise to each other that if we ever find ourselves in a position where we throw off the shackles of oppression, we'll leave them off and stay in charge of ourselves. Not just pick some new shackles with Nike on them and get on with our subjugation.

This requires diligence. As David Graeber said, any authoritative measures supposedly for our benefit must be resisted. We must insist on total self-governance.

The American constitution was designed to keep rich men in charge; the only significant change was the accent and crowns. They swapped a lion for an eagle and crowns for hair cream. The same people that were shafted then are shafted now. Any country that puts the word 'United' in its title has got something to hide, and I would suggest that its conflict. In the United Kingdom, the Scottish want out, the Welsh want out, even the English want nothing to do with it. The United States is anything but. Descendants of slaves, Europeans of every description, Latino folk, forever condemned for crossing a line that didn't used to be there. The nation state is a relatively modern idea and I don't think we're getting a lot out of it except for flags and World Cups.

It's odd that those in power condemn people who want change for being whimsical and impractical but actually what is being demanded is pragmatism, systems that function. People get the resources they need, the resources are managed efficiently, and the conditions required to create resources are respected. None of that happens. It can't because they've prioritised a bizarre, selfish and destructive idea over common sense.

We've already, thanks to Helena Norberg-Hodge, had a cursory glance at the gluttonous absurdity of global trade agreements and the profligacy and inefficiency of industrialised agriculture, neither of which have any place in a world built on common sense. They are only advantageous to the elite organisations that implemented them. Anyone who tells you different is on the make. In fact we are at the point where the catastrophic failings of the system are so gallingly obvious that anyone who supports it, or denies change is needed, is verbally daubing themselves with the black cross of the damned. As soon as someone pipes up with 'There ain't no climate change' or 'Compassionate capitalism could work' we should just nod, smile and lead them to the sanitarium to begin their re-education.

Redemption is possible and compassion a prerequisite. If we don't allow people to change, then how can we change the world?

My dad, Ron Brand, was an entrepreneurial Essex man. Del Boy'd up to the hilt on Thatcher's creed, he was a self-made and self-destructive man and intermittently tumbled either side of the line. The prevailing mentality of the time, the eighties, was 'every man for himself'. Unions were crushed, state interests were carved up and flogged and council houses were sold back to the people whose efforts had built them. One of the great venture capitalist heroes of this time who epitomised this bucca-neering spirit was Sir James Goldsmith, Tory hero, Thatcher crush, scourge of *Private Eye* and demon of the left. My dad and a lot of people from modest backgrounds admired him: there was something appealingly anti-establishment and daring in the aggressive and ingenious ways that James Goldsmith exploited the system. Now I am tribally obligated to loathe James Goldsmith, with his individualistic, asset-stripping, Thatcher-loving ways; however, recent events demanded I revise this disdain, and as usual, the truth was a little more complicated.

CHAPTER 26

Conversion?

If my jaunt to Hollywood and pop-star nuptials represented the penetration of one establishment, the show-business machine, then unavoidably I must address the alliance I have since been in. I have occasionally been in the company of people at the upper echelons of the British establishment. I met a Rothschild the other day, a Rothschild! I still go on websites that say they might be lizard illuminati. One website accused me of being illuminati – me, ol' Russ! I was so flabbergasted, I squashed one of the eggs I was incubating.

Let me tell you now if there is an illuminati (and I hope there is, it gives us a clear target), and they ask me to join, I will sprint out of that Masonic temple and announce it on the Internet. I can't imagine the Rothschild lady I met was in it either; she seemed kind of sweet and erratic. That's not to say other members of the family aren't attending Bilderberg meetings and giggling at the back of the fun bus. My mate Gee says you can't make love from hate. There is enough antipathy, judgment and bile, pop Fox News on, they're giving it away. Perhaps even the Bilderbergers, illuminati and lizards can be guided back to humanity. My attitude to the establishment is comparable to my feelings towards the police. Of course I feel a visceral clench of antipathy when I encounter them but if our objective is harmony we must ensure its presence in the one place we can control, ourselves.

Usually when I've met the people who are meant to be in a position of power I've always made sure to give them a damn good soul-stare, y'know, look right in their eyes, through the blackness of the pupils and into whatever conscious field exists within. Then lock the eyes on, but let them gently defocus so that the defined parameters of the visual physical goes blurry and you can feel the energy behind it, the unseeable energy that isn't made of photons. Then, if your mind is quiet, you will be informed of the quality of their essence, or at least of the manifest persona that they believe themselves to be.

Gordon Brown: kind, bewildered. Prince Charles: lost jocundity. George Osborne: naive heat. Ed Miliband: earnest angst.

I'm beginning to recognise a pattern here: in each case they seemed edgy and they were all meeting me. If an observed electron alters its behaviour when it interacts with the consciousness of the observer, how the fuck are we meant to get an honest reaction out of George Osborne? Impossible. Especially if you're bogging at him like Derren Brown; that'd make anyone clammy.

My point is, of course, they are human beings who were born and will die. All on a journey to oneness with the source, dealing with varying degrees of distraction.

If, in my heart of hearts, I know the only productive attitude to have towards a paedophile is one of loving, inclusive, rehabilitative tolerance, how can I not afford the same stance to George Osborne? Well, he has fucked over more kids than the average nonce.

At some posh do that I recently attended – all the way there justifying it to myself, trying to find a way to say it wasn't hypocritical – I discovered on arrival that Prince Andrew was in the house. What am I meant to do? Smack him in the mouth? Knock over a teapot and tell him he's at the heart of an institution that's responsible for the death and suffering of millions of normal people? Wipe my bum on a tenner, say 'That's what I think of your old tit' and throw it at him? What would my ex've said? Thank God, the answer lies in spirituality: an attitude of loving tolerance on our mutual journey to manifesting divine will.

I mean if Gandhi can write a letter to Hitler, lovingly requesting that he step back from genocide (that went well!), then surely I can have a polite crumpet with Airforce Andy without wanking in the sugar bowl.

Here's what I can tell you from the Establishment's dark heart: they're lost too, they're as lost as me and you. Looking for love and redemption, waddling toddlers in their mum's high-heeled shoes, trying to look like they know what to do. A lady went to the loo and left me and Andrew, one on one, and we were both stumped; neither of us knew what to do.

Just scratch the record off, we're naked under our clothes, we both know what it's like to need to fart and hold it in, or not be able to get a hard-on, or worry that a bloke across the room might be looking at your bird and you might have to fight him but he looks well hard. Well, he might not get the last one – he can call MI5 and get the bloke killed.

Who does a baby think it is before it can recognise its face in a mirror, before it's taught its name, before it's drummed into stagnant separation, cordoned off from the infinite oneness?

Love is innate. We must be taught to hate, and now we must unlearn it; as the Buddhists say, let it burn, that which needs to burn, let it burn.

The class system isn't fair on them either, poor little sods, packed off to school, weaned on privatised maternity shopped in from a northern spinster. Trying to find love in the tangle of dismantled family. No one can be happy imbibing a poisoned brew. It's poisonous for us all. They'll gratefully sigh when we unlock them from their opulent penitentiaries, they'll be grateful when their fallow lands and empty chambers feed the hungry and house the poor. They know contentment cannot be enjoyed when stolen. They need the Revolution as much as we do.

The whole of human history is nothing new, the whole of your personal story is nothing true, you can do with it whatever you want to do, flick a switch, scratch the record off, look behind the veil. Anything you don't want discard, anything that hurts let go. None of it's real you know, all that pain, all that regret, all that doubt, not thin enough, not a good enough mum, not a good enough son, not a good enough bum. You are enough, you're enough, there's nothing you can buy or try on that's going to make you any better, because you couldn't be any better than you are.

Drag your past around if you like, an old dead decaying ox of what you think they might've thought, or what might've been if you'd done what you ought. That which needs to burn let it burn. If the idea doesn't serve you, let it go. If it separates you from the moment, from others, from yourself, let it go.

James Goldsmith, who spent his life as a kind of ultra capitalist, destroying manufacturing industries and working class unity, in his twilight years, in a Damascene flash, realised that it was a broken system dragging the planet towards destruction. In his book *The Trap* he explains with perspicacity gained from a lifetime's front-line experience how global free trade and transnational corporations would inevitably bring about a kind of economic and ecological Armageddon.

All the more pertinent because we're hardly talking about Karl Marx here; he played the game of capitalism like a mercantile Pelé, but in *The Trap* he disavows free-market economics as a suicidal system. He also explains that GNP, Gross National Product, which is the economic thermometer by which the health of a nation is assessed, is a profoundly flawed, in fact bloody stupid, instrument. GNP commends nations that have had disasters, like a hurricane or whatever, because that requires them to spend money on aid and reparation, which in GNP lingo is good.

It commends nations where crime and cancer are rife, because dealing with those problems requires industry and expenditure. He explains that the qualities GNP is measuring and evaluating as successful are not only divorced from but often detrimental to the happiness of the population.

In other words, the lenses of the glasses through which success is viewed are dirty. GNP is still the measure that we use. Goldsmith explains that the king of Bhutan eschews this system, favouring instead a measure that takes into account – get this – the happiness of the people who live in the country.

Goldsmith then dissects free trade, observing that a system that enables transnational corporations to flit around the world, exploiting labour, benefits only the corporations themselves and not the consumers, the purported beneficiaries. 'When Nike moved from the US to Asia shoe prices did not drop, instead profit margins rose. The real cost to consumers is that they will lose their jobs, get paid less and have higher taxes to cover the social cost of increased unemployment.'

Or as Flight of the Conchords put it, 'We're turning kids into slaves just to make cheaper sneakers, but what's the real cost cos the sneakers don't seem that much cheaper. Why are we still paying so much for sneakers when they're made by little slave-kids; what are your overheads?'*

---

* Nike have doubtless stopped using kids now, after all the publicity they got a while back and the 'chords wicked song, so let's rush out and buy some Nikes.**
** Legally, I am obliged to say 'Nike have never used slave kids'. If you want that legally required sentence to remain unchallenged in your mind, never google 'Nike slave kids' or you'll struggle.

This is globalisation described by a man who knew the system inside out, explained from an informed and honest perspective.

We are given biased, censored information, and even when the consequences of their mad, greedy dabblings become apparent they deny it.

Goldsmith describes the institutions that benefit from this doomed ideology as 'winners of a poker game on the *Titanic*', explaining that this mentality unimpeded will deeply wound our societies and lead to brutal consequences.

He expresses fears around the mass industrialisation of agriculture, which aligns with what Helena Norberg-Hodge told us earlier, that we need to return to localised, organic farming. Everyone is saying the same thing, in fact: return to a more harmonious way of living. Since industrialisation we have moved rapidly out of synchronicity with nature and our own nature. We were told this would be a better way of life, and it is. It's a better way of life for people that subscribe to the ideology that capitalist apostate James Goldsmith here attacks.

Mass production, synthesisation, global trade arrangements are all brilliant ideas for concentrating power in the hands of a few. Well done, it worked, you fooled us. Now can we have our ball back, please? Capitalism has brought us many useful tools and systems: the laptop I type this on, the money I bought it with, the fame that means you've heard of me and are reading this. We are nothing if not adaptive, and if these systems and tools have now fulfilled their function, or have become a hindrance, we owe them no loyalty, we must move on; it's not an unconditional commitment, we're not talking devotion to West Ham United here, a dumb affiliation that we're just stuck with.

By the end of the book Goldsmith, who I'd always regarded as a fundamentalist free-marketeer, is mellifluously espousing on paganism and environmentalism, quoting Buddhist tracts and Black Elk, the Native American chief who wrote a now famous letter to President Franklin Pierce in 1854. This letter is a belated and, it turned out, utterly ignored appeal for 'the white man' to recognise his role as 'a strand in the web of life' to overcome our need to dominate and exploit the land and see all the earth's resources merely as commodities for the advancement of the few.

This ideology is so antithetical to the business pursuits of Goldsmith or any powerful capitalist that his inclusion of the letter as the denouement to his book amounts to a deathbed conversion to the Revolution.

It is a shame that the means for achieving status and honour are so irrevocably entrenched within toxic structures, that it is hard to find expression for that kind of dynamism in this mercantile culture.

I wonder if Donald Trump has any tingling epiphanies that he cudgels back to slumber as he goose-steps towards the grave.

I met Trump once and was surprised mostly by his daftness. He was peculiarly juvenile; I thought at the time that he was like a dimwit with a prodigious skill that happens to be highly valued: making money. He had no curiosity about consciousness, spirituality, interconnectivity, the micro or the macro or anything except in how it might relate to making money; it was odd. That someone whose mind rattles around within such limited borders had made such a lot of money. It's almost like being an athlete, ordinary but for one lucrative skill, irrelevant in a parallel world.

Like a world built around excellence at a niche bagatelle, or a dumb parlour trick, or board game; the masters of the universe are just experts at Hungry Hippo.

Instead of vying to be heavyweight champion of a cannibalistic and stupid game, we must attune now to a clearer, shared objective. Like Daniel Pinchbeck earlier outlined, or as

Buckminster Fuller succinctly described, 'To make the world work for 100% of humanity in the shortest possible time through spontaneous cooperation, without ecological offense or the disadvantage of anyone.'

CHAPTER 27

Es Mejor Morir de Pie . . .

The American Revolution laid the way for a new kind of imperialism, a new kind of colonisation. An expansionist, militant ideology that is only now expiring, we have to decide if what replaces it will be better or worse.

Noam Chomsky, Adam Curtis and *The Godfather* films have all been trying to tell us, sometimes subtly through story, sometimes wittily through archive and arch voiceover, and sometimes through being Noam Chomsky, that 'America' is not a land mass, a country, some stars 'n' stripes and a song. It is a violent mad gang enforcing the interests of its corporate clients on to a terrified globe. Look at the heroes of its folk tales: the cowboy, a lone, justice-dispensing maverick; the gangster, a surly outlaw playing by his own rules; or the gangsta, a bejewelled misogynist making money by moving ice.

All the good things about America either came from the counter-culture or were there already when the white people arrived.

What they've really mastered, like all good racketeers, is the business of scaring the shit out of people and then telling 'em that they'll take care of them. They've also co-opted a bit too much ideology and technology from the Nazis for my liking.

Sure, get their scientists to build you rockets, if the moon means that much to you, but check this bit of social technology from everyone's favourite founder of the Gestapo, Hermann Göring, 'The people can always be brought to the bidding of the leaders. That is easy. All you have to do is tell them they are being attacked and denounce the pacifists for lack of patriotism and exposing the country to danger. It works the same way in any country.'

The Americans and their allies, which means the British of course, have been using this Nazi skullduggery on us for ages. I grew up worried sick about nuclear attack, forever peering out the window when a plane went over. It turns out the threat of nuclear attack comes primarily from the people that got me worrying about it in the first place; it's the apocalyptic version of 'who smelt it dealt it'.

Chomsky, who must have one of the most satisfying names to say in the world, which is apposite for a linguist, explains how this technique has been used to validate US terror, domestically and abroad, since 1823. This is when the Monroe Doctrine was established. Because you are childish, you think the Monroe Doctrine is a pledge to act all sexy and emphysemic, lifting up yer frock, going, 'Poo-poo-pee-doo.' It ain't. It was a diplomatic commitment from a century and a half ago when the Americans decided that they intended to 'dominate the hemisphere', which is an outlandish objective. It sounds like the sort of devilish intention that kept the British paedo establishment occupied: 'I'd like to dominate your hemisphere,' they hollered into hospital wards and children's homes.

The US have achieved this domination primarily by scaring us all witless and starting wars either explicitly or by proxy, primarily in countries where they were really confident they would win.

I'm not saying I'm as clever as Chomsky – that would be mad, obnoxious, off-putting and untrue – but, as is always the case with a prefix of this nature, here is something that makes it seem like what I'm trying to suggest is exactly that. When I was quite young I realised that the primary motivation for secrecy within powerful structures was not the protection of the people they had power over but the preservation of their own power. I think I've even mentioned as much in a previous book (y wook): those 'Top Secret' files at the CIA or MI5 are not full of devious ways to trump the Russians and the Chinese, they're full of information that is so incendiary that if we read it we'd be so aghast that we'd go, 'Fuck this lot, let's have a Revolution.'

In this essay on US foreign policy Chomsky says the same thing. So if anything Chomsky is nicking my ideas, likely from my defining work on the subject of propaganda, 'The Manufacture of Consenty-Went'. In his essay Chomsky explains that for years the US used the threat of Russian attack as a palliative to hustle through any ideas that impaired the freedom of the domestic population, contravened international law or increased the power and wealth of their corporate clientele. Chomsky observes that if the real motivation behind this conduct was the Soviet threat, then it would have ceased when the Soviet threat did in 1989, when the Berlin Wall came down. It didn't. In fact their behaviour became far more militant, particularly in Latin America and the Middle East.

The fall of the Berlin Wall is perhaps the most significant political event in my lifetime, but even though I was fourteen at the time I remember not especially caring about it, other than when Knight Rider turned up and sang a song on the rubble. Surely an indication of a nation with a bewildered and damaged sense of self is that the first thing they think of when years of enforced segregation end is to enlist David Hasselhoff.

Perhaps I've missed something, he might be a vocalist healer – we should've got him along for 9/11 or Lockerbie.

After the fall of the wall and lots of images of communists

queuing up for McDonald's, America was able to more freely pursue its agenda to 'corporatise' the world by force. They waded into Panama, killed thousands of people and installed a 'client regime'. The media, which shares the same ideology as the US government, always supports them. This could be, as Julian Assange says, the cooperation of separate entities with a shared agenda, or a more Bilderberg, illuminati, shadowy, evil, clandestine thing – I don't know, it actually doesn't matter, the results are the same: government, transnational corporations and the media cooperate to advance and maintain an agenda that is detrimental to the majority of us and the planet.

With the excuse of Soviet threat gone, the US (and I am at pains to point out, I mean not the American people, who are lovely, kind passionate folk; the same as when I talk of the UK's sycophantic, clammy-palmed support, like a rapist's impotent sidekick, holding his glove, I don't mean us, the people, I mean the Establishment) had to dream up new reasons to act in the same way. Like when your girlfriend wants to have a row because she's got PMT but instead of saying that creates some bizarre reason to thump you, like, I dunno, nose-picking.

The US said there was an 'increased threat from Third World nations who were developing technology' that could disrupt US domestic serenity – really they mean economic hegemony.

The US acts like an army that enforces the business interests of the corporations it is allied to. I didn't know before I read this Chomsky piece that the American government subsidises the development of weapons. They literally give massive companies grants to make missiles and whatnot, as well as creating ridiculously favourable tax conditions for them to prosper in. That's state-funded industry; America does believe in communism, but just communism for the rich.

In spite of creating this corporate kindergarten environment for their pals, if anyone else tries doing it, especially Arabs or

Latinos, America will fuck them up. In El Salvador, along with Israel and Egypt one of the countries that gets a lot of US military aid and, in a common corollary, has one of the worst human rights records, the US trained a military unit at their facilities to wipe out half a dozen Latin American intellectuals, mostly Jesuit priests who were opposing the El Salvadorian government.

When Mikhail Gorbachev, who it turns out was a lovely fella who bent over backwards to prevent nuclear war and deserved to be remembered for more than that birthmark on his head, allowed a unified Germany to enter NATO, a hostile military alliance, on the condition that 'NATO would not expand one inch to the east', the US agreed. Then they expanded right into East Germany, likely giggling as they went. This dunder-headed truculence persisted under every US regime change. Just to reiterate the irrelevance of bi-party democracy: we all get excited by the Blairs, Obamas and Clintons with their well-rehearsed gestures and photo-op affability, but when push comes to shove we're dealing with cunts. Clinton in his tenure expanded NATO right up to Russia's borders. Chomsky says all this aggro we're having today in the Crimea and Ukraine is because of these unreported acts of military expansionism by the West.

The US government acts to prevent any ideology that opposes corporate dominance emerging. That is why they are constantly meddling with the internal affairs of their neighbours to the south. Latin American people, like the indigenous people whose land they nicked and the Spanish people who nicked it, have some inherent and potent inward drift towards socialism. Socialism isn't a dirty word, it just means sharing; really it's just the bureaucratic arm of Christianity.

Chomsky explains that any country that nurtures a national identity that conflicts with US interest is regarded as hostile and if possible overthrown. The people of Iran have been under constant attack since their regime change in the early fifties and in Guatemala anyone who opposes the interests of the United Fruit Company is likely to be jailed or killed. The United Fruit Company sound so friendly as well, like a posse of bananas and lemons all just trying to get along.

In the fifties President Eisenhower and Secretary of State John Foster Dulles came perilously close to understanding the allure of socialism when they observed communists had an unfair advantage as their ethos – sharing, equality, community, economic parity and stability achieved through redistributing the resources of elites – would always be more appealing to poor people than an ideology that exploits poor people and makes the rich unassailable.

I like that they felt it an unfair advantage, like the disgruntlement felt by Philip Morris that their profits were declining because their customers were dying.

The reason Cuba are the object of such unrelenting antagonism from the US is that their very existence is a rallying cry to other nations that corporatism can be beaten. Ever since the Monroe Doctrine the US had intended to colonise Cuba; in 1898 they invaded it under the now familiar guise of liberating it. Until the Revolution in 1959 the US ran it as a virtual colony, – mostly, as far as I can work out, with casinos and Bacardi rum. Fidel Castro, a law student in the early fifties, started kicking off, along with his brother Raul, after initially petitioning for change through diplomatic channels, decided to form a militia from Havana's disillusioned working class. Their first round of attacks on military targets were a shoddy affair and ended with Raul and Fidel banged up for fifteen years apiece and their small band of followers either nutted off or incarcerated.

Fidel whilst being sentenced delivered a four-hour speech in which he came across as double cool, telling the judge he'd do his time standing on his head and '*la historia me absolverá*' – that when people look back at this they'll think I'm great.

After a few years of jailtime, campaigners managed to get the brothers released, they scarpered to Mexico to cook up a new scheme. Whilst there they met Che Guevara, an Argentinian aristocrat who was seriously up for a row. Guevera said he'd join the pair in overthrowing the corrupt Batista regime. I've agreed to some crazy things with people I've met on holiday myself, but I've never gone as far as saying I'd help a couple of lads take their country back, so respect to Che for that.

Also present in Mexico was Alberto Bayo, who had fought on the side of the socialists during the civil war that followed the Spanish Revolution. He gave the lads guerrilla training to toughen them up. They took to it like ducks to water and within a few months with a crew of eighty other like-minded revolutionaries they set off back to Cuba on a yacht called *Granma*, a vessel seemingly designed to undermine the whole enterprise. A yacht – posh – called *Granma*: bit lame.

The nautical aspect of the Revolution was a right nalls-up: when they practised sailing they'd done it with only a few people on board, so when they set off the boat was much slower. Also some dope fell in the drink and that put the mockers on things. Castro insisted the boat stop and rescue the chump, which really slowed things down but also created a real sense of morale and cohesion. I suppose if Fidel had just looked over at the spluttering prat, tugged on his cigar and gone, 'Fuck him,' the others might've felt that their leader lacked compassion.

Due to all the maritime calamities they arrived in Cuba two days late, meaning their allies in the harbour weren't there. Instead Batista's troops were and knocked off 60 per cent of the rebels, including, I bet, that nitwit who fell in. The surviving revolutionaries fled into the Sierra Maestra mountains and hung out there for ages: it was a total shambles. They recruited peasants that they met in the mountains that were sympathetic to the cause and trained them in warfare. Obviously they did a good job because they won a few battles where the odds were heavily stacked against them, Sparta-style, like the film *300*.

Che Guevara identified how a comparatively small resistance can overcome a national military:

> The enemy soldier in the Cuban example, which at present concerns us, is the junior partner of the dictator; he is the man who gets the last crumb left by a long line of profiteers that begins in Wall Street and ends with him. He is disposed to defend his privileges, but he is disposed to defend them only to the degree that they are important to him. His salary and his pension are worth some suffering and some dangers, but they are never worth his life. If the price of maintaining them will cost it, he is better off giving them up; that is to say, withdrawing from the face of the guerrilla danger.

Amazing to hear that the domination of sovereign governments by Wall Street was already an established pattern; also encouraging is Che's verdict that people won't fight to the death to protect a wage and a pension. Eventually, the unavoidable conclusion that Revolution will benefit the people hired to prop the state up cannot be ignored.

CHAPTER 28

Stick Your Blue Flag

Soldiers are given a terrible time in the UK and US: I am always surprised by how many homeless people have been in the services in both countries. There are almost 60,000 homeless veterans in the US, 12 per cent of all homeless people. In the UK it could be as high as 25 per cent. I chat to homeless people a lot. Partly because it makes me look nice, but also out of a genuine concern for people that are, as I've already indicated, living in conditions that for most of us would be regarded as apocalyptic, the end of the world.

The people that are in poverty, pain, prison, those that are suffering, I feel like they carry the burden for us all, like troops on a foreign front to ensure our freedom.

Homelessness is a bit of a scourge on our society, a shrill whistle from the canary in the cage of our collective conscience that all is not well. Recent studies have shown that it's not cost-effective for a society to have human beings scattered around like living litter and the economic argument is surely the only one that people are averring. 'It would cost too much to house them,' people might say. Well, that's not true: according to separate research in Florida, North Carolina and Utah, hardly enclaves of pie-eyed hippiedom, it's proven to be three times as expensive to leave people lying around like half-finished suicides than to stick them in a flat.

We know it's wrong, we all feel a bit of a cramp of entanglement when we walk past a rough sleeper, especially when alone, like it's an ex-lover or something. Is there anyone who strides mightily by, untroubled with a smile? I bet even Trump or Murdoch or Boris feel something.

Louis CK does a brilliant bit of stand-up in which a friend's cousin who has never been to a city first encounters a homeless person. Louis describes how the man is 'particularly homeless' and that he and his New Yorker friend habitually ignore the man but the out-of-towner is overwhelmed with compassion and attempts to help: 'Sir, are you okay?' Louis and his cousin correct her behaviour, like hers is wrong. The woman asks the man, 'What happened?' 'America happened,' is Louis's proxy response.

This is a beautifully executed demonstration of how an extraordinary attitude has been incrementally inculcated. It is also useful to see how astonishing transgressions are normalised, as it helps us to see more obvious violations in a different light.

The Oscar-nominated documentary *The Act of Killing* tells the story of the gangster leaders who carried out anti-communist purges in Indonesia in 1965 to usher in the regime of Suharto.

The film's hook, which makes it compelling and accessible, is that the film-makers get Anwar, one of the death-squad leaders who murdered around a thousand communists using a wire rope, and his acolytes to re-enact the killings and events around them on film in a variety of genres of their choosing.

In the film's most memorable sequence Anwar, who is old now and actually really likeable, a bit like Nelson Mandela, all soft and wrinkly with nice fuzzy grey hair, for the purposes of a scene plays the role of a victim in one of the murders that he, in real life carried out.

A little way into it he gets a bit tearful and distressed, and when discussing it with the film-maker on camera in the next scene reveals that he found the scene upsetting. The off-camera director asks the poignant question 'What do you think your victims must've felt like?' and Anwar initially almost fails to see the connection. Eventually when the bloody obvious correlation hits him, he thinks it unlikely that his victims were as upset as he was because he was 'really' upset. The director, pressing the film's point home, says 'Yeah, but it must've been worse for them because we were just pretending, for them it was real.'

Evidently at this point the reality of the cruelty he has inflicted hits Anwar, because when they return to the concrete garden where the executions had taken place years before he, on camera, begins to violently gag.

This makes incredible viewing, as this literally visceral ejection of his self and sickness at his previous actions is a vivid catharsis. He gagged at what he'd done.

After watching the film I thought, as probably everyone who saw it did, how can people carry out violent murders by the thousand without it ever occurring to them that it is causing suffering? Surely someone with piano wire round their neck, being asphyxiated, must give off some recognisable signs? Like going 'ouch' or 'stop' or having blood come out of their throats while twitching and spluttering into perpetual slumber?

What it must be is that in order to carry out that kind of brutal murder you have to disengage with the empathetic aspect of your nature and cultivate an idea of the victim as different, inferior and subhuman. The only way to understand how such inhumane behaviour could be unthinkingly conducted is to look for comparable examples from our own lives. Our attitude to homelessness is apposite here.

295

It isn't difficult to envisage a species like us, only slightly more evolved, being universally appalled by our acceptance of homelessness.

'What? You had sufficient housing, it cost less money to house them, and you just ignored the problem?'

They'd be as astonished by our indifference as we are by the disconnected cruelty of Anwar. Maybe as they talked us through the suffering our indifference caused we'd gag too.

'I've got plenty of room in my flat,' I think as I pass Jason, the lad who sleeps under the bridge at the end of my street. 'I could just let him live here with me.' Why don't I? I did once, as a younger and more chaotic man, take that line of enquiry to its natural conclusion and moved James, a homeless Scottish bloke, into my flat.

It was a fucking disaster actually. He slept in my bed with me, I had a bath with him, it was a total nightmare. Most disturbing of all is the fact that he got tired of the arrangement before I did, and fucked off. I had to book him a cab, which was bloody stupid because he was home as soon as he stepped out the flat, that's the only benefit of being homeless. The point of the experiment was obviously to do something shocking on TV – I lived for that in those days – but also to humanise a homeless man because it's appalling that they've been dehumanised in the first place. This, though, is a necessary negotiation to enable the aberrance to continue. We all routinely do it, we make a learned moral evaluation: 'This is fine,' we tell ourselves as we pass, ignoring the gentle tug of the angel within. 'Don't give them any money; they'll only spend it on drugs.' Jesus, so what? I find it hard enough to not take smack sleeping in my cosy flat, take that away and I'll need at least a ten-pound bag of brown warmth to take the edge off.

If, as the Washington DC meditation experiment implies, we

are all invisibly connected, then this suffering is dragging us all down. We don't need even to look at academic studies; just feel what happens to you when you walk past, some inner alarm goes off to remind you that there is a problem, and it's your problem.

'The problem is . . .' I tell myself as I squintily smile at Jason, key in hand, 'that he's bloody disagreeable. He's not like a jolly tramp in a Quentin Blake book. He's a junkie and he's stinky and he's slippery.' I issue an inner evaluation that makes my inaction acceptable. It is not.

We are nearing the apex. Global change requires social change, and social change requires personal change.

'You've got all that money – give it to the homeless if you care so much': it's a fair point.

Are we all doing all we can? Interestingly, those of us with less give more: people with an annual income below £5,000 give an average of 4.5 per cent, but the proportion falls as income increases. People earning £40,000 or more donate just over 2 per cent to charity.

'From each according to his means, to each according to his needs' is a maxim that won't leave after a century-long saccharine rinse, capitalist lies and communist misadventure. Why is the idea that the pursuit of self-centred happiness will lead to contentment so adhesive? I wake up every day newly baptised into the cult of individualism. I wish I was more like my mum or my nan, who find joy in nourishing others; they've sussed it.

I daily renew my pledge to adorn, forgetting again in the light of the morning what lessons I'd learned as I stretch out and yawn. The greed is reborn, the crucifix fallen and again with a groan the greed rises and the heart is overthrown, the dissonant drone resumes: what can I do for me? My mind runs commercials for the tingling gut. What can I do for me? A jingling I can't unhear, or a fractal screensaver, burrowing down like a tick on my collarbone that I dug out with scissors in a shaving mirror.

What would happen if I brought Jason home, if I brought him across the fifty yards that separates his squalor from my splendour? Would the inconvenience and disruption be compensated for by some holy glow?

I saw a woman on Stamford bridge, broken down and embarrassed as the traffic stacked behind her. She stood in a gesture of impotence at the rear passenger door where her young child waited. 'You alright, love?' I enquired, and she told me in English more reliable than her car, but only just, that someone was coming. A passing cyclist heard the exchange and said, 'Shall we push it to the side of the road?' I agreed and he propped up his bike on the iron railings and we assumed the Sisyphean position at the rear, prematurely crouched. 'Is the handbrake off?' says Tom, who's trim and posh and is taking the lead in all this. We roll the car initially uphill – it's on a humpback bridge – then to the crest and downhill from there, and with the job done, Tom and I, unified by our momentary endeavour, shake hands. The woman seems pleased too as she waves from the driver's seat.

Tom, as he departed, said he'd started a new business venture that day, he'd been debating whether to stick to his initial plan to give a third of all profits away. 'Sometimes there are things like this,' he said, 'y'know, signs.' Off he cycled, and subsequent to this minor act of public spiritedness, as I marched down Kings Road, I felt like Jesus.

I know, it was nothing, but some gland or neurological zone saw fit to flood me with rewarding endorphins. I felt better. In that moment I was better. It was a connection between the three of us. My last consumer purchase, a pair of orange-rimmed Paul Smith sunglasses, didn't give me as good a kick as that did. Maybe a life of devotion doesn't need to be robes and chanting; maybe it's just going through life with open eyes and an open mind, looking out for chances to help people and buzz on the altruistic zip it gives, like coins in Mario Land.

CHAPTER 29

Granma We Love You

As we approach the book's conclusion the answer to the question 'What would this Revolution look like?' begins to emerge.

It is defined and achieved by a sustained, mass-supported attack on the hegemony of corporations and the regulations that allow them to dominate us. It is the radical decentralisation of power, whether private or state. It is the return of power to us, the people at the level of community. It is the assertion of spirituality, of whatever form, to the heart of our social structures.

We do eat food, so we need a reassessment of global trade agreements to make them favourable to localised, organic farming, not reckless profiteering.

Economics is at the heart of our nation-state philosophy. The nation state may have served its purpose and have to be dissolved; it's not a big deal – ask the Bavarians or Persians or Mesopotamians.

A measure other than GNP to judge a nation's success, as in Bhutan; revocation of corporate charters for corporations that have behaved criminally, e.g. Monsanto, General Motors, Philip Morris, Pfizer. The assets of 'killed' corporations handed over to the people who work in them, to become worker-run cooperatives.

State power to dissolve wherever possible to empower autonomous, democratic communities.

Remember, the people who tell you this can't work, in government, on Fox News or MSNBC, or in op-eds in the *Guardian* or the *Spectator*, or wherever, are people with a vested interest in things staying the same.

I'll level with you: you know me, when I started this book I really thought I might be able to write my version of, I dunno, *Mein Kampf* (whatever happened to that guy?) or *Das Kapital*, that I'd contrive some brilliant manifesto where I would, on a wave of roaring adulation, be carried from celebrity to political office. Now I know that nobody should ever be in that position; the structures that elevate, rarefy or in any way concentrate power have to themselves be eradicated.

There is no heroic revolutionary figure in whom we can invest hope, except for ourselves as individuals together.

I really hate it when I think I'm on the precipice of saying something deep and empowering when it's actually more or less a quote from *Rocky IV* ('If you can change and I can change, maybe the whole damn world can change') or a lyric from an M People song ('search for the hero inside yourself'), but I've really got very little to add to these scattered and perennial pop-cultural artefacts.

There's no dearth of alternatives, there just aren't many people in power who want things to change. Buckminster Fuller is the fella to return to on the practical stuff: he is only interested in the efficacy of systems and the truth of our situation. Capitalism isn't irreducible and absolute; the depletion of earth's resources due to the free market is. Do we ditch capitalism or the planet? We can't have both. Obviously we know capitalism has to go, everyone does, especially the elites that benefit from it most. They know that the majority of people would benefit from radical change and the implementation of the type of systems we have been discussing. This means they do two things: they disparage our viable alternatives to prevent us pursuing them actively and collectively; and, in the event that their propaganda and distractions don't work, they are prepared for confrontation. They are prepared for activism, protest and moaning. They aren't prepared for Revolution.

The Cuban Revolution was a remarkable success in many respects: it was recent, it was initiated by a small number of people, and it scared the shit out of America.

Che Guevara was unusually fond of making pronouncements seemingly designed to ensure his eventual CIA execution. Soon after the Revolution he said, 'Our Revolution is endangering all American possessions in Latin America. We are telling these countries to make their own Revolution.' Which is basically revolutionary for 'Come on then, you mugs.'

After numerous victories in the mountains and jungles, including one incredible strategic victory where Castro negotiated a ceasefire when his troops were surrounded, then snuck 'em out, the rebels made their way to the major cities of Cuba, forming alliances as they went with other militias and kicking ass.

Batista, the corrupt US puppet, bricked it and legged it at the first sign of aggro, and Castro marched victoriously into Havana on 8 January 1959, just over two years after he'd arrived on a yacht called *Granma* with a bunch of shit sailors.

In one notable speech given by Castro a white dove landed on his shoulder, anointing him divinely with a globally recognised totem of unity between man and a higher ideal.

The revolutionary movement did some pretty cool things which you'll never really hear about because most of them were a real kick in the balls to US foreign policy (in fact, when you look at it, the US military's reputation for being invincible is a bit shaky: WW2 – unpunctual; Vietnam – nil–nil draw; Gulf

2 – cock-up; Cuba – decked in their own back yard). All private corporations were booted out of the country and 75 per cent of privately owned land was renationalised and given over to collectives, including in a 'practice what you preach' move of epic proportions, Castro handing his own family's land over. The priorities of the new government were land reform (sharing land) and making sure everyone had food and literacy, making sure the population was educated.

Now I'm a big fan of Castro and Guevara and all their beret-wearing, gun-toting, cigar-chuffing pals. They were sexy, cool, tough and they won, they fuckin' won a Revolution against America, which is to say, the big companies that America runs rackets for.

However, in the interests of balance I am obliged to tell you they are not as pure and innocent as the dove that alighted on Fidel's shoulder as he addressed the devoted Havana crowd. In way of mitigation I will say this: the Cuban people and their Revolution became a bit of a pawn in a game of international eyeballing between Russia and America and communism and capitalism. This skewed their ideals. It became necessary, under intense military and economic pressure, for Cuba to form an alliance with the Soviet Union, who had wandered way off track with their own Revolution, which started off as a lovely ritualistic murder of the royal family and empowerment of the serf class but went a bit mad and dictatorial.

So the Cubans did shut down all the churches, which is a bit of a drag, because we all need somebody to lean on. Again this lot were dealing with a version of organised religion that had become crazily exploitative and corrupt, so I suppose Fidel and the gang thought, 'Knock it on the head. Less said, soonest mended.' This attitude of 'nipping problems in the bud' led to a bit too much of the ol' execution of 'traitors' and 'counter-revolutionaries'. This is notoriously the big problem of ideologues: the forcible imposition of the ideal. 'My idea is fantastic, but it's complicated and I haven't got time to explain it to everyone, but if you knew what I know, you'd do what I'm telling you. However, we are in a bit of a rush, so anyone who gets in the way of the idea might get a little bit murdered in cold blood.'

This is what Dave Graeber is keen to avoid. 'Can there be an intermittent regime that imposes the changes that give birth to utopia?' I ask him. 'No,' he says, 'those operations always end up clinging to power and dispatching brutal justice.'

Then they start taking short cuts, like 'Probably all Jews/gays/gypsies/Muslims/women/fat people are as bad as each other; to save time, let's do them as a job lot.'

This is why revolutions require a spiritual creed. It doesn't matter who is doing violence or to what end. Violence is wrong. It's not that violence by the people we disagree with is wrong but our violence in overthrowing them in order to assert our brilliant idea is 'a means to an end'; all violence is wrong.

This leads to some challenging and absolute ideas: capital punishment is wrong, torture is wrong, armed struggle is wrong, revenge is wrong. The only way to grasp this idea is by transcending the individual or material expression of violence and regarding violence in and of itself as taboo. Non-violent Palestinians and non-violent Israelis have to non-violently unite to oppose violence.

So all my class-war rhetoric about lopping off the Queen's bonce is counterproductive – counter-revolutionary, in fact. The rounding up and execution of executives at J. P. Morgan and Goldman Sachs is counter-revolutionary.

Political rhetoric cannot ever solve these conflicts; it doesn't have the language. Religion does. When Jesus, or whoever, says, 'The lion will lay down with the lamb,' what this symbol infers is a time where the shared act of 'lying down' is given pre-eminence over the distinct, temporary forms of 'lion' or 'lamb'.

When people get all worked up about which religion is superior, that is not religion, that is individualistic, materialistic, territorial ideology asserted through the language of religion. As Joseph Campbell says, 'All religions are true, in that the metaphor is true,' and all religions have a bit in them where it says, 'Don't kill other people.'

All that fire and brimstone, blood and thunder, jihadi, crusade stuff is expedient materialism.

The point of religion is to remind us that we are a temporary expression of a subtler and connected electromagnetic realm unknowable on our narrow bandwidth of consciousness. The defining principle is oneness, not division, not opposition. Regard geometry: circles, spheres, spirals, from the subatomic realm to Jupiter and beyond; not a single right angle or square to be found. We are fractally dissolving and reconfiguring into infinite oneness; harmonise it here, now, 'on earth as it is in heaven'.

If one autonomous collective wants to live as the most extreme and fundamentalist version of Muslims conceivable, cool – they can. As long as it doesn't contravene the autonomy and self-governance of any other collective or damage the planet we share.

If another autonomous collective wants to live as an orgiastic, homoerotic, polygamous cult, cool. As long as it doesn't contravene the autonomy or self-governance of any other collective or the planet and the members all voted for it, it's no one's business but theirs.

Same for the bankers' collective. Or the Zapatista collective, or even the secular, mixed, ecologically responsible, electronically democratic collectives that I secretly hope will be most prominent.

The Cuban Revolution did a lot right – education for everyone, land sharing, emancipation of women and equal rights for black Cubans – but they went a bit wayward with the homophobia and authoritarianism. I've got a bit of a soft spot for them – don't throw the baby out with the bathwater. Take the stuff we like; leave the stuff we don't. It's our collective future we're building, and the sanctity of those yet born, as long as we return to Buckminster's theorem: 'To make the world work for 100% of humanity in the shortest possible time through spontaneous cooperation, without ecological offense or the disadvantage of anyone.'

Remember, too, we are not trying to supplant a perfect system, we are not competing with justice, we are intervening in a gallingly unequal and corrupt system on the brink of Armageddon.

As Chomsky's essay on enforced corporatisation makes clear, the head of the serpent that must be severed is the United States as defined by the Monroe Doctrine and 'Manifest Destiny'. You hear this phrase a lot, but unless you're an American schoolchild or a potential immigrant undergoing rigorous exams, you're unlikely to know what it means.

One of the myths that America built itself on, and perhaps any nation builds itself on, is the idea that it has a sublime, even divine, reason to exist. Otherwise it looks like it's just a hashed-together construct that serves the interest of elites. No one wants to belong to a nation that overtly and clinically states, 'This land mass/concept having a pinnacle that is controlled by an elite is a convenient way of harvesting resources both material and human, so shut the fuck up and salute.' It's not a very inspiring message. Better to tell people that God likes your land mass and mountain ranges and flag, and that the leaders are just interpreting his wishes.

In the opening scenes of *Monty Python and the Holy Grail*, Graham Chapman's King Arthur addresses some serfs he encounters as his subordinates. The serf, played by Michael Palin, asserts that he doesn't know that he's a Briton, that no one has explained the concept of nation to him or his position in a hierarchy, and he believes himself to be a member of an anarcho-syndicalist democracy, much like the ones I'm advocating. The scene is well funny because it comedically demonstrates the absurdity of nation and feudalism, ideas that are so familiar to us that we don't question their validity.

The only thing that makes Britain Britain is our consent; the only thing that makes money money is our consent.

My mate Gee told me – and I choose to believe him, and I happen to be in a very research-dense part of the book and can't be fucked to check this particular fact, especially as it works as a metaphor, even if it ain't true – that the Dutch used to dominate the global economy in colonial times, in part because of the value of tulips and they had the tulip market by the balls. Then one day, I like to think apropos of nothing, everyone went, 'Fuck tulips, they're bullshit,' and the whole caper fell apart.

CHAPTER 30

Manifest Destiny

Manifest Destiny is an ideological pillar of expansionist America that proposes they have a divine right, beyond right, a duty to take over nameless land and impose American values on it. They had this idea midway through the nineteenth century and a glance at your TV set will show you that they're still into it. The people of Finland don't just get into boats, sail to New Zealand and tell them they're making a pig's ear of it; they just get on with their Finnish gear.

You could argue that the majority of people in New Zealand are only there as a result of Britannia and our bowler-hatted version of 'we know best', so if the Finnish did turn up and start, I dunno, insisting they eat blubber, it'd be little more than they deserve.

These are broadly agreed to be the tenets of Manifest Destiny:

1. The special virtues of the American people and their institutions
This literally means they think they're better. Even though there was no such thing as American people a few hundred years ago, they think that by moving to a new bit of this tiny rock in infinite space they have acquired supremacy and a colonial imperative.

2. America's mission to redeem and remake the West in the image of agrarian America

America has a mission – mission is a word that is connected with doing God's work. Also, of course, missionary position, which is apparently so called because when Christian ministers went to tribal regions in newly colonised lands the folk that lived there fucked in a variety of ways, like all people, but because the missionaries were basically vicars they thought the whole spectacle to be a stomach-churning display.

Firstly, why were they watching people having it off in the first place? Seems a bit of a cheek to me, and how is it an ecumenical matter? How did they even broach the subject? 'Chief Umbohkoo, I'd like to watch you mating with Mrs Umbohkoo, if I may?'

'Why reverend?'

'Good question. Mostly it's to offer tips.'

'I thought you were celibate.'

'You're right, sorry, I've just been lonely since I left Surrey and would like to watch a bit of howsyerfather.'

'Well, I'd like to help, but it's private.'

So America is on a mission to make the West in the image of agrarian America. Who else is it that makes things in 'his image' that you can think of? It's God, isn't it. It's one of his most cherished skills. America has an image of itself as a place run, apparently, by farmers and it wants to impose that on other people. I suppose the farm bit is okay; I imagine that having control over your own food is important for a formerly colonised nation. What did we do to them? America is like an abused child that grows up to become an abuser.

3. An irresistible destiny to accomplish this essential duty

I like that one the best. It's irresistible, this destiny – that wording really hammers home the notion that it isn't an idea that's convenient for the people who propose it; no, it's an external magnetic force, that, even if you disagree with it, will suck you in, to fulfil a duty, and the duty is essential, the very basis of being, and at its deepest and most indivisible level. America invading Iraq is as unquestionable as gravity or carbon. Don't think about it, it just is.

Manifest Destiny, while a uniquely American imperialist term, is derived from the colonial concepts, and obviously ideas that precede even that, like 'Romantic Nationalism, the form of nationalism in which the state derives its political legitimacy as an organic consequence of the unity of those it governs'. Well, we're all guilty of that.

As I write, Brazil have just been thrashed out of the World Cup they are hosting and they are now 'a nation in mourning'.

Brazil is an agreement in the mind; football is an arbitrary, temporary, consensual structure; and today, as a consequence of the result of a football match, hundreds of millions of people are feeling real emotions: grief, regret, humiliation. Emotions perhaps exacerbated by the destructive economic and social impact of staging the event: homes were demolished, money was squandered.

We are voluntarily subscribing to belief systems that are punishing us and enabling us to be exploited. Surely ultimately an external affiliation to place should be manageable? Is patriotism essentially any different, other than in scale, to me making a decision to consecrate the room I'm now typing in? To declare it superior to other rooms, to give it a crest, an anthem, an ideology? People might go, 'Russell, you idiot, that's just the spare bedroom, your only relationship with it is that you're in it.'

'No,' I'll reply, 'God put me here. What's more, he told me this is better than other rooms and I have a duty, an essential

311

duty, to go to other rooms and build them in the image of the spare room; God told me to.' God told me to! Isn't that what every lunatic who ever murdered a woman working as a prostitute has declared as his excuse?

So Chomsky explains that America has always seen itself as a nation of capitalist Christian soldiers 'marching as to war', ostensibly to protect its divinely chosen populace (all of whom are immigrants, except for the poor bastards who were there in the first place, or the people they kidnapped to do all the work) from 'evil'. When evil in the form of Soviet communism evaporated, did America revise its military expansionist programmes in Latin America or the Middle East? The answer is no. They became more aggressive and promoted the idea of new ideological opponents. I'm not saying 9/11 was an inside job. The mysterious, ignored third tower – 'Building Seven' – the signs of 'controlled demolition', the nationality of all the terrorists, are all cause for question. What is irrefutable is that America has a long history of carrying out invasions to impose the will of its corporate clientele, there is documentation of a plan to invade Iraq prior to 9/11, and the reasons they said they were invading Iraq have all since been proved untrue.

Henry Kissinger regarded conflicting national identity as a virus that had to be subdued and inoculated against. When Chile elected a socialist leader, Salvador Allende, America deposed him and replaced him with one who fitted in with their thinking, that cuddly ol' Thatcher chum General Pinochet, although if you ask me he wasn't that general, he was specifically a bit of a bastard. They also used Chile to pilot some of the financial ideologies that have recently been crashing down around us in our markets.

America's support of Israel continues to destabilise the Middle East; Chomsky says they like it unstable. Also he points out that Saudi Arabia, the most hard core of the Islamic nations, is America's tightest Arab ally in the region, and that the US, like the UK, quite likes fundamentalist Muslim states, preferring them in fact to secular Arab societies, as I suppose oppressive regimes, regardless of aesthetics, are easier to do business with because they don't have to respond to an empowered electorate.

Chomsky concludes that 'security in the conventional sense' plays very little part in the formation of policy. By which he means the security of the population. The security that they are interested in preserving is the security for state power.

America have a well dodgy bit of legislation, known as the Netherlands Invasion Act, that means that should any American citizen ever be tried at The Hague, which is where they try war criminals like George W. Bush, America can storm in with helicopters and motorbikes and whisk him out the dock to freedom. Although given their recent history with foreign wars they'd probably end up bombing Anne Frank's house, torching the Van Gogh Museum and running over Tony Blair on the way out.

Chomsky, in his lifelong audition speech for assassination, continues that the security that is claimed to be 'for the people' is actually security 'from the people', which is where me and ol' Chompers (as I've just started calling him) align.

Like I said, 'Top Secret' means in practice 'Don't let that lot find out what we're up to, they'll go nuts.' The military and police force are primarily there as insurance for when we do finally rise up. Chompskerooney uses a quote from the prominent liberal scholar and government adviser Samuel Huntington to make his – let's say 'our' – point: 'The architects of power in the United States must create a force that can be felt but not seen. Power remains strong when it remains in the dark; exposed to the sunlight it begins to evaporate.' Blimey, a bit heavy that, then Chomsky adds, 'State power has to be protected from its domestic enemy; in sharp contrast, the population is not secure from state power.'

We're the domestic enemy! Us and our mums and our little dreams of freedom. What the blazes is going on? We can't trust our leaders at all, they're all at it. When Edward Snowden, the nerdy, techno-hero, Milky Bar, Harry Potter, speccy Neo, exposed the NSA surveillance programme because it made him feel all sick in his gutty-wuts that we were all being secretly spied on to an incomprehensible degree, how did Obama's administration respond? What was their justification? 'We're doing it for your security' plus 'If you want privacy or freedom, it can only mean you've got something to hide and you're probably a paedo.'

Fucking hell, that's amazing, like we're the ones who've done something wrong when they have broken the laws that we elect them to uphold. Of course the Americans were quick to label Snowden a traitor: 'You bloody traitor, informing hundreds of millions of people that their government was spying on them – we were only doing that to stop terrorists.' It's like when you catch someone acting suspicious on their phone and lying, and they go all pious and outraged and say, 'Actually I was only trying to arrange a surprise party for YOU and now YOU'VE spoiled it.' Actually I think that's a soap opera cliché, not real life, but you get the point. It's also what Göring said to do in his 'how to be a Nazi' formula.

True to form, as Professor Chomsky points out in his article, that I'm basically nicking, when Snowden exposed these unthinkable violations on the privacy and freedom of its popu-lation, the officials responsible hit back with the classic anti-terror narrative, claiming that the NSA's measures had prevented fifty-four acts of terrorism.

When pressed on the matter, they went, 'Alright, twelve.' Then when the suspicious inquisitor insisted on checking, it turned out that all that aggro and spying, the non-consensual compilation of oceans of private data, had revealed, wait for it, one – yes, one – dubious transaction: somebody had sent eight and a half grand to Somalia. That's slim pickings. That's like in *Life of Brian* when that Roman garrison searches the HQ of the People's Front of Judea and turns up one spoon.

Chomsky explains that the trade agreements – that we've seen are the administrative assurances that we're all doomed, so people can turn a profit flogging goods that will be reciprocally imported – are being replicated and expanded.

Trans-Pacific and transatlantic pacts are being negotiated in secret with the collusion of squads of corporate lawyers. These pacts, like the pacts contrived in the past, are not free trade agreements, they are investor rights agreements, insurance for corporations that the conditions being created will guarantee profit. Why does this need to be done in secret? Because the conditions that benefit them fuck us right over.

They spy on us, they lie to us, they control us with violence, they sell us shit food and annihilate the planet, and all for a little bit of money. I wish they *were* lizards; that would make more sense. Certainly they are manifesting a reality that comes from reptilian consciousness in that selfishness and greed are short-sighted, survivalist impulses that are outmoded and must now be upgraded. This next bit of Chomskers is so wicked I'm not even going to patronisingly translate it into colloquial prose, just mainline neat Noam, straight into your synapses. Here he just gives it to us straight:

'There is, in other words, ample evidence that securing state power from the domestic population and securing concentrated private power are driving forces in policy formation.'

What Chomsky has done is spelled out for us, like we're children or layabouts or P. G. Wodehouse characters who'd sooner pootle about in our jalopies than stare the stark reality of our virtual slavery in the face, is that we're being fed porkie pies by a bunch of hell-bent swines.

Chomsky demands that we accept our role as sentient adults, citizens; with fearless, ruthless, mechanical dexterity he exposes the absurdity and disingenuousness of the dominant narrative. In this next paragraph, another that I'm loathe to meddle with, he very simply demonstrates that our authorities, those in power, those who set the agenda, are not acting out of the paternal benevolence that they claim guides them. Check it:

'Take two prominent current examples, global warming and nuclear weapons. As any literate person is doubtless aware, these are dire threats to the security of the population. Turning to state policy, we find that it is committed to accelerating each of those threats – in the interests of the primary concerns, protection of state power and of the concentrated private power that largely determines state policy.'

Global warming is totally real, it has been empirically proven, and the only people who tell you it's not real are, yes, people who make money from creating the conditions that cause it.

We're reaching the end of Professor Chomsky's contribution. I was intrigued by his inclusion in his essay of this quote from General Lee Butler, the last commander of the Strategic Air Command, which was armed with nuclear weapons. 'We have so far survived the nuclear age by some combination of skill, luck, and divine intervention, and I suspect the latter in greatest proportion.'

Whether you believe in God or not it is interesting to hear a military general in charge of nuclear weapons ascribing our avoidance of Armageddon to a Higher Power. I do believe in God, as must surely be abundantly clear. The more I learn, the more I experience, the more certain I become. Perhaps the persistent belief that there is 'something else', some force that supersedes and governs, is simply derived from the ghostly knowledge that behind our own being is a separate and auton-omous system that digests our food and pumps our heart and converts oxygen. It seems that those that reach the higher echelons of our man-made structures, or delve deeply into science, become initiated into an awareness of a nameless beyond. Indeterminate human cells suddenly and invisibly triggered into purpose – no one knows why. No one knows when the soul alights upon these cells. No one knows the formula for consciousness, no one knows why our destruction has as yet not been permitted, and even the men with their fingers on the button ascribe it to God.

Noam Chomsky is too fastidious, diligent and brilliant a man to, at this time, in his life of peerless truth-telling, cry 'Revolution!' But this final paragraph, to me, suggests but one course of action:

'As we are all surely aware, we now face the most ominous decisions in human history. There are many problems that must be addressed, but two are overwhelming in their significance: environmental destruction and nuclear war. For the first time in history, we face the possibility of destroying the prospects for decent existence – and not in the distant future. For this reason alone, it is imperative to sweep away the ideological clouds and face honestly and realistically the question of how policy decisions are made, and what we can do to alter them before it is too late.'

Thanks, Noam, I'll take it from here: so we're fucked unless we organise and disobey. They've got this sewn up. They own both the teams that are competing, the stadium they play in, the grass they play on, and we're the ball they're kicking around. They have removed all possibility for reform or redirection within the system; the change must come from us. Our only hope of survival is to overthrow their structures and take our power back.

CHAPTER 31

Be The Change

Of the successful revolutions we've thus far discussed, the one we ought most emulate is the Spanish Revolution. One thing we don't want to do is replace one ruling class with another; we want power to be shared, not concentrated, and the role of the diminished state to be administrative and responsive. The means by which we achieve this, too, is important. Perhaps there is a corollary between the violence that brings about Revolution and the corruption that tends to follow.

The Indian Revolution was a roaring success but took ages. I always thought that the British colonised India and thought of it as being tied up with our empire, which in spite of everything I've written, I still am programmed to be a bit proud of; however, it was a blag. India was controlled by the East India Company.

Queen Victoria an' all that mob were just the Ronald McDonalds of the day, weirdly dressed clowns to look at while the real caper took place out of view. Or maybe she was a brand ambassador like Scarlett Johannsen knocking out SodaStreams on the West Bank to make the persecution of Palestinians seem sexy and fizzy.*

* Scarlet Johannsen has sued people before for defaming her. I bet she's a lovely, well intentioned human being and, for a number of reasons, I wouldn't like her to feel that I am criticising her. It just shows how tangled the entertainment world and corporate world are.**

I think with brands and their branding that if you want to understand the truth of what they are, you have to first look at what they're telling you, then track back from that point as far as you can and you'll be closer to reality. So with a monarch like Queen Victoria, representing the brand of Britain and its economic interests, what is the message they're giving us? Firstly, respectability: this woman is super-stiff, she never smiles, she's serious and well behaved. Secondly, authority: listen to their jingle, 'God Save Our Queen' – she's tied up with God, that means divinely sanctioned; the Americans must've nicked that idea when they took the lingo. Everything about the empire screams respectability, legitimacy, authority and permanence. Using my theory, we must move as far away from that as possible and we'll be closer to the reality that they are masking, like a tramp smothered in deodorant.

So, then, the British Empire was not respectable – we know that now, they were vicious thugs using violence to get their way, reneging on deals and nicking the resources of whole nations. Are they legit? Of course not, the whole Christian mythology they loosely appropriated, whilst still clinging on to bizarre pagan symbols like lions and unicorns and pyramids, is all about empathy and sharing – what a swizz. Is there any real authority? No, only that which is achieved through coercion and violence, and as for permanence, where the fuck is it now?

The same is true for Coke or Apple or any of them. If they sell you community, they are in fact individualistic; if they sell you youth, they're steeped in decaying tradition and antiquated

** Scarlett Johannsen sued a French novel because the lead character was 'too like her', so we have to be super careful. To be clear, and as far as I know, she ain't sued anyone re SodaStream. I am not criticising Scarlett, I am a man and have the same motivations as all men when addressing her. She is pretty and I want her to like me. Please can this matter rest.

ideas like materialism. How can Coke, a brown drink with too much sugar in it, represent coolness or youth or America or sex? How can Apple, a bunch of needlessly elaborate, too frequently updated, deliberately expiring* digital pools for cyber-narcissism, do anything but lock us into binary solipsism? How does it create community?

Any corporation selling us products on the basis of anything other than utility should be revoked and shut down. Any corporation that at this time of fast-diminishing resources designs products that have inbuilt doomsday devices, planned obsolescence**, should be shut down. All this glamour and clamour and blagging and skanking has to end.

'This drink. This drink will fuck you from your gums to your guts, but cold enough, the sugar and fizz will provide a blip, just long enough to stop you opening a vein. Coke. Or Pepsi, doesn't matter.'

---

* Our lawyer Roger, who's decent, says Apple do not make deliberately expiring goods. Online there are many accounts of glitchy downloads that appear to make iPhones stop working correctly. I have a terrible time personally with my iPhone, he's like an evil Knight Rider, losing emails, sending nude photos into cyber space. A proper troublemaker. Legally, though, I cannot prove that Apple engage in planned obsolescence, though this practice is extremely common in the tech industry. Like most things in this book, you can do your own research, and draw on your own experience. But so you can see, once more, how powerful this system is and how it's parameters are rigidly enforced, not by masked illuminati but by nice professional people, just doing their jobs at a publishing house, I am obliged to tell you candidly that Apple do not make deliberately expiring products.**

** In God's Holy name, by all the saints, I swear by the blood of Christ, that I am not referring to Apple here but to other companies, who I will not name as not to add to the complications that you encounter when trying to confront Mammon. You will see the companies' names when you search 'planned obsolescence'. Also, like me, you will be astonished how frequently Apple's name comes back in the results, especially as you weren't even searching for it. There must be some reason for that other than Apple engaging in planned obsolescence though, as we all know, and I swear, by the name of Allah, that there is no proof that Apple have ever engaged in any of that.

'This phone will connect you to people everywhere except for where you are and sever you from God for ever. Apple.'

You've seen their logo, it's an apple with a bite taken out of it; that bite is the symbol of the moment mankind broke their pact with God, transgressed their own innocent nature and chewed into consuming and consumerism. We have externalised all wonder, materialised our inherent magic.

There is an old river where I write; it's grimy and dirty and ancient. From a distance it's all very chocolate box: swans and cygnets, willows weeping and long grasses. When you stand on the bank, though, it's brown and full of pungent gunk and natural funk and it's cold, British cold.

As I plunge in my skin tightens and I stare, I reach for strangled breath. Forgotten capacities stir and a noise I've never heard emerges, a roar, an animal roar, unrefined and naked. Unexplored depths and vibrations neglected and unstirred. We are nature; we are nature as we munch gum and check the phone; we are nature as we queasily regret our imperfection, turning the glossy page, turning our glossy stomachs; we are nature as we hear them witter inanely on the radio, desecrating the silence with the violence of their idiocy and dumb verdicts, chattering and grooming, picking through the ticks in their hair, marvelling at new minutia.

These boys that throw off Birmingham for Baghdad, what are they looking for there? What's in that crimson desert that they can't find in the Bullring? Untangled from Spaghetti Junction and aspiring to spaghetti westerns, these loaded kids of Charlton Heston declaring their jihad.

To end this hapless meander through a mapless expanse, a hopeful and myopic grope, a listless disconnected kiss smothered, like Magritte's shrouded lovers, whose hand can guide us through this abyss, what cartographers of consciousness can we look to now?

I'd take Gandhi over Isis when it comes to making maps for new worlds. Gandhi is a bit of a placeholder hero for me, a kind of unthinking grab for an easily identifiable brand of hero. Einstein said of him, 'Future generations will scarce believe one such as he existed.' My own love of him is founded upon early exposure to the film, in which scene after scene he challenges authority and stands up to corruption and bullying. Gandhi knew too that defiance had to come from somewhere other than rage. That you can't build love from hate, that the world we live in is the manifestation of a sublime source. The most practical application of what a lot of people would regard as wishy-washy claptrap was his popularisation of non-violent protest.

Gandhi organised the Indian people around this principle: total civil disobedience and non-violence. Gandhi deplored violence but hated cowardice more, so walked face first into a bloody good hiding from British colonial forces during his decades-long leadership of the campaign for self-rule.

When we think about former colonial nations campaigning for self-rule, we can see the legitimacy of their demands. They only want to determine their own lives without constantly being exploited and controlled by an invading economic power – perfectly reasonable, we conclude.

Today in our apparently free Western secular democracies we live under a tyranny that is only superficially distinct. The only connection that, say, David Cameron can claim is that he was born on the same land mass as the majority of the people his party governs. But as we now know from the contributions of Chomsky, Graeber, Norberg-Hodge and Goldsmith, and our intuitive understanding of life, our governments are not account-able to us but to transnational corporations. Is that really any different from the Indian people being exploited by the East India Company, give or take a few Xboxes?

There's a lovely bit of Pathé newsreel footage of Gandhi in Lancashire and east London when he came to Britain in the forties to mug off Churchill and everyone with his pithy lyrics and demands for self-rule.

'What do you think of Western civilisation, Mr Gandhi?'

'I think it'd be a good idea,' he said, the rascal.

Like any dignitary, they've dragged him round the joint, meeting folk and seeing sights. I like to think Gandhi went, 'Yeah, I like the Tower of London and that, can I meet some real people now?'

Who knows? Regardless, when you see Gandhi with the female mill workers of Lancashire, whose livelihoods his ideas threatened – he didn't want pointless importation of textiles from Britain that had been sent from India, manufactured, then sent back, for profit; he wanted Indian folk to make their own stuff – you can see the workers really dig him. Even though he's a mad-looking little Indian bloke all dressed up in a nappy, only in England to fuck off the empire, and superficially negatively impact them, the women know a kindred spirit when they see one. They know that Gandhi is fighting for the rights of the oppressed against the powerful, a struggle they know well. The insight of these women, the inherent connection shared between the world's exploited people in the struggle for autonomy, matters now more than ever.

We can no longer dopily believe that we have more in common with billionaire warlords and their slick white political acolytes than the populations of the nations that they're up for bombing this week.

'Shoplifters of the world, unite and take over': Morrissey's mid-eighties wail, the administratively unlikely rallying cry for the world's dispossessed to organise, the way they have organised to ensure their hymn sheet is the one we end up singing from.

According to Chomsky, the hijacked ghostwriter of the last

chapter, revolutions that concentrate power in the hands of a new elite are pointless; revolutions that spread power across society succeed.

So let's review the situation. We know the world needs to change – we're on the brink of destruction. We know the majority of people – I would argue, everyone – would benefit from Revolution, and we know what has to change: corporate tyranny, ecological irresponsibility and economic inequality. We know how to change them: remove all systems that contravene Buckminster Fuller's theorem – trade agreements, monopolies, unrepresentative democratic institutions. We know to a degree what will replace them: localised, self-governing communities and businesses.

Do we know 100 per cent what this will look like? No, we don't know if there will still be some inequality, some hierarchies, some conflict. We do know that there are alternatives and we can no longer remain pallid and listless in the cellar like Fritzl's kids, unaware that there's a big wide world out there where getting raped by your dad isn't mandatory.

The democratic models that some of our contributors have mentioned are contingent on participation; this is where we really address the accusation that the withdrawal of participation in fraudulent democracy is apathetic. It's not 'Don't vote, watch porn'; it's 'Don't vote, build your own system'.

Have you ever participated in any horizontal, non-hierarchal organisations as they make plans? I have, it's really challenging. Everyone has something to say and everyone has their own version of what would be best. After about ten minutes of trying to fairly and democratically organise a charity event in a committee of twelve where everyone has an equal voice, I want to shout, 'Fuck you lot! I know what I'm doing, we're doing it my way.' The ego marches to the forefront and tries to seize control, and it's not just my ego, they all have egos too, everybody's ego wants to be heard. It's like a dog park where we, the human owners, stand back and our canine representatives sniff arse and yap.

Quickly you realise that your job is to negotiate with your own ego and let collective power that is not allied to any individual govern. Hand over your power; trust the common consciousness, guided by consensual, trusted principles, to be the authority. This is not a lethargic and laissez-faire process; it is dynamic, time-consuming and requires patience. We will probably always require some form of representative democracy, it just has to be the two things that conjunction implies: representative – the people's will is represented; and democratic – entirely answerable to the electorate.

When you look at the House of Commons, or Congress, the reason you feel bored and disengaged is because you know it is a masquerade. The exceptions, the Tony Benns and Caroline Lucases, are well-intentioned dinghies bobbing along in an ocean of treachery.

That is why I do not vote, that is why I will never vote, let's instead participate in a system that is truly representative. In the next chapter we are going to look at some stuff that if we don't really concentrate and determinedly remain upbeat could get all boring, and we hate that. The fact is, though, if we're to shut up Paxman and the naysayers (good name for a band) we have to show our working out. Like in a boring maths GCSE, which I knew was pointless even as I was failing it.

CHAPTER 32

Help Me, Help You

Here are the principles of a successful, worldwide, leaderless, anarchist collective with millions of members, that, helps people to deal with substance misuse issues and is defined by anonymity so, as you will see when you read it, I am forbidden to declare whether I belong to or not. They are known as the Twelve Traditions. I believe that this social code has much in it that we can replicate and benefit from.

1. Our common welfare should come first; personal recovery depends upon our unity.

This first edict establishes an important spiritual principle: our power is in unity, we must always prioritise our collective well-being above individual advantage. If you look at the way the world is currently governed it runs almost diametrically averse to this mandate: individual success and happiness is prioritised through the prevailing consumer mentality and the dominant, elitist capitalist system.

These shady, secret trade deals that Chomsky told us about are like white phosphorous-tipped arrows in the heart of this principle: 'Fuck the world, fuck community, show me the money.'

So when we're holding a group meeting on how our community

should be managed, no individual would have the right to do anything that fucks on a micro level with the group or on a macro level with the planet.

On a lighter note, I was once in the back of a limo with Tom Cruise – oh yeah, I've lived, baby – and he was talking to me about acting and he told me how he approached the character of Jerry Maguire, who said the famous 'show me the money' line. His kids were opposite and we were trapped in a luxurious carriage of beige leather. He said the comedy of Jerry came from his frustrated enthusiasm, a man who believed powerfully in what he was doing but was constantly thwarted. 'Help me, help you,' said Tom all passionately. In this moment I thought, 'Wow, I'm in a car with Tom Cruise and he's doing bits from his films – how cool.' I looked round the car to see if I could get a reciprocal bit of eye contact from someone, y'know, like, 'Hey guys! This is mad, he's doing that thing!' but everyone else in the car was either Tom Cruise or Tom Cruise's kids, so they weren't as impressed by it; in fact they didn't notice it, so I changed my 'wow' face to a normal nodding, smiling face and thought, 'I'll just have to put this in a book one day if I'm going to get any juice out of it. I hope, when I do, it doesn't seem like an extraneous name drop.'

2. For our group purpose there is but one ultimate authority – a loving God as He may express Himself in our group conscience. Our leaders are but trusted servants; they do not govern.

I love this idea: no individual has authority; the group has authority, the group conscience is expressed through voting. If I turn up and say, 'I'd like a big statue of me erected in the town square, and as leader of the group, I'm going ahead with it,' everyone else can say, 'Well, that's a nice idea, Russell, you've been a good leader, arguing our case at the regional meetings and nationwide meetings, let's see if a statue is a winner. All those in favour, press the green button; all those against, press red.' If for some crazy reason there are more red votes than greens, I don't get my fuckin' statue and that's that. This principle reminds Rumsfeld, or Ed Balls, or whichever risible dope in a suit trying to wangle a conservatory or new pair of shoes out of their role in public office,* that we, not they, are in charge and you only get to act on the will of the people, so if the people don't want a war in Iraq, no war in Iraq. The bosses, the people, through the group conscience, have spoken.

3. The only requirement for membership is a desire to stop drinking.

This requires a bit of translation. What it means is it don't matter what gender, sexual persuasion, colour, religion or class you are, if you want to join the group, you can. I suppose on a global level there will be groups that want to define themselves through specificity and exclusion – the English Defence League or the Nation of Islam might want their own set-up. I suppose we'd have to tolerate that. I mean, we can't phone up the Nation and say Bill O'Reilly wants to join up, you've got to let him. That might be antagonistic.

---

* Ed Balls didn't specifically get a conservatory or a pair of shoes. For all I know he didn't claim anything dodgy. I was joking. I happen to know that Ed Balls is in politics as a result of a powerful yearning to help others. He is a political Saint Francis (he did charge his £2,000 removal van to expenses and flipped his home three times in two years. Sort of thing St. Francis might've done).

4. Each group should be autonomous except in matters affecting other groups or our organisation as a whole.

This tradition deftly deals with the above problem: have a racially, religiously or sexually defined and exclusive group if you want, but you can't mess with our necessary, overall objective of ecological responsibility and economic equality.

5. Each group has but one primary purpose – to carry its message to the alcoholic who still suffers.

Our primary purpose is the preservation of our environment and the creation of a harmonious and inclusive democracy. We can likely only achieve this through small, self-determined communities that are run voluntarily and democratically.

6. A group ought never endorse, finance, or lend our name to any related facility or outside enterprise, lest problems of money, property and prestige divert us from our primary purpose.

This prevents people trying to profit from communities designed with spirituality in mind. We're all flawed and greedy and egotistical, so we have regulations in place that acknowledge that and guide us back to the better part of our individual and communal nature: our altruism, our empathy, our creativity.

7. Every group ought to be fully self-supporting, declining outside contributions.

This is designed to prevent top-down authority asserting itself. The group is independent and democratically run. This tradition – even the word 'tradition' is nicer and less incendiary than the word 'rule' – prevents swaggering capitalists and glamorous nitwits acquiring authority through financial means.

8. Our organisation should remain forever non-professional, but our service centres may employ special workers.

This reminds me of Matt Stoller's 'No Titles' policy: no one can suddenly claim to be a Professor of Revolution or an Admiral of Equality. To quote myself, always the sign of a well-managed ego, those in government are administrators, those in municipal positions are servants; our relationship to 'police' or 'traffic wardens', should the community vote for such institutions, are not subordinate, they are horizontal.

9. Our organisation, as such, ought never be organised; but we may create service boards or committees directly responsible to those they serve.

Remember what *Adbusters* said about corporations? They used to be set up to do a job, then disbanded. Then for no other reason than profit and individual advancement, they became ongoing immortal money-guzzling entities. This tradition prevents that: we set up a committee to build a nice juice bar or hold a World Cup, and when it's finished, it's disbanded. 'Ta da, Sepp, glad you enjoyed it. You can stand for re-election in four years, we'll let you know.'

10. Our organisation has no opinion on outside issues; hence the name ought never be drawn into public controversy.

This principle ensures the autonomy of other groups. Clearly our ideology is defined not by us wanting to be free from boozing, one day at a time, but free from our addiction to a corrupt and corrosive system. We are addicted to destructive ideas. When consent is achieved on our collective agenda, we can then determine what 'the incontrovertibles' are; likely they are based on ecological responsibility and individual freedom. I know what I'd like, but that is probably different from your requirements. As long as we both know neither of us has a hotline to God or inherent superiority, we should be cool.

11. Our public relations policy is based on attraction rather than promotion; we need always maintain personal anonymity at the level of press, radio and films.

This principle is dangerously close to being transgressed right now. You'll note that I haven't declared my affiliation, because were I a member of organisations defined by these traditions, I'd have no right to. What is implicit in this principle is the obligation to make your primary focus your own conduct, not telling other people what to do. Another big challenge for me personally. I love giving advice on how to change the world, it's much harder to get on and live like a good man. How effective and beautiful to have a tradition to remind us of this.

12. Anonymity is the spiritual foundation of all our Traditions, ever reminding us to place principles before personalities.

Here we see that the titular anonymity which defines these organisations is not solely in place to prevent sloshed old drunkards getting embarrassed by their condition, rather to emphasise that individuals are all equally valuable and equally expendable. I like this principle very much, as it returns to the primary battlefield where revolutions must be waged, our own consciousness. It's not that I want to oust David Cameron or Barack

Obama or Angela Merkel, it's that we must collectively over-come the structures that promote the egocentric in all of us.

Me and you and David Cameron and everyone else have to individually yield to the divine within us so that collectively we can manifest a society worthy of beautiful beings. One day, David Cameron's ego might be playing up, but that'll be okay because collectively we have a system that can avert that. Another day, I might get flash – that doesn't matter because we have principles in place which prevent anybody's negative nature becoming dominant.

'Tyranny is the deliberate removal of nuance,' said the film-maker Albert Maysles, when an institution or an individual oppresses truth to ensure that their version of reality dominates.

Whether that's Philip Morris removing the nuance of the carcinogenic properties of different types of fags to perpetuate sales, or me deceptively managing information within my own relationships, or the gun lobby insisting that guns shoot peace out of them, not lead.

We have a culture where principles mean nothing and person-alities mean everything. And I can see why it caught on. I've done very well out of it, my personality allows me to get away with all sorts of rubbish – riding the wrong way up a one-way street on a stolen bicycle (I didn't steal it though, I bought it off a dodgy bloke), winking at the police as I pass, years of trouble-free promiscuity, tables at restaurants – but without principles I was freewheeling away from God.

Here are some more examples of ideologies that flout the Establishment's insistent jingle that their way is the only way.

So, many corporations will be 'killed' according to *Adbusters'* excellent suggestion. Perhaps we should use the word 'cull', like people do when they want to kill something cute.

'Are you killing that badger?'

'No, sir, culling it.'

'When you've finished "culling" it, will it be dead?'

'A bit, yes.'

'So explain the difference between killing and culling.'

'Well it's a 'u' – and a sort of tuneful sense that the creature is being gently lulled to death rather than killed with a hammer.'

'And what's the hammer you're holding for?'

'Culling.'

So maybe we should cull some corporations.

Once we've culled them, their resources and materials can be returned to communities to run themselves. Outlined here is a suggestion for how a corporation could be structured more fairly.

Employee Investment Funds – Sweden, 1970s

- Every large Swedish corporation had to give its employees shares equivalent to 20 per cent of its profits every year.

Well, that's novel, the empowerment of workers within a corporate structure. Sure, it's limited, 20 per cent isn't enough; the workers should have 100 per cent and there should be no hierarchical distinction between any of the workers, regardless of their costume; title abolition will help towards that. We've begun negotiations, good. Well done, Sweden.

- The shares were not owned by individuals but were controlled by regional management boards which were democratically accountable.

Fair enough, we're not after a new elite, collectivisation and lateral autonomy. Cool. No wonder Volvos are so safe.

334

- The boards had to use the shares 'for social priorities and the public interest'.

That's good. I mean, I think huge sectors of the financial industry would be entirely dispensed with, given that the whole thing is an elaborate mathematical metaphor designed to legitimise fraud and theft. Nice to know that if any form of market did remain, there'd be no unaccountable bankers getting bonuses during an economic crisis that they caused. Viva IKEA.

- As the shares in the companies grew, so did the influence of the workers management boards on corporate decision-making.

Clever, the destiny of the board and workers are inextricably linked. From what we've discovered so far, this structure still seems a bit hierarchical, but at least it proposes a form of empowerment for workers, which we could easily amplify. Abba for ever.

- Unfortunately this scheme was never put into place due to widespread hostility from employers.

Oh right, they never actually did it. It was a hypothetical corporate Revolution. Typical; the sauna-dwelling, porn-watching, suicide-committing pervs.

Understandable, really. It's a method of financial reform that could never be imposed without union power and regulation that modifies the power of corporations. Bloody ironic.

Even though I think this measure is too modest, look at how it would have an impact in a country like Britain on a company like Tesco.

- In 2014 Tesco posted profits of £3.3 billion. Under the aforementioned system they would have to transfer £660 million
  to the employee share trust, meaning they would still keep
  £2.64 billion.

Well, they can't moan about that, can they? They'd still get billions in profit. Let's pause to recall that profit means surfeit money that you don't actually need after all your costs have been covered. We know that for profit to exist in one place, deficit has to exist elsewhere, so I don't think this goes nearly far enough. None the less, let's look at how this modest reform would impact Britain.

- The Queen Elizabeth Hospital in Birmingham cost £545
  million to build in 2010. You'd have more than that amount
  to spend every year just from one company, and they'd still
  get to keep 80 per cent of their profits.

Wow. That means that corporations that make huge profits, with a modest amendment, could be making life-saving contributions to the society they profiteer within. That seems so reasonable, fair, apposite and just.

Hey, how come not one mainstream democratic party anywhere in the world has policies like that? Why could that be? Why aren't Labour or the Democrats or even self-declared people's parties (they're ALL meant to be people's parties) like Ukip proposing gentle, effective regulation of corporations? Unless . . . they're all utterly supplicant to corporate tyranny. Ah yes, that's it.

So that's one idea, that in my view is a piece of pipsqueak reformism and not worth dying for, that no party in the 'democratic' space would ever propose because it conflicts with what Chomsky outlined for us earlier as the true function of power: to protect itself and to control us. What the above example does is demonstrate another alternative to 'the way things are' and shatters the convenient lie that there are no alternatives.

Here's another example of things being run differently. This time it's truly representative democracy – that means 'something worth voting for', a system that actually means the will of the people can be manifested.

It's called participatory democracy.

In Porto Alegre in Brazil, a city with a population of 1.3 million, 22 per cent of whom live in shanty towns and slums where typically people aren't that well educated or affluent, large-scale participatory democracy has proven to be very successful.

Since 1989 the expenditure for the whole city has been designed as an annual participatory budget so people can decide how the money is spent. That seems unfeasible: all these slum-dwelling, City-of-Gold-emulating, barefoot-with-an-orange-football-on-the-beach folk are each year involved in the economics of their community – it can't be done. Alright, how is it done?

- In March, there are micro-level discussions in preparation held all over the city.

Okay, so people understand that they are part of a community and can take part in its management.

- In April and May, assemblies are held to decide on priorities for the coming year.

I see, so the first meeting is to establish priorities: some people might want to have more regular refuse collection, others might want more community housing, others might be worried about immigration. Bring it up at the micro meeting, work it through, then take it to the assembly the following month.

- Forty-eight delegates are elected from the assemblies to attend the budget council.

So there's a representative element, but it doesn't feel as dislocated as our politics, there's a sense that you are making decisions that will affect your life. I bet if we were able to present that information interestingly, people would be as engaged by that as they are in *Dancing on Ice*.

- The requests of the citizens arising from the assembly meetings are handed to the mayor.

Mayor, hey? How did he get that gig? I don't remember voting for him. The title 'mayor' would have to go in Matt Stoller's utopia and the incumbent of the role entirely beholden to the people in Dave DeGraw's. Like with the revolutions we've read about, we're under no obligation to replicate their ideologies wholesale, we can democratically cultivate our world together.

- The budget council meets from September and the delegates, councillors and administrators work through the budget, which is adopted by the mayor at the end of the year.

Sounds like a lot of bureaucracy, and I bet it fucking is. That's what politics should be: admin. No power, just clerical work, enacting the will of the people. The mayor doesn't get to make any crafty moves to help out his banker pals or get bikes named after him, it's just graft and service.

- The procedure is aided by a team of coordinators who liaise with the community throughout the process.

Real-life democracy, where the issues that you care about are addressed. Me, I don't see immigration as a real issue. For me, an immigrant is just someone who used to be somewhere else and the sooner we unite and organise to dismantle the structures that prevent all of us being free, the better I'll feel.

You might feel differently though. You might want strict border controls like Bill O'Reilly or Nigel Farage.

Now, whilst I'd argue that the only reason we even think stuff like that is because we've been given duff and manipulative information, you may not care. In a truly representative democracy, we'd be presented with the arguments, then we'd vote. If after all the pleading and exposure of actually culpable bankers and corrupt politicians there was still a determination to blame immigrants, some crazy racist deal could be voted in.

Given that we're all meant to be deeply apathetic, our refusal to vote regarded as slovenliness rather than an unwillingness to participate in a system that knowingly harbours and protects political paedophiles, the concern would be that no one would bother to take part in this new, empowering system.

Well, 31,300 people took part in the process in Porto Alegre in 2002, up from 1,300 in 1989. This goes to show that participation escalates when people see that they're not wasting their time. Also, it clearly wasn't as boring as I worried it would be; it caught on like Rubik's Cube or, if you're young, and I hope you are, loom bands.

That's a huge number, positive in itself but imagine the increased sense of community and connection. Compare this to what we're mugged off with by way of democracy:

- In London, twenty-five elected members of the GLA and the Mayor of London decide how to spend a budget of £14.6 billion.

Sounds like there's a bit of wiggle room there.

When this new type of democracy was implemented in Brazil – let's call it actual democracy – the majority of participants were women and 'poor people'. Isn't that what we need in all democracy? Under-represented groups to come to the forefront? I think our communities would greatly improve if more women, and blokes that hadn't all gone to the same school, got stuck in to running them.

What happened when they got involved in Porto Alegre?

- Spending on health and education rose from 13 per cent to 40 per cent.
- 98 per cent of houses were connected to mains water and the sewage system.
- The number of schools increased by four times.

That's what happens in representative democracy: people get represented, instead of mad policies that allow spying, new water cannons, arms deals and the carving up of health services. Generally speaking, when empowered as a community, or common mind, our common spirit, our common sense, reaches conclusions that are beneficial for our community. Our common unity.

CHAPTER 33

Worth Voting For?

These models already exist. They are already working. We know the current system isn't, shrug, 'not perfect, but the best we can do': it's fucked and it's fucking us and it's obsolete. Now there are alternatives. We have the means, we just haven't used our power to assert our will. The technology that enables us to vote for TV talent shows can be used for truly representative, localised democratic process – that's common sense.

The trade agreements that benefit transnational corporations can be rewritten to provide food and resources for the people of the world.

The utilities and facilities of major corporations – Monsanto, Apple, Time Warner – can be confiscated and given to democratic collectives so we can have food, technology and communication on a local level without needless global tariffs, Mickey Mouse product updates, and senseless ecological damage.

The US writer Walter Mosley said, 'We have the formal structure of a democracy, but not the substance.'

The structures exist, the resources exist, the only thing that stands in the way of this necessary Revolution is the venal entitlement and self-interest of the people who benefit from things staying as they are.

Now, as David Graeber said to me once, these people aren't going to just stand aside, say 'We see your point' and let us get on with the Revolution. When fear and propaganda finally fail and that process has begun, they will, of course, use force.

Military force, police force and private security. The good news is, as Che Guevara pointed out, the people that do all the work in those institutions are getting shafted like the rest of us and will only go so far for a pension. Their compliance is kind of a habit. Habits are hard to break but – and this I know from personal experience – you are more inclined to break them when they stop working for you.

As the degeneration of our governing institutions becomes more blatant, more and more of the brave men and women that have sworn to protect and serve the people are going to see that oath runs directly adverse to what they're being paid to do.

The battalions of ex-service people living on the city streets of the UK and USA are a cruel testimony to the true sentiments of our governments towards those that are willing to give their lives. Sixty thousand homeless people in the USA, and 25 per cent of all London's homeless, have formerly served the country that now does them such a rank disservice.

What would happen if we tried to create regional participatory democracy? What would happen if we tried this out in London, New York or Barcelona? What would it be like?

What if in London we used the existing democratic structure to return power to the population of London?

Every major decision within the current jurisdiction of the mayoralty could be voted on directly by the people, like in Porto Alegre. In actual fact the Mayor of London, thank God, has only limited power, but we could all vote on issues that would immediately change the vibe of the place like:

- Should all development contracts given out by the mayor and the city of London be to non-profit cooperatives, whose workers elect their bosses, and reinvest all the money they make in London, and guarantee the living wage?

One of the things the mayor could do – and the one London has now would never do – is only grant development contracts to ethical businesses that behave themselves. My feeling is, even with the above stipulations, like paying people properly, empowering your workforce and responsible reinvestment, these exciting new enterprises could give snidey outfits like Boots, Starbucks and Vodafone a run for their money.* We as a community might prefer to get our stuff from outlets that aren't ripping us off and not contributing. I'd vote for it.

- Should all new housing developments be required by law to consist of at least 70 per cent affordable housing?

London doesn't have enough affordable homes. The Mayor of London could ensure new developers addressed this by building some. It'd also go some way to alleviating the spiritual stain of urban homelessness. That'd be cool.

- Should we be arresting drug users?

The Mayor of London has power over the Metropolitan Police Force and could ask them to stop bugging casual drug users. In fact all drug users. The War on Drugs has been lost. People take drugs and that's that; all we can do is create conditions that are as safe as possible and result in as little criminal activity as possible for something that remains illegal. Most police I've

* I'm not saying their products are substandard, I don't have a view on that. I'm saying that they in collusion with a compliant government avoid paying tax that pays for the social structures that allow their compamies to profit.

343

chatted to think it's a ball-ache nicking drug users and would be glad to drop it. We could have a vote on that.

- Should we abandon stop and search and the harassment of the homeless?

This is another area where the mayor's authority over the police could save a lot of aggravation for them and the community. Actually given the mayoralty's power over development contracts how about a vote for the city's residents on this subject:

- Should all businesses granted development contracts support a city-wide fund to provide shelter for all?

Imagine that! No homelessness, an end to the inhuman twitch required to steel ourselves for the guilty march past street sleepers.

- Should we subsidise the creation of democratic media and an online dialogue with the electorate?

Even though 10 per cent of Londoners don't have Internet access, which seems mad to me in my bubble, it would be good if the relationship between city administrators and the electorate became complete and ongoing. In fact, given that one fifth of the population are offline, how about:

- City-wide free Wi-Fi for all residents, subsidised by commercial and financial interests?

The advantage of using the pre-existing infrastructure of a metropolis like London is it gives us the opportunity to demonstrate a

344

new politics. A politics that spreads power as widely as possible and represents people directly.

As we have seen from the US's treatment of any nation that tries to step outside of the capitalist paradigm, any attempt to reduce corporate influence and empower people is met by extreme external pressure. That would probably happen to any public official who sought to truly devolve power.

That's why the chance this office gives to rally for wider change ought to be exploited. Regular referenda could be held to form a powerful 'people's lobby' to pressure national government and international organisations to align with the needs of the people they claim to represent.

London could become a paragon of advancing consciousness, an awakened society that organises a good, fair, empowered life for its citizens and campaigns for global change for everyone.

The ideas I've collated in this book are clear, simple and necessary. This is continually obfuscated by the representatives of a dying system that requires our docility for their ludicrous prosperity.

The feeling you have of anger is real and just; the feelings of hopelessness and despair are not.

We all have a choice; we are the creators of our reality. All we have to do is make a decision to take collective responsibility for change. Do you really think that the Revolution is a ridiculous proposition? That we cannot engineer our own structures?

What's ridiculous is the system we have now. If we were starting society anew, who among us would propose a monarchy, an aristocracy, a financial elite that exploits the earth and farms its population?

If at one of the local or regional meetings that we have to govern our community someone proposed, instead of equality, that all of us, including the poorest among us, donated a percentage of our income to a super-rich family with a little old lady at its helm who would turn up annually in our parliament, draped in jewels and finery, to tell us that austerity had to continue, you'd tell them they were mental.

If someone said that we should give 64 per cent of British land to 0.28 per cent of the population, we would not vote for it.

If trade agreements were proposed that meant local businesses were shackled so that transnational corporations could create a farcical tyrannical economy where produce was needlessly transported around the world for their gain and to the detriment of everyone else, it would be forbidden.

If energy companies said they wanted to be run for huge profit, without regulation, whilst harming the environment, we wouldn't allow it.

That pharmaceutical and food companies could run their own governing bodies, flood the world with inferior and harmful products that damage and even kill the people that use them, we would not tolerate it.

Here is the truth that they fight so hard to suppress: to create a better world the priority is not the implementation of new systems, though that is necessary, it is a refusal to cooperate with the obsolete and harmful structures that are already in place. The Revolution will be easily enacted and beneficial to all. It is time to wake up.

In a survey that YouGov conducted among non-voters (that we paid for and they still refused to skew so that it gave damned lying statistical answers) a third said they wanted outright Revolution, 54 per cent said they didn't vote because big businesses run Britain, and 96 per cent thought the voting public had no influence at all on the way the country was run.

Incredible that the vast majority of non-voters have found their way to the truth given that 70 per cent of the UK press is controlled by just three companies and have a vested interest in ensuring that this truth only appears fleetingly, usually masked by tits and bingo.

Six corporations own 90 per cent of all media in the US. If you want the truth, you're not going to get it there.

The people that own the means for conveying information, who decide what knowledge enters our minds, are on the fun bus.

My personal Revolution is to live by spiritual principles and to serve this wider change in any way I can.

It's early in the process for me, but my infatuation with fame is waning, my need for external approval and the control of other people's opinions is expiring.

Practically I've decided that profits from this book will go towards creating a place where recovering addicts like me can run a business based on the ideas in this book. A cafe and production company run to create community, not money, democratically managed by the workforce. No bosses. No profit. No bullshit.

Selling food sourced ethically, grown locally and served by people who have had a Revolution in their own lives and are now able to learn and give back.

Supporting modest creative projects, building a community of people who want to be part of something other than the toxic hegemony.

We will start small but we will grow quickly because we have a limitless resource and we are providing an alternative to a dying system. There are no limits to what we can achieve if we behave collectively, responsibly and humanely.

The world is changing and we are awakening. These statistics give us a numerical glimpse at the visceral dissatisfaction that most of us feel. Now is the time to express it. These corrupt structures cannot be maintained without our compliance. You could vote against them if there was anything to vote for, but there isn't, or you could stop paying your mortgage, stop paying your taxes, stop buying stuff you don't need. When we, the majority, unite and demonstrate our new intention, we will be invincible. If we who are complicit by our silence become active and disobedient.

This is a pivotal time in the history of our species. We are transitioning from an ideology that places power and responsibility in the hands of the few to one where we all collectively have power. It is important that we clarify in a manner accessible to all which institutions and systems are beneficial and which ones have to go. It is important that we propose ideas and systems that will be advantageous, like the handful in this book, and ensure that they are presented properly. When they are inevitably disparaged by the fearful enemies of change, we must remain unified and insistent. At this climactic time, we have no choice but change.

This book, written by a twerp, with minimal interaction with brilliant thinkers and uncorrupted minds, demonstrates that.

Now what are you going to do about it?

For The Benefit Of The Tape

I went back to Lakeside to see if its lustre remained or if it would be like meeting an old lover, the magic drained by time. Whilst it may architecturally resemble St Paul's Cathedral rebooted by a Kardashian, on arrival there's very little to slap nostalgia on. For a place so dependent on superficial splendour and opulence it's peculiarly bleak, a barren edifice.

The process of parking the car is almost enough to get your gander up. By the time we'd ditched the vehicle in a gloomy, low-ceilinged multi-storey, but no real plot, car park, I was so irritated by the lack of spaces and incessant checkpoints that I needed to have a fight or buy a pair of trainers just to let off some steam.

True beauty binds you to it; ugliness in art, architecture or people makes you unwittingly recoil. When I watch a bit of shit theatre, suddenly I'm painfully aware that I'm in a humid room, watching people gesticulate and gurn for no bloody good reason. 'They're just pretending,' I think, and feel a bit embarrassed for me and for them. Where do I situate my nostalgia on the pitiless and blank walls of Lakeside? No concession to the human is made. I bet the corporation that built Lakeside, and six malls just like it, could just as easily turn their hand to building prisons. It's not a place for people, for public life; it's a vacuum in a suburb that empties more than your pockets.

I ask one or two people why they're there and no one seems to know. There is no purposeful stride, rolled-up paper under the arm, fag on, tapping the hedge as you go, a sense of civic participation. This is mass hypnosis. When a pigeon flies in it seems obscene, like an unzipped fly in a wedding photograph. What the fuck are you doing in here? Here the birdsong is piped in, the plants are doing their best to synthetically photosynthesise but their hearts aren't in it as they pose in their Guantánamo urns.

I can see the absurdity of the wayward bird or the indentured flora, but really their presence is no more ridiculous than mine, or any of the others interned in this fluorescent volt. How sparse must our hope be to come looking here.

What must I have been like to willingly subject myself to this context where nature itself seems superfluous, like pubes on a mannequin?

A wrist-slashing adolescent, escaped from pudgy and hysterical childhood until delivered into the secondary cradle of addiction.

As hapless as the pigeon and as forlorn as Wilde in Reading Jail without even the little tent of blue sky, we are severed from ourselves, severed from God. The geometry that Lakeside mocks that's found in every church and mosque, is the material representation of the invisible connection that we've lost only to walk these glistening yards.

Later you will search 'rice resonance' on YouTube and be shocked at the sublimely choreographed rice particles performing miraculous crop circles on top of a panel vibrating to a gradually increasing frequency. You will see that the invisible waves that sound is made of form the shapes and patterns that define our world, that perfect geometry fills the spaces between us. The unknown is constantly addressing us, it doesn't use our language, but it's here, quite clear among us.

N,N-Dimethyltryptamine (DMT), a drug which I mentioned earlier, when administered in high doses gives with eerie consistency, to those who take it, the experience of hidden realms where new consciousness is experienced. Beings are encountered that commune and reassure. DMT occurs naturally in many plants, all mammals and in the human brain. No one knows its neurological function but many assume it's connected to dreaming. Dreams, more immersive and psychedelic than any drug and occurring whenever we sleep, unbidden, a nightly reminder that mystery reigns within.

Incrementally indoctrinated, we have forgotten how to dream, we have forgotten who we are. We have abandoned our connection to wonder and placed our destiny in unclean hands. Look closely next time a world leader is on your TV. Look at their face from deep within yourself. Is that the face of someone you can trust? Either a mask of Plasticine smugness, or wrought and befuddled sincerity, or smug bellicosity. Should we allow these men to govern?

On I went to Grays and was actually a bit embarrassed by how lovely the library was and how sweet the people were, as in my head I'd rendered it as a suburban South Central with myself as a white Ice Tea. Nik, who was with me, on leaving the Thameside Musuem judged it to be a 'centre of excellence', an estuary Oxford. Harvard with fake tan.

In fact I must mention that I was interviewed by the police during the writing of this book, and the WPC who questioned me was so resolutely lovely, judicious and kind, I nearly gave up on the whole revolutionary caper. There were cups of tea and codes of conduct and tales of public marches in her former life. In fact, though, this just confirms my thesis that people are beautiful, and Revolution inevitable. We don't need to grow compassion in a Petri dish, everyone's fine, we just have to scrape away a few repellent systems.

351

Thankfully, in Grays Park (once we'd passed the immaculately tended roses) I ran into the now grown-up child of a girl I'd dated when I was a teenager; this child, now twenty, had a baby of her own (making my former paramour a grandmother and me inwardly wince) and she looked like she'd had a hard time.

In the short exchange between us it was clear that in the intervening years she'd been subject to the ordinary tragedy that bludgeons normal people. The girl I used to date, who I remember as being imbued with a powerful and adventurous spirit, the kind of girl who's in grave danger in a small town (in Salem she'd've been burned), was in a wheelchair now.

Administered the wrong drug at the wrong time by a knackered nurse during a routine visit, she'll never walk again. All around us lives are squandered and dreams are unfulfilled.

We condition our children and ourselves to enter into this spectacle, confining ourselves to a prescribed path. My mate Matt says when he takes his two-year-old son down the park he has to fight not to impose a predefined version of the experience on to the spontaneous boy, who not knowing the script may wander off after an ant or pick daisies when he's supposed to be playing football. Is there a limited number of times that a child will insist on remaining wedded to the moment? Do we eventually all become cowed and beat down and just sit in the swings like we're supposed to?

Eckhart Tolle told me that to be free of suffering I must, in the moment of temptation, when I want to yield to anger or jealousy or self-pity, to recognise that the ego that these fleeting interlopers serve, is an illusion.

When in conflict with a partner, I see myself as the sole defender of some superior truth, that I must impose this truth for some higher cause. I asked Eckhart why.

'We adopt a mental position,' he told me, 'then we identify with that mental position and it becomes invested with self.'

The self is a construction: some memories, some feelings, some opinions, a name, a bunch of photographs, real and imaginary. This conglomerate that we hold in our consciousness is temporary, it is an illusion.

The boundless energy, the hidden energy, that invisibly performs its geometric dance is real. The unified energy that is behind all diversity is real. The moment of conception, individual or universal, is real. Behind all phenomena, thoughts, things, animals, life itself, is an awareness. 'Move into this awareness,' said Eckhart.

When you are in conflict or doubt, or afraid, when you lose hope or lose people that you depend upon, move beyond the pain and fear, there is an awareness there. An awareness that has always been there. In your loneliness and suffering and darkness and fear, silently behind it the awareness is waiting for us to return. This awareness is the field of consciousness from which all life came, the absolute energy that precedes all and is beyond all and is within all. It is within you.

We all have this in common but we have been convinced that we are alone, but this energy that compels one cell to become two, that heals wounds, that spins quarks and planets, is within us all. And all language can do is rest on top of it, or point to it, never really describing it, this force, this undeniable compulsion to come together, we all know that it's there and we all know when it's absent and we all know that we must be open to it now. And in spite of its ethereal and indefinable nature, we all know that it's love.

INDEX

RB indicates Russell Brand.